Course in General Linguistics

Course in General Linguistics

Ferdinand de Saussure

Translated by Wade Baskin

Edited by Perry Meisel and Haun Saussy

Columbia University Press
New York

Columbia University Press
Publishers Since 1893
New York Chichester, West Sussex

Library of Congress Cataloging-in-Publication Data
Saussure, Ferdinand de, 1857–1913.
[Cours de linguistique generale. English]
Course in general linguistics / Ferdinand de Saussure ; translated by Wade Baskin ; edited by Perry Meisel and Haun Saussy.
p. cm.
Translation of Cours de linguistique generale.
Includes bibliographical references and index.
ISBN 978-0-231-15726-1 (cloth : alk. paper)—ISBN 978-0-231-15727-8 (pbk. : alk. paper)—ISBN 978-0-231-52795-8 (e-book)
1. Language and languages. 2. Comparative linguistics. I. Baskin, Wade. II. Meisel, Perry. III. Saussy, Haun, 1960– IV. Title.
P121.S363 2011
410—dc22 2010053912

∞

Columbia University Press books are printed on permanent and durable acid-free paper.
This book is printed on paper with recycled content.
Printed in the United States of America

c 10 9 8 7 6 5 4 3 2
p 10 9 8 7 6 5 4

Contents

PART ONE

GENERAL PRINCIPLES

PART TWO

SYNCHRONIC LINGUISTICS

PART THREE

DIACHRONIC LINGUISTICS

PART FOUR

GEOGRAPHICAL LINGUISTICS

PART FIVE

CONCERNING RETROSPECTIVE LINGUISTICS

Editors' Preface and Acknowledgments

A new English text of Saussure's *Course in General Linguistics* (1916) is long overdue. Wade Baskin's splendid original translation (1959) is now unavailable, and a proper edition of the *Course* in English has never been done. Saussure was granted full-scale academic editions first in Italian (1967) and German (1968, 1974), and, with a French translation of de Mauro's apparatus, at last in French (de Mauro 1972). Baskin's modest translation was his doctoral dissertation at Columbia (1956) and sports only a brief translator's introduction appended to the unornamented first French text of 1916, which contains only the brief introductory commentary by those students of Saussure who assembled the text of the *Course* from the notes of his lectures (Bally and Sechehaye 1916). Roy Harris's English translation of 1983 also presents Saussure's text unornamented except for polemical annotations.

Our labors have been divided as follows: Perry Meisel has written the principal parts of the introduction. Haun Saussy has provided a sketch of Saussure's life and described in detail the many versions of the *Course* discovered in other sources since 1916, including the consequences each one has for understanding, and misunderstanding, what Saussure has to say. Saussy's notes to this new edition widen the traditional focus on Saussure as linguist to include his epochal influence on the human sciences as a whole. An annotated textual note follows this preface outlining reference protocols for this new edition.

We wish to thank our editor, Jennifer Crewe; Jonathan Culler; Regeen Runes Najar; and Wade Baskin Jr. Thanks also to Natalie Adler, Naomi McDougall Jones, Michael Miller, Rachel Tanner, and Lindsay Welsch. Thanks to Chris Gisonny for preparation of the manuscript.

Textual Note

The following editions of work by Ferdinand de Saussure are cited. Each is preceded by an abbreviation and date of first publication:

CLG (1916)	*Cours de linguistique générale.* Charles Bally and Albert Sechehaye, eds., with the assistance of Albert Riedlinger. Lausanne and Paris: Payot. Second edition, repaginated, 1922; third edition, 1931; subsequent editions closely follow this last.
Recueil (1922)	*Recueil des publications scientifiques de Ferdinand de Saussure.* Charles Bally and Léopold Gautier, eds. Lausanne: Payot.
Godel (1957)	Godel, Robert. *Les sources manuscrites du Cours de linguistique générale de F. de Saussure.* Geneva: Droz. A study, with abundant quotation of excerpts, of the materials that Bally and Sechehaye used in compiling *CLG* 1916.
CGL (1959)	*Course in General Linguistics.* Wade Baskin, trans. New York: Philosophical Library. An English translation of *CLG* 1916. Reprinted 1968, New York: McGraw-Hill.
CLG (1967)	*Corso di linguistica generale.* Tullio de Mauro, trans. and annot. Bari: Laterza. French edition cited below as *CLG* 1972.
CLG (1968–1974)	*Ferdinand de Saussure, Cours de linguistique générale, édition critique.* Rudolf Engler, ed. Wiesbaden: Harrassowitz. Engler's critical edition provides

	transcriptions of the student notes used (and some not used) in the composition of *CLG* 1916, keyed to the corresponding paragraphs of the *CLG* 1916/1922 published texts. Émile Constantin's detailed notes on version III of the course, not known to the 1916 editors but supplied here, provide a check on their work.
CLG (1972)	*Cours de linguistique générale.* Charles Bally and Albert Sechehaye, eds., with the assistance of Albert Riedlinger; annotated by Tullio de Mauro. Frequently reprinted. The notes by de Mauro, keyed to passages of the text, provide a large linguistic and intellectual background.
CGL (1983)	*Course in General Linguistics.* Roy Harris, trans. and annot. London: Duckworth.
Komatsu (1993)	*Troisième cours de linguistique générale (1910–1911) d'après les cahiers d'Émile Constantin / Saussure's Third Course of Lectures on General Linguistics (1910–1911) from the Notebooks of Emile Constantin.* Eisuke Komatsu, ed., Roy Harris, trans. Oxford: Pergamon Press.
Komatsu (1996)	*Premier cours de linguistique générale (1907) d'après les cahiers d'Albert Riedlinger / Saussure's First Course of Lectures on General Linguistics (1907) from the Notebooks of Albert Riedlinger.* Eisuke Komatsu, ed., George Wolf, trans. Oxford: Pergamon Press.
Komatsu (1997)	*Deuxième cours de linguistique générale (1908–1909) d'après les cahiers d'Albert Riedlinger et Charles Patois / Saussure's Second Course of Lectures on General Linguistics (1908–1909) from the Notebooks of Albert Riedlinger and Charles*

	Patois. Eisuke Komatsu, ed., George Wolf, trans. Oxford: Pergamon Press. Unlike *CLG* (1968–1974), the editions of student notes by Komatsu retain the original continuity and paragraph order.
ELG (2002)	*Écrits de linguistique générale.* Simon Bouquet and Rudolf Engler, eds. Paris: Gallimard. A collection of manuscript notes and drafts left behind by Saussure at his death, some of them rediscovered only in 1996. These notes afford our best glimpse of Saussure's developing thoughts about linguistic theory.
WGL (2006)	*Writings in General Linguistics.* Carol Sanders and Matthew Pires, trans. New York: Oxford University Press. English translation of *ELG* (2002).

Introduction: Saussure and His Contexts

"Signifier" and "Signified": Reclaiming Saussure's Legacy

This new edition of Saussure's *Course in General Linguistics* (1916) restores the Saussure that generations of English readers grew up on: Wade Baskin's 1959 translation. In addition to its inherent elegance, Baskin's translation of the lectures Saussure gave at the end of his life at the University of Geneva is indispensable for a very particular reason, one that Roy Harris's 1983 translation wholly obscures: the rendition of Saussure's terms "*signifiant*" and "*signifié*" (*CLG* 1972, 99) as "signifier" and "signified" (*CGL* 1959, 67). These equivalent neologisms in French and English embody precisely what is revolutionary about Saussure's thought and what is specific to it. Baskin's translation makes this revolution clear. Saussure presents the solution to a problem in the history of ideas that stretches back to Plato and that reached crisis proportions in the late nineteenth century: the problem of reference. Most familiar as a problem in poetics, it is a problem in all media, including the life sciences, which is why Saussure reconceived the problem of reference as one of signification. Many false starts delayed Saussure's discovery until the end of his life, daunted as he was by the numerous historical contexts in which he had to test his ideas in order to ensure their durability. Traditionally cast as the problem of mimesis—of language as imitating or representing what it refers to—the problem of reference is put on an entirely different footing by what Saussure eventually achieved.

Regarding Saussure in this way situates his achievement not only specifically but also outside of linguistics proper, where he has never been accorded an especially happy position. Saussure is not a system builder, and his findings are not easy to apply to the ambitions of scientific projects. Rather, as his position in the history of ideas suggests, he is a philosopher, however unwillingly, and a philosopher with the particular mission of solving a problem in poetics. It is no surprise that structuralism faded when it tried to become a systematic semiology. The philosophical consequences of Saussure's inventiveness are more indirect and profound than they are programmatic. Roland Barthes, Michel Foucault, Jacques Derrida, and Jacques Lacan are the surest proofs. By reconceiving reference as signification rather than as mimesis, Saussure and his disciples no longer allow one to take for granted the assumptions that mimesis as a notion traditionally puts in place: the separation of word and thing, subject and object, self and world. Saussure requires a reimagination of these categories and a makeover of the way we think.

Decisive, of course, are the notions of signifier and signified. Despite Saussure's own lucidity, what these terms mean requires repetition and constant clarification. The notion of the "signifier" is presumably assimilable to our notion of the "vehicle" of reference, to use I. A. Richards's term in *The Philosophy of Rhetoric* (1936, 96). It is what in Richards's theory of metaphor indicates that an act of reference has occurred. The notion of the "signified," however, is not assimilable to Richards's term "tenor" (96), or what it is, exactly, to which the "signifier," or the "vehicle" of signification, refers. Though a metaphor is, in Richards's phrase, "a transaction between contexts" (94)—what Umberto Eco will describe as a match between items in the semantic inventories of both "tenor" and "vehicle" that the reader has been "entitled" to discover (1976, 284)—"the tenor," says Richards, is, by the same token, "the underlying idea or principal subject which the vehicle or figure means" (1936, 97). "Idea," "subject," "means"—these cannot be synonyms in so rigorous an analysis. In *The Meaning of Meaning* (1923), C. K. Ogden and Richards flatly call reference a reference to "things" (1923, 6), deriding Saussure in the process (8). Even Émile Benveniste, a good Saussurean, requires a third term in addition to "signifier" and "signified" and proposes, scandalously, that "this third term" is, quite simply, "the thing itself, reality" (1939, 44). But the "signified" is a "concept," says Saussure, and "psychological" (*CGL*

1959, 66; *CLG* 1972, 98). It is not a "thing in itself," or an object in the world distinct from language, or even an "idea" that may, as it does in Richards, preexist its verbal expression. Derrida's term "logocentrism" (1967a) well describes this classical assumption about reference—the very assumption that Saussure overrides. Derrida's notion of the "signified" as simply another signifier (1967a, 7, 71) is the clearest way of showing why it is a problematic assumption to have.

Roman Jakobson's assaults upon Saussure feature prominently in the flurry of discontent that Derrida resolves. Jakobson claims that Saussure is inclined to "isolate" the "sensible" and the "intelligible" (1949a, 396), but this is exactly what he does not do. The reciprocity of the "sensible" and "intelligible" is the hinge upon which the economy of the sign turns (*CGL* 1959, 66, 112, 120). Nor are *langue* and *parole*, language and speech, "fixed" (1949b, 54) in relation to each other. Bakhtin, writing as his friend Vološinov (1929), had already taken Saussure to task for the same reason. Saussure, he says, neglects the very dialectic between *langue* and *parole* that he shows. Many years later, Pierre Bourdieu actually reconstitutes the Saussurean system that he degrades as formal and ahistorical (1980, 1992) by transforming *langue* and *parole* into "field" and "*habitus*" (1972, 1979). No wonder Leonard Bloomfield was generous to Saussure, recognizing in his review of the *Course* in 1923 that Saussure shows how changes in *parole* accumulate over time and sink deeply enough into the fabric of speech so as to create changes in *langue*.

That Saussure's "signified" is conceptual and psychological does not mean that it is any more "abstract," to use Bakhtin's term (1929, 58), than the plainly "sensory" or "material" status of Saussure's "signifier" (*CGL* 1959, 66; *CLG* 1972, 98). Above all, it does not mean that it is not in the world or part of its history. In their reciprocity, signifier and signified produce a world that is both wholly concrete and wholly conceptual at one and the same time. Indeed, the world itself—the real, external world—is a matrix of signification, real because it is symbolic and symbolic because it is real. Language and the world are continuous. The object-world, including nature and our own bodies, is a web of signs continuous with the languages and images with which we describe them. Saussure's belief that the object of linguistic study is the structure of language does not mean that language is placed outside of history. Far from it. Language is "evolutionary," a function of ceaseless "change" (*CGL* 1959, 98; *CLG* 1972, 138). "Every time an *event* of whatever magnitude," says Saussure, "occurs within a language system, the evident consequence is that the reciprocal state of the terms after the event is not the same as it was before" (*WGL* 2006, 156). Saussure invents a new kind of historicism.

This is because Saussure's signification is a process, not a product. Language is part of the reality to which it refers. It does not resemble social or organic life, nor is it simply a part of social or organic life. It is identical with them both. Language is a vast interactive project, an exchange with the environment that puts the world in focus only to the extent that the world puts language in focus. As Samuel Johnson observes in the preface to his *Dictionary* (1755), life and language are standardized in relation to each other. No lexicographer, says Johnson, can "lash the wind" (1755, 239). Language is both subject and object in relation to itself, something to which it responds as much as something that it uses. Neither Johnson in the *Dictionary* nor Saussure in the *Course* attempt to bind its vicissitudes. Eschewing a universal estimation of language, Saussure gives us instead a picture of how language functions at any particular moment, introducing by contrast and necessity a picture also of the pressures of time upon it.

To replace Baskin's "signifier" and "signified," as Harris does, with "signification" and "signal" (*CGL* 1983, 67; *CLG* 1972, 98) foils Saussure's decided intent. Harris's translation, like his pugnacious study, *Saussure and His Interpreters* (2001), fights hard to foil this clarity. So trenchant is this clarity, however, that *Saussure and His Interpreters* is, quite ironically, an excellent, if inadvertent, history of Saussure's many discipleships and misreadings, from Jakobson to Derrida. As a linguist, Harris is little interested in Saussure's philosophical breakthroughs, and he is desperate to show how unfit Saussure is as the engineer of an applied, technical linguistics. Saussure's belated similarities to

Bloomfield's structural linguistics are legion, but they contribute a philosophical justification for Bloomfield's project more than they provide it a methodological supplement (Bloomfield 1922, 56). Saussure's wholesale difference in assumption from later linguists, Noam Chomsky in particular, despite Chomsky's borrowings from Saussure, suggests even more plainly just how little Saussure's real context is linguistics proper.

Saussure's sedentary life in Geneva after his years teaching in Paris contrasts with Baskin's rather more active life as a teacher of language and literature in Oklahoma. A Christian existentialist devoted to Sartre, whom he also translated, Baskin was personal secretary to Dwight D. Eisenhower when Eisenhower was president of Columbia University and Baskin was a graduate student there. Baskin's translation of Saussure was originally his doctoral dissertation in Teachers College in 1956. Both veterans of World War II (a medic, Baskin stayed on in Europe after the war to study at the Sorbonne), Eisenhower and Baskin found in the New York of the 1950s rich ground for developing an egalitarian and global approach to life, one in politics, the other in literature and the land. Born in the Ozarks, Baskin returned to the region to teach language and literature at Southeast Oklahoma State. He also established a bilingual education program for the Choctaw nation, teaching English while also compiling a vocabulary of the endangered Choctaw tongue. Baskin's lifelong interest in Native American speech was part of a tradition of American thinking about language. Franz Boas's *Handbook of American Indian Languages* (1911), one of many published by the Bureau of American Ethnology, is the principal scholarly benchmark.

This edition of Saussure is therefore not oriented toward linguistics but toward literature, philosophy, and cultural criticism. Unlike Tullio de Mauro's notes to the French edition (*CLG* 1972), the notes that follow Baskin's translation here do not trace the many criticisms of Saussure leveled at him by linguists over the years. Rather, they trace Saussure's reception, good and bad, among literary critics, philosophers, and cultural theorists. Nor does our introduction aim to reestablish the possibility of a general semiology. Our account of the contexts that lie behind

Saussure's revolutionary achievement is designed instead to show how precise Saussure's solution is to a series of familiar, and presumably intractable, problems in the history of ideas.

Life and Afterlife

A plaque on the side of the Saussure family's neoclassical town house in rue de la Cité, Geneva, depicts the linguist in profile and quotes the sentences from the *Course in General Linguistics* that proclaim the discipline of semiology. Two blocks up the street, another plaque announces the birthplace of Jean-Jacques Rousseau; another three or four blocks bring the visitor to John Calvin's former seat in the cathedral of St. Peter. Calvin, Rousseau, Saussure: three distinguished Genevois, each in his own way a reformer, all three concerned with the right relation between words and things.

Saussure was born into a prominent family of alternating bankers and scientists (for a detailed biography, see Joseph in press). Though he left to study in Paris and Leipzig and later taught for ten years in Paris, he returned to Geneva and married a cousin (as the Saussures usually did). His father, known for publications in entomology, was plagued by financial worries following a series of poor investments but encouraged his children's intellectual interests. Already captivated by languages as an adolescent, Saussure at first planned to study physics and chemistry at the University of Geneva but soon changed his direction to comparative philology. In Leipzig, he studied with the leading exponents of the then-emerging "neogrammatical tendency" and published, at twenty-one, a study of the ancient Indo-European vowels. This study already exhibited his way of conceiving of features of language as interdependent functions of a system. Thereafter, he joined the Linguistic Society of Paris, taught at the École Pratique des Hautes Études, and stretched his bare professorial salary through almost nightly poker games with the best Parisian society.

His rare publications of this period bore on questions of etymology and phonetic change. Returning in 1891 to Geneva, he taught smaller audiences Sanskrit, phonology, Greek, Latin, and Germanic languages, and, starting in 1907, general linguistics.

Early in his second Geneva period, he began to write a book about terms and methods in linguistics but, unsatisfied, abandoned the project. Manuscript sketches relating to this book were rediscovered over a hundred years later and published in 2002. Less and less frequently in contact with his Parisian associates, he opened investigations into apparent patterns of anagrams in Latin poetry and into early Germanic legends—projects abandoned midway. He died of heart failure in February 1913, coincidentally with a struggle in the university and in the Genevan press over the introduction of practical business courses. The first edition of the *Course in General Linguistics* appeared three years later.

As a document, Saussure's *Course in General Linguistics* is a lost original, the lectures that Saussure pronounced to a small audience in a Geneva auditorium for which no written text exists. After Saussure's death, his students, Charles Bally, Albert Sechehaye, and Albert Riedlinger, wishing to perpetuate his teaching, looked for the master's notes but found little. As a substitute, they collected the notebooks of students who had taken Saussure's class. They found that Saussure's oral teaching survived in several transcriptions. These, however, bore on three versions of the course (1907, 1908–1909, and 1910–1911), taken down by several auditors, each transcription incomplete, and some of them contradicting the others on various points. The editors established a table of contents on the basis of the third version of the course, which none of them had actually heard. Riedlinger had attended the first two versions; Mrs. Sechehaye had attended the third (*CLG* 1968–1974; see x–xii for a list of manuscript materials used in the compilation of the 1916 *CLG*). But they changed the order of topics, practically reversing the order in which they were given in 1910–1911 (Godel 1957, 77–92, 95–102; on the editorial process generally, see Harris 2001, 15–58). Engler's critical edition (*CLG* 1968–1974) provides transcriptions of the course notes used (and some not used) in the composition of the *CLG*, keyed to the corresponding paragraphs of the 1916 text. Émile Constantin's detailed notes on version III of the course, not known to the 1916 editors, provide a check on their work (*CLG* 1968–1974, xi). These notes have been published in full (Komatsu 1993). The chapters "The Students' Saussure" and "The Editors' Saussure" in Harris's *Saussure and His Interpreters* (2001, 15–58) narrate the process that resulted in the 1916 text. For each paragraph, the editors collated and condensed the students' notes, sometimes adding other material left behind by Saussure and in a few places inventing what they thought Saussure should have said. Though the original editors were convinced that their work was a reverent reconstruction, later manuscript discoveries have shown that they are responsible for a number of Saussurean myths. Thus Saussure the Semiologist, like a medieval saint or hero, survives in a legend compiled from diverse written sources recording a vanished oral tradition. Not every piece of the legend is equally authentic, and some of its best-known passages may be the least trustworthy, precisely because they seemed so apposite to its compilers (Vansina 1961, 76–87).

The text translated by Wade Baskin in 1959 is, for most English speakers, the home of this legendary Saussure. Why republish it? Why not publish a corrected edition, one taking into account as far as possible the differences between what Bally, Sechehaye, and Riedlinger wrote in Saussure's name and what he said or wrote himself? While we are now aware that Saussure is not identical with the presumed author of the posthumous 1916 publication, it is the 1916 Saussure who has exerted the immense influence on twentieth-century linguistics, literary study, and social science for which he has come to be known as much by the emulation of his ideas as by their rejection. The legendary Saussure is the effective Saussure, the Saussure of record, for most contexts in which "Saussure" is mentioned. The Saussure known to Saussure specialists substitutes for the figure of legend as little as St. Nicholas of Myra can replace Santa Claus. From this point of view, the Wade Baskin translation, too, has its specific merits and its place in Saussure's reception. This introduction and the notes following the main text will locate the linguist that Baskin translated—the Saussure of the 1916 *Course*—in relation to some of the other earlier and subsequent Saussures and point out the ways in which the 1916 Saussure, even in its inauthenticities, caught the temper of its times.

One of the editors' most successful "duck eggs" (cf. *CGL* 1959, 76; *CLG* 1972, 111) comes at the very end of the 1916 book. There the lecturer states, "the fundamental idea of this course: *the true and unique object of linguistics is language studied in and for itself*" (*CGL* 1959, 232; *CLG* 1972, 317). This sentence appears to establish linguistics as a separate domain of knowledge that should distinguish itself from every other science; furthermore, it should ratify its independence by identifying as its object of study *langue*, the language system, as distinguished both from external factors and from *parole*, the performance of acts of language by individuals in particular situations. Hence Saussure the formalist straw man who turns his back on history, geography, psychology, physiology, sociology, and so on. But Robert Godel long ago pointed out that "this final sentence, often cited . . . does not come from Saussure, but from the editors" (1957, 181), who rewrote and transposed a paragraph from Saussure's introductory section on the history of linguistic ideas. How did Saussure conclude his course in 1911? The fullest set of notes from this third and last version of the course, taken down by Constantin, shows that the last topic covered was the theory of linguistic "value" (now located at *CLG* 1959, 114–120; *CLG* 1972, 158–166). Then followed a few lines situating more precisely the content of the *Course* within Saussure's conception of linguistics:

> In this course only the external part is more or less complete.
>
> In the internal part, evolutionary linguistics has been neglected in favor of synchronic linguistics and I have dealt with only a few general principles of linguistics.
>
> These general principles provide the basis for a productive approach to the details of a static state or the law of static states.
>
> (Komatsu 1993, 143)

"The external part" (dialectology, sociolinguistics, the place of language among other human institutions) corresponds to the less-read sections of *CLG* 1916; Saussure acknowledges his neglect of historical change and explains his emphasis on "static" linguistics as a pedagogical choice. The aims of the 1910–1911 course, then, were far from consecrating "a true and unique object of linguistics" or urging that language be studied "in and for itself." Nonetheless, the editors' concluding sentence has been quoted often enough to have become Saussure's decisive formulation of the essence of his teaching. Another of Bourdieu's adversarial formulations well summarizes the stakes of the common reception of the 1916 text:

> The whole fate of modern linguistics was decided, in effect, by the inaugural move whereby Saussure separated "external linguistics" from "internal linguistics" and, reserving the name of linguistics for this second discipline, excluded from it all forms of research that put a language in contact with the ethnology or political history of those who speak it, or the geography of the area where it is spoken, on the grounds that these factors would bring nothing to the knowledge of language taken in itself. Structural linguistics, born from the autonomization of language from its social conditions of production, reproduction and utilization, could not become the dominant field among the social sciences without exerting an ideological effect by giving an appearance of scientificity to the naturalization of symbolic objects, those products of history. The transfer of the phonological model to fields other than linguistics had the effect of generalizing to the totality of symbolic products (taxonomies of kinship, mythical systems or works of art) the inaugural operation that makes linguistics *the most natural of social sciences.*
>
> (Bourdieu 1982, 8–9)

A similar repudiation of Saussure's "abstract objectivism" inspires Bakhtin, writing under Vološinov's name (1929, 52–61).

Saussure, in this view, excludes from linguistics everything that is historical, individual, conscious, voluntary, contextual, or, in Terry Eagleton's desperate formulation, "actual" (1983, 40, 97). Whatever accuracy this may have as a portrayal of Saussureanism or structuralism, it is plainly a projection from the simplifications of the 1916 text. Not only did the 1916 editors make Saussure conclude with an appeal to "language studied in and for itself," but they also designed the published *Course* to foreground the analysis of linguistic "system," the synchronic representation of what Saussure called "*langue*." Its introduction, giving a first exposure to the concepts of semiology, *langue* and *parole*, and the two first parts expounding general principles and synchronic linguistics, occupy the greater number of pages in the book and have received the greater part of the attention of readers. These are the chapters that most people know as containing Saussure's linguistic thought. The sections on diachronic linguistics and dialectology come later in the book. Less original in their formulations, proceeding through the enumeration of examples rather than through striking metaphors, they seem to have been read by only a few specialists, and, in any case, they are followed (and seemingly dismissed) by the editors' ringing internalist conclusion.

But when Saussure taught his course, he put its stresses differently. In the third version, after an opening set of lessons defining *langue* as a semiological institution, Saussure spent from late October 1910 to late April 1911 describing linguistic diversity, with excursuses on phonology and writing. From April 25 to July 4, Saussure talked about *langue*, the nature of the sign, diachronic versus synchronic, and value as a result of difference within a system. The editors, by reversing this order, made history and geography appear to be a mere annex to the real business of linguistics, which would be capturing and describing systems of differentially opposed elements at particular moments in time. As for the exclusion of history, geography, and society from linguistics, Riedlinger's notes from the second course show that although Saussure insisted that the "essential" (Komatsu 1997, 11, 13) or "central" (17) features of language for the linguist are those relating to the nature of the sign and the economy of sign systems, he was hardly adamant about the separation of linguistics from other human sciences:

> We must first of all put on one side everything that we call the external side of linguistics, everything that is not directly related to the internal organism of language. Objections have been made to the use of the term *organism*: language cannot be compared to a living being! . . . Can we speak of external linguistics? If one hesitates by scrupulousness to do so, one might say: the internal and external *study* of linguistics. What goes into the external side: history and external description. This side includes important things. The word "linguistics" [at the present time] makes people think primarily of this set of things. This is the side by which linguistics touches on a number of domains that do not belong to it; this side is not linguistics in the pure or proper sense. Thus our definition [of linguistics] is entirely negative.
>
> (Komatsu 1997, 25, translation modified)

The relation of linguistics to the other sciences of human behavior must then be "oppositive, relative and negative" (*CGL* 1959, 119; *CLG* 1972, 164)—a relation nonetheless implying membership in a set of comparable entities, not isolation and exclusion. Linguistics will have as its main feature that of being what the neighboring sciences are not. As Harris observes, the *Course* is "the great masterpiece" of its own method (1987, 15). The method, however, was deformed in its application: to assert priority for "internal linguistics" is not to reject the "external" from the field of linguistics. Indeed, a good half of the third version of the course as Saussure taught it bore on those "external" questions, and the "internal" theorems such as the *langue/parole* distinction emerge from the discussion of historical and analogical change (see, for example, Komatsu 1996, 65). Moreover, Saussure's lively interest in sociology, economics, psychology, politics, natural science, and history shows on nearly every page, yielding, in a characteristic paradox, the very metaphors and technical terms whereby to capture the specificity of linguistics (see

Koerner 1973, 45–71; Aarsleff 1982, 356–371; and compare Bouquet 1997, 29–53).

The very suggestion that linguistics could have a "*true and unique object*" would have made Saussure smile. As he put it in the opening words of the second course, "linguistics is not simple . . . because language is not simple" (Komatsu 1997, 1, translation modified). Not simple, but (as the recently rediscovered notes for a book on linguistic theory put it) "dual." Language has a "dual essence":

> There is no linguistic entity among those available to us which is simple, since even when reduced to its simplest expression it requires that account be taken simultaneously of a sign and a meaning . . . [and] if the unity of each linguistic entity itself results from a complex reality consisting of a union of elements, it results moreover from a union of a very particular sort in that there is nothing in common in essence between a sign and that which it signifies.
>
> (*WGL* 2006, 5; *ELG* 2002, 20)

If language's essence is "dual," and if Saussure means what he says here, then there is no essence of language. "Dual essence" is an almost ungrammatical statement in the language of Aristotelian philosophy from which the word "essence" comes: the essence of a thing should be single; otherwise, it is a mere lumping together of separate essences. Would it not be more fitting to concede that in language two "essences" are conjoined? But to divide language into its subparts is to lose what makes it language. Language is primarily a relation between two sets of things that have "nothing in common in essence" between them. Their binding is obligatory but irrational. This relation is brought out much more strongly in the manuscript notes than in the *Course* of 1916:

> A linguistic entity is unique in that it involves the association of two distinct elements. If we were invited first to determine the chemical classification of a sheet of iron, gold, or

> copper, and then the zoological species of a horse, cow, or sheep, these would be two easy tasks. But if we were asked to determine what "species" is represented by the odd combination of an iron plaque attached to a horse, a gold plate on a cow, or a sheep adorned with something copper, we would exclaim that the task is absurd. The linguist has to realize that it is precisely this absurd task that faces him right from the very outset.
>
> (*WLG* 2006, 3; *ELG* 2002, 18)

"What species?" That is, "what essence"? This combination of gold and cow yields two separate and unrelated essences. A dual essence is no essence at all. An analogous passage in the *CLG* of 1916, long thought to be a result of misunderstanding by Saussure's hearers, deliberately misemploys another set of terms from the Aristotelian vocabulary: "in language, a concept is a quality of its phonic substance just as a particular slice of sound is a quality of the concept" (*CGL* 1959, 103; *CLG* 1972, 144–145). The students heard correctly, and the editors did not swerve, as Engler's edition confirms (*CLG* 1968–1974, xi, 232–233). In this passage, an apparently loose and vague expression gives rise, when taken in a sharper sense, to a scandal in the house of science. For qualities normally adhere in substances: mortality is part of Socrates; hardness belongs to a stone (Aristotle 1984, 14–16). Thus nasality might, without startling anyone, be a "quality of the phonic substance" of a syllable. But Saussure here makes the concept a quality of the sound and the sound a quality of the thought, as if, to take up the manuscript's analogy, the iron were to be horselike, the gold to exhibit bovine characteristics, and the sheep, cuprous ones. The philosophical malapropism of the 1916 sentence hints that language is the object of an unnatural science, where qualities are found wandering outside the material envelopes of their substances.

Such anomalies are a normal part of linguistic epistemology. Saussure will be their critic, but he will also present them as irreducible to any superior method:

Having named a certain object, instituted the point of view A, which has absolutely no existence except in the A category, and which would not even be a delimited thing except in the A category, it is perhaps possible (in certain cases) to look at how this object is presented in the A category, as seen from the viewpoint of B.

In that instance, is one seeing things from viewpoint A, or viewpoint B? . . . The most difficult, but the most salutary, of linguistic truths to grasp, is to comprehend that in such a case one has on the contrary not ceased to remain basically within the A point of view, by the very fact that one is making use of a term in the A category, the very notion of which would escape us if seen from B.

Thus, many linguists believe that they have positioned themselves within the physiological-acoustics field when they abstract from the meaning of a word so as to consider its vocal elements. Thus, they state that from the vocal point of view the [French] word *champ* is identical to the word *chant*, saying that a word is made up of a vocal aspect, which is to be examined, plus another aspect, etc. But where does the idea come from in the first place that there is a *word* which has then to be considered from different points of view? . . .

Hence in linguistics one constantly considers in the B category *a* objects which really belong to A and not to B; and in the A category *b* objects which belong to B but not to A, etc. . . . [To illustrate with the example given: in order to express the phonetic identity of *champ* and *chant*, the linguist must refer to them as "words"—though the "word" is a unit without reality for phonetics.]

A vast vicious circle which cannot be broken except by replacing once and for all in linguistics the discussion of "facts" with the discussion of points of view.

(*WGL* 2006, 9; *ELG* 2002, 23–24)

To be a speaker of a language means, first of all, adopting a "point of view" for which the cow and the plaque of gold form a single thing: a sign, the forced combination of a signifier (a group of vocal sounds; an arrangement of carved, painted, or printed lines; a sequence of semaphore flags; a gesture; a string of zeroes and ones) with a signified (a name, a concept, an impression, an emotion). Moreover, any signifier can be the signified of another signifier. The written word can be the signifier of the spoken word, or vice versa. *A* can be the signifier of a certain speech sound, of the first item in a series, of a musical note, of an exhibit, of a long poem by Louis Zukofsky, and so forth. What holds the signified and signifier together is a relation, and this relation is nothing other than the sign; the sign is nothing other than this relation.

On the sign, the *CLG* of 1916 is more discreet than the manuscript notes and therefore invites misunderstanding. "The linguistic sign unites, not a thing and a name"—this crucial formulation is worth repeating—"but a concept and a sound-image" (*CGL* 1959, 66; *CLG* 1972, 98). No one will object to a thesis so gently put, but, despite it, Saussure's readers are always sliding back into the error of "nomenclature." The little drawings representing the sign as a bubble divided into two halves, signified on top, signifier on the bottom, suggest that the sign is a whole that can be analytically divided into parts (as if *sign* = *signifier* + *signified*) and that these parts fit together like two halves of a split egg. Symmetrical to each other, these halves seem as inseparable as the front and back sides of a single "sheet of paper" (*CGL* 1959, 113; *CLG* 1972, 157). But this would be to naturalize the sign, to make it into a thing, to offer it a position in reality that would confer on it an essence. Such optimistic visions of the sign are commonplace in paraphrases of Saussure, easily found by searching for class notes on the Internet. The surreal combinations of farm animals and metals that the manuscript notes present as typical of the sign do a much better job of bringing to mind the profoundly contingent, irrational, historical character of the sign-relation (cf. de Mauro in *CLG* 1972, 448). Somebody had to go out and hang the plaque of iron on that horse, but why?

Yet once the sign is established, it becomes indivisible (this is the context to which the famous sheet of paper applies). The "certain slice of sound" becomes the outline of a "certain concept" *because*, not although, there is no basis in reason for the two to cohere. Speaking a language is a steady matter of considering "in the A category *b* objects which belong to B but not to A," using sound to leverage thought.

As Simon Bouquet has shown in great detail, the epistemology of linguistics in Saussure threatened to cut him off, as a matter of conscience, from the assumptions that guided the kind of linguistics he did in the first part of his career. To a radical skeptic like Saussure, what legitimated linguistics as a positive field of knowledge is indistinguishable from its methodological blunders. The great philologists of the nineteenth century studied the history of words and worked out comparisons among languages belonging to a few families (starting with Indo-European). But in order to make this enterprise possible, they had to grant the entities of language—words, roots, conjugation patterns, sound—a persistent identity over time and space. This assumption Saussure was unable to make. The distinction he proposed in the *Course* between diachrony and synchrony was not intended to split linguistics down the middle and create a profession of linguists who know nothing about history and philology but rather to solve a problem that had never been recognized as such or had always been leapt over by faith and intuition. To take seriously a small matter, it is nonsense to say, for example, that the *a* of Latin *facio* ("I make") "turns into" an *i* when the verb is extended by a prefix to become *conficio* ("I bring together"). It is only on the blackboard that the *a* turns into an *i*. In the past, presumably, people said *facio* side by side with *confacio*, and then after a time they were saying *facio* side by side with *conficio*, the shortened form. But at no moment could anyone have observed *facio* turning into *-ficio*. When recognized for what it is, a useful shorthand rule that the learner can generalize to cover a number of other cases of Latin compound verbs, there is no harm in it, but if thought to be a description of the behavior of speakers, it projects into history a process that happens inside our minds. The literature of historical linguistics is full of such retrojections.

To refrain from substantializing analogies as events, Saussure would rewrite any historical or diachronic proposition as a series of synchronic states, each of which exhibits a somewhat different organization from those before and after it. In this way, rather than saying that Latin *civitas* became French *cité* and Spanish *ciudad*, or the like, the linguist would represent the term "city" as a node in a double network of ever-changing sound-patterns (*CGL* 1959, 66; *CLG* 1972, 98) and semantic units, three phases of which have just been enumerated, with many more needing to be added before we can have anything like an account of the "changes" that produced *cité* and *ciudad*.

Far from being a "binary opposition" that would impose an exclusionary taboo on linguists, the difference between synchronic and diachronic linguistics should have resolved into a distinction between representation that fits into a single synchronic frame and representation that requires a series of such frames. Here again the editors of the *CLG* of 1916 damaged Saussure's argument by overstating it. Were we to take the editors at their word, historical linguistics would be inaccessible to the linguist attentive to structure: they make Saussure say, "Since changes never affect the system as a whole but rather one or another of its elements, they can be studied only outside the system" (*CGL* 1959, 87; *CLG* 1972, 124). But Georges Dégallier's notes say at the corresponding point: "Language is a system, and in any system, one must consider the whole; that is what makes the system. But changes never operate on the entirety of a system, but on partial points. The change will make itself felt on the system by solidarity, but the fact will have occurred on a special point. Language being a system, one cannot follow the two things simultaneously" (*CLG* 1968–1974, 191). This does not mean that one cannot follow the two things and still be a linguist.

The effort to do without convenient illusions and describe accurately what is going on in the odd realm of language, or in the minds that try to observe it, gave Saussure little satisfaction. His critique of linguistic reason joined the other projects of his Geneva years in terminal incompleteness. The Saussure of the *CLG* of 1916 is a reconstruction and a projection. Not only a memory in the minds of his former students, he became what they wanted him to be, if that will serve as an explanation for the overdrawn contrasts, the excluded middles, the categorical affirmations and denials that have survived in some of the most vigorously disseminated versions of Saussure. The fallacious, self-contradictory Saussure is also, it must be admitted, exactly what his opponents wanted him to be: an exemplar of scholarly hubris. Among the many possible Saussures, the Saussure some readers have long desired to meet, the conjectural "real Saussure," the *Saussure who understands Saussure* emerges hesitantly from the variant notes and the manuscript materials. A reprinting of the 1959 translation of the 1916 *Course* cannot fail to evoke him.

The Materiality of the Sign: Solving the Problem of "Sensations" and "Ideas"

No reader of the *Course* can fail to see that the signifier is "material," says Saussure, because it is "sensory" (*CGL* 1959, 66; *CLG* 1972, 98). Viewing Saussure within the history of the philosophy of sense, as Hans Aarsleff does (1982), makes Saussure's materiality a foregone conclusion. But Saussure's materiality is, in good sensory tradition, impressionistic, not objective. Its emphasis on the physical is of a "psychological character" (*CGL* 1959, 66; *CLG* 1972, 98). The signifier is "not the material sound, a purely physical thing, but the psychological imprint of the sound, the impression that it makes on our senses" (*CGL* 1959, 66; *CLG* 1972, 98). In this sense, the signifier is always already a signified, just as the signified, *mutatis mutandis*, is always another signifier.

The psychological note should remind us that the history of the philosophy of sense that begins with Locke finds its resolution not only with Saussure himself but also with Freud. Bergson is the turning point or crisis moment in this history. For Saussure's student Charles Bally, the path from Bergson to Saussure was plain (Médina 1985). Bergson functions as precursor for Saussure and Freud alike, both of whom solve the problems he cannot. They put them on a securely impressionistic plane, and with good precedent. With Hume, Locke's ban on the Platonic notion of inherent ideas to explain thinking finds new working terms, which derive, with good humor on Hume's part, from the vocabulary of medieval medicine. The medieval distinction between body and soul had its medical counterpart in the difference between "sensations" and "ideas." Hume turns this distinction into a fresh way of thinking about the relationship between the sensory and the conceptual. This is the simple manner in which he structures the history of sensory philosophy that makes Saussure's place in it abundantly clear. "Sensations" and "ideas"—"sensations" and "impressions" (1748, 99) in Hume's own vocabulary—become "signifier" and "signified." Hume's concern with how associations between the sensory and the conceptual take place centers on how to find a mechanism or dynamic—an "economy," to use the term Freud will use—that joins them. This Hume himself accomplishes by showing how "resemblance" and "contiguity" (101)—metaphor and metonymy—are the chief mechanisms in what is already a notion of the sign, or what Hume calls a "necessary connexion" (145).

"Necessary connexion" is, as it will be for Pater, "habit": "The mind," says Hume, "is carried by habit, upon the appearance of one event, to expect its usual attendant, and to believe, that it will exist. This connexion, therefore, which we feel in the mind, this customary transition of the imagination from one object to its usual attendant, is the sentiment or impression, from which we form the idea of power or necessary connexion" (145).

In order to explain "fresh" impressions, "necessary connexion" becomes a part of what Hume calls "a customary connexion" (147) in a hierarchy of association. "Customary connexion" is really a recognition of sameness in a field of otherwise slightly different "impressions" (147): the second-order construction of ideas that have many contributing originals but no single or unique one. As in Derrida's description of the Freudian psychical apparatus (1967b), "fresh" impressions may occur simultaneously with the retention of past ones. This is hardly a philosophy of consciousness. Consciousness is supererogatory. Hume has, like Saussure and like Freud, invented a doctrine of the unconscious, together with a new notion of time.

The philosophy of sense includes in its history the history of literary criticism, too. Our example from Samuel Johnson well represents eighteenth-century thinking about reference as a question of "association" between a sense perception and an "idea." Like his contemporary Hume, Johnson is by no means Saussure's sole precursor in English in pointing out the materiality of signification. Wordsworth makes this dimension of Johnson's thinking even sharper in his own prefatory remarks to *Lyrical Ballads* (1800–1802). As with Johnson in the preface to the *Dictionary*, what is important to Wordsworth in the preface to *Lyrical Ballads* is that the reader sees that writing is not mimetic. It is made up—at least with the birth of the novel and with Wordsworth's own poetry—of "the real language of men in a state of vivid sensation" (1800–1802, 241). "The real language of men" and literary language are, says Wordsworth, "of the same substance" (253). The material metaphor—"substance"—is noteworthy. Like the words of an eighteenth-century novel or newspaper, or like Wordsworth's own verse, endlessly revised until the end of his life in the case of *The Prelude* (1850), literary language and what it represents do not stand in a hierarchical relation to each other. Literary language does not, from a summit, copy life below. Johnson jests about this pretension in his reflections on the garret (1751), whose loftlike views of the street below represent the pretensions of the self-exiled artist who disdainfully surveys the crowd beneath him. For Wordsworth, literary language and the life it describes are, as they are in Johnson, continuous. They both reside on the ground floor. They are in "substance" one and the same. They are made up of the same material: "the real language of men." Baudelaire will make this belief concrete by taking the artist out of the loft and into the street in "The Painter of Modern Life" (1863).

Wordsworth's achievement is dauntingly ambitious philosophically, and in a way that one does not expect from him. Like Hume, he provides us with an epistemology of perception, an epistemology of epistemology. No determinist, Wordsworth wonders "in what manner language and the human mind act and react" (1800–1802, 243). This is really to ask what the nature of the reciprocity is between species and environment, in the human case a reciprocity not between "mind" and "nature" but between "mind" and "language." They are, materially, of a piece, but it is their exchange as "impressions" one upon the other that both creates and separates them. Indeed, it separates them by joining them, just as it joins them by means of their separation. Like Freud's *Beyond the Pleasure Principle* (1920), Wordsworth's preface shows the organism emerging from the environment in a defensive posture. It does so in order to protect itself from the stimulation that continually threatens it. It becomes alienated from the environment in order to survive. "The primary laws of our nature" (1800–1802, 245), as a seemingly naturalist Wordsworth calls them, are actually a system of exchange between species and landscape, mind and language. The key remains impressionistic—"the manner in which we associate ideas in a state of excitement" (245). As with Coleridge, Wordsworth's philosophical origins are in the associative tradition of Hume and David Hartley. The relation between "ideas" and "sensations" (258), as nineteenth-century science will also call them, is precisely what custom structures. Custom structures nothing less than this interrelationship. "Continued influxes of feeling," says Wordsworth, are "modified and directed by our thoughts, which are"—here is the surprise—"the representatives of all our past feelings" (246). The formulation of a series of buffers is a refinement of Hume's doctrine of association and a good example of it. Prior experience or predilection affects how we receive new feelings or stimulation. "Thought"—majestic "thought"—is no more than "the representative . . . of all"—all—"our past feelings." The prophecy of Freud's equally surprising definition of "instinct" in 1915 is astonishing: "the psychical representative of the stimuli originating from within the organism and reaching the mind" (14:122). The implication here is also astonishing, well before the Freudian fact. For Wordsworth, "thought" is not only "feeling"; "feeling," necessarily, is also "thought." And custom—the new lord, custom—structures thought and feeling alike because it is custom that structures whatever historical interrelationship thought and feeling, sensation and idea may have. This is already Saussure to a fault.

Saussure's largely unexamined relation to Bergson later in the nineteenth century very clearly places him, as it does Freud, at the conclusion of this history. The need to solve the question of the nature of the bond between "sensations" and "ideas" comes to a head with the pressure that experimental psychology brings to bear on philosophical thinking about sense and meaning with Gustav Fechner's *Elements of Psychophysics* in 1860. A professor of philosophy at Leipzig, also the center of linguistics where Saussure had taken his doctorate in 1880, Fechner's influence was widespread, particularly the way in which he raised, for the first time, questions regarding the relation between thought and perception from a clinical point of view. Its penumbra well prepared Saussure for what he would encounter when he moved to Paris later that same year. Saussure was resident in Paris from 1880 to 1891, the years of Bergson's ascendance. Like Freud, who attended Charcot's lectures in Paris in 1885 and 1886, Saussure was doubtless versed in the terms of Bergson's attempt to provide a mechanism for the relation between "sensations" and "ideas" in his influential dissertation, which was published as the *Essay on Time and Consciousness* in 1889. With a fine rigor, Bergson invents, before the fact, an almost psychoanalytic distinction between what he calls the "affective" and the "representative" (1889, 42) or, in a Freudian vocabulary, "affect" and "idea." It is also a Saussurean invention, a distinction between signifier and signified. The *Essay*'s formulation of the relation between "sensations" and "ideas" is in retrospect very familiar: "I do not see how . . . differences of sensation would be interpreted by our consciousness as differences of quantity unless we connected them with the reactions which usually accompany them, and which are more or less extended and more or less important" (37–38).

Bergson has already established not only Saussure's distinction between signifier and signified but also Freud's distinction between "quantity" and "quality." But he requires "consciousness" to validate the link between "quantity" and our "reactions" to it in order to know that the link has occurred. Here is the final step—the Saussurean step—that Bergson cannot take. He requires, unlike Saussure or Freud, the category of consciousness to vouchsafe the link between signifier and signified, even though the practical life of language assures us that the ease with which language is used makes unconscious life necessary to assume. This Bergson admits when he says that meaning is simply "convention" (64). Yet his philosophy of consciousness prohibits him from accepting the Saussurean consequences. That the idea that is linked to a sensation is arbitrary because it is conventional is what disturbs Bergson most of all.

Saussure's relation to Bergson makes his relation to Freud inevitable. Freud's neurological background and the model it provides for psychical representation is the widest frame we have for understanding Saussure's own materiality. It also allows us to see how Freud and Saussure alike solve the problem of "sensations" and "ideas" that Bergson cannot. No wonder the young Lévi-Strauss reports a deep frustration that his teachers lionized Bergson rather than Saussure and Freud when attempting to solve problems of method:

> They were more intent on Bergson's *Essai sur les données immédiates de la conscience* than on F. de Saussure's *Cours de linguistique générale*. Next, Freud's work showed me that the oppositions did not really exist in this form, since it is precisely the most apparently emotional behavior, the least rational procedures and so-called pre-logical manifestations which are at the same time the most meaningful.
>
> (1955, 55)

Lévi-Strauss saw that Freud and Saussure both invent vocabularies to describe what Bergson does not. For Freud, beginning with the *Project for a Scientific Psychology* (1895), "quantity" is the "signifier," "quality" the "signified." The signifier is the physical, the impact or "impression" of stimuli on the senses, whether the rush of the wind, or the word. The signified is the "idea" with which it is joined by "association" and that rises up as though within it. Signifier and signified are always already each other. In *The Interpretation of Dreams* (1900, 5:528), the signified is a "memory-trace," as Freud calls it, of a prior sensory experience, or cluster of them. These associations, moreover, are a function of what a Saussurean Freud and Breuer have already called "chance coincidences" in the sign systems of conversion hysteria in 1895. "Chance coincidences," writes Breuer of the first great "hysteric," Anna O., "set up pathological associations and sensory or motor disturbances which thenceforward appeared along with the affect" (Freud 1895, 2:43). The association of signifier and signified is "arbitrary," to use Saussure's word (*CGL* 1959, 67; *CLG* 1972, 100), because it is only circumstantially determined. Emmy Von N.'s nervous cough in *Studies on Hysteria* is simply "the accident," as Freud puts it there, of its "connection" to its "precipitating cause" (1895, 2:4–5); Anna O.'s inability to drink is the result of her seeing the family dog drink from her English lady-companion's glass. "Because the sign is arbitrary," says Saussure in the *Course*, "it follows no law other than that of tradition, and because it is based on tradition, it is arbitrary" (*CGL* 1959, 74; *CLG* 1972, 108). No natural link attends the relation between signifier and signified, only a historical one. The sign is metaphysically arbitrary, but it is socially determined.

Saussure calls the systems of "unconscious" association (*CGL* 1959, 165; *CLG* 1972, 227) that link "sensations" and "ideas" a "storehouse" (*CGL* 1959, 15; *CLG* 1972, 32), "a social institution" (*CGL* 1959, 15; *CLG* 1972, 33), as he puts it, borrowing the latter term from the American linguist William Dwight Whitney, with whom he had allied himself in moving beyond his Neogrammarian teachers. Saussure's "storehouse" is a political unconscious. Like Freud's, Saussure's unconscious is a bustling thoroughfare, a perpetually shifting series of "pathways," to use Freud's term, with the resources of a lifetime at its disposal. Freud's unconscious transforms signs into "memory-traces," each of which is structured by the historical association of signifier and signified, "affect" or somatic stimulation, particularly anxiety, and "idea." "A trace is left in our psychical apparatus," writes Freud in the seventh chapter of *The Interpretation of Dreams*, "of the perceptions which impinge upon it. This we may describe as a 'memory-trace'; and to the function relating to it we give the name of 'memory.'" Not only that. "Memory-traces can only consist in permanent modifications of the elements of the system" (1900, 5:538). The "storehouse" of the unconscious is not only residual. If every new memory modifies those that precede it, then, like Saussure's view of change in language, the unconscious is structured by its cumulative differences from itself. It is a sponge, in Derrida's metaphor (1976), or, in Freud's, a "crust" (1920, 18:26). Languages, too, absorb events, to use Saussure's term, and transform their features over time. This is how phylogeny, in Freud's apothegm, recapitulates ontogeny. "French," says a hilarious Saussure, "does not *come* from Latin, it *is* Latin" (*WGL* 2006, 101; *ELG* 2002, 153). Nor does this process rob the subject of its history or its prehistory. It is what gives the subject both. In Freud's model, "sensation," especially in its earliest incarnations, is entirely somatic, although it is still impressionistic and memorial in its structure. Embryologically and during infancy, its signifiers as well as its signifieds—its "sensations" and its "ideas"—are made up of histological and neurological sign systems that generate and sustain cognition, long before unconscious language acquisition or even socially designated behavior make the organism psychological. This is the passage that Lacan calls the passage from need to desire. Nor is the later life of the psychological or speaking subject particularly conscious. Saussure himself abrogates the distinction between consciousness and the unconscious by using the term "signification" to account for both behavior and assumption. Freud does so in *The Ego and the Id* (1923) by declaring that the ego, too—once the seat of consciousness in Freud's own earlier thinking—is also largely unconscious.

Like Freud's unconscious systems of memory, Saussure's "storehouse" solves not only the problems accumulated by the history of the philosophy of sense. Once these problems are solved, the "storehouse" also joins the history of the philosophy of sense with the tradition of Hegel's philosophy of mind. Neurology gives way to psychology because "sensation" begins to associate with "idea." Soma gives way to cognition in a succession that makes cognition psychological in retrospect. The infant reacts to survival anxiety regarding the parents, particularly the mother, by creating a world of psychological fantasy that puts in place a belatedly psychologized family environment that was initially only sensory. Propped upon the cognitive, the psyche transforms it into the psychological, seeking recognition where it once sought only succor. The infant stipulates a dialectic with its parents as a defense against the mortal rigors it faces in order to endure their care. Desire emerges from need, and the psychological subject emerges from the biological one. As with Freud, Saussure's solution to the problem of the association of "sensations" and "ideas" that assures competent cognitive functioning is also a solution to the problem of the subject. Like Freud, Saussure requires a psychological subject to interpret, belatedly and unconsciously, the exigencies of sensory survival as a drama of love and hate, recognition and nonrecognition. The itinerary of the subject leads us to recognize, too, the temporal conditions that underwrite Saussure's dynamic world.

The Temporality of the Sign: Dialectic of Langue *and* Parole

Saussurean temporality is not a notion of time in the traditional sense of either human development or historical process. It is not linear but recursive. It is, however, deeply historicist and dialectical, though in a way that has not been clarified by New Historicism, a reaction-formation to both structuralism and psychoanalysis despite its own vexed relation to Michel Foucault, a consummate Saussurean and Freudian in his own right. Foucault's stately historiographies of difference well describe how it is semiotic negation that puts in place assumptions about life and behavior. What even Foucault lacks, however, as Sartre pointed out (1966), is an account of historical agency and, by definition, of historical process, a criticism typically leveled at Saussure (Jameson 1972; Eagleton 1983, 40, 97) but which Saussure himself easily engages and solves. What, then, is the real status of time in Saussure's work? It emerges in two registers, one hypothetical and heuristic, the other existential and, quite surprisingly, also didactic. The first is the relation between *langue* and *parole*, or language and speech, in Baskin's translation. The second is the relation of signifier and signified in the active life of the speaking subject, for whom the conditions required by the relationship of *langue* and *parole* impart a strangeness—an "uncanniness," to use Freud's word—to the lived experience of signification. They give it a relationship to time that links Saussure not only to psychoanalysis but also, and in a renewed way, to historiography and environmentalism. Both relationships hinge on the splendid notion of "reciprocal delimitation" (*CGL* 1959, 112; *CLG* 1972, 156), or double articulation, the way in which signifier and signified are associated, which lends an austere clarity to the homologous way in which *langue* and *parole* also intersect. Between them, they give an unsuspected power to Saussure's notion of both the subject in history and history in the subject.

Saussure's posthumously published work from the years prior to the lectures that make up the *Course* show him struggling to find a vocabulary appropriate to describe the reciprocal relationship of both *langue* and *parole* and signifier and signified, particularly in the broken odds and ends of the draft for the awkwardly titled *De l'essence double du langage* (*ELG* 2002, 15–88; *WGL* 2006, 1–60). Such a vocabulary would also solve the problem of how to represent the subject and how to represent historical process. Solving the problem of reference always comes first for Saussure, and it is the precondition for the solution to the problem of both the subject and of history. The reciprocity of *langue* and *parole*, signifier and signified, requires admitting time into the picture. It is the road to the understanding of Saussure's notion of the sign as an economy or dialectic. This economy or dialectic is, as de Mauro puts it, "*un jeu*," or "a play" (*CLG* 1972, 403), between signifier and signified, speech and language. Much as "sensations" and "ideas" come into being because of one another, *langue* and *parole*, signifier and signified also require each other to be what they are. This, of course, cannot be conceived of by means of a conventional, chronological notion of cause and effect but by a wholly different conception of time and how it works.

Saussure's work as a young linguist had led him, in his 1878 monograph on vowels and in his dissertation in 1880, to a notion of difference along the signifying chain that constitutes the signifier as a differential event, particularly in the way vowels shift in Sanskrit. It was the less mechanistic problem of difference in the signified that preoccupied him in subsequent years, leading, both in Paris and, later, in Geneva, to a similar though more startling solution regarding how we think and feel. Ever fearful of a lapse into a belief in "pre-existing ideas," as he puts it in the *Course* (*CGL* 1959, 112; *CLG* 1972, 155), Saussure is quick to point out in the *Écrits* that signifier and signified do not merely "correspond" (*WGL* 2006, 41; *ELG* 2002, 64). Their interplay is, as he puts it, "not so simple as that" (*WGL* 2006, 41; *ELG* 2002, 64). They are structured not as cause and effect but as a *chiasmus*, or crossing over. Signifier and signified are mutually constitutive, not mimetic, in their relationship. It is not a question of which comes first. "Each," says Saussure in the *Course*, "recalls the other" (*CGL* 1959, 66; *CLG* 1972, 99).

This investigation is what preoccupied Saussure more than any other in the years between his work on vowels and his coming to terms with the epistemological status of the signified in the *Course*. He came to reject the notion of a "correspondence" between signifier and signified, or of a word's "representing" an "idea," a notion that haunts him in the *Écrits* and that he exorcises in the *Course*:

> *Langue* has a physical side and a psychological side. But the unforgivable error which is found in every paragraph of the grammars is the belief that the psychological side is the *idea*, while the physical side is the *sound*, the *form*, the *word*.
>
> Things are rather more complicated than that.
>
> It is not true, indeed it is extremely false to imagine there to be a distinction between the sound and the idea. These are in fact inseparably one in our minds.
>
> (*WGL* 2006, 41; *ELG* 2002, 64)

Concepts function no differently from sound images. There is no signified as such, nothing to which a signifier simply "corresponds." Like the signifier, the signified is also produced by difference, a function of contrasts and comparisons among ideas that shift in time and that shift in relation to the different sensors with which they are associated. Signification is not, as he is quick to insist, one of simple but of "complicated" association. The word recalls Hume's "complex": "A first-order DIFFERENCE is constantly incorporated into a second-order difference and vice versa" (*WGL* 2006, 49; *ELG* 2002, 73). This kind of "complex" or "complicated" association makes room for the histories of difference that constitute the signified as well as the signifier—that is, of the history of accumulated signifiers that put signifieds in place. These proceed from "first-order" to "second-order" ones in an increasingly denser history of both the subject and the linguistic community in which he dwells. Saussure's vocabulary recalls Freud's and looks forward to Barthes's. It is no wonder, then, that "every sign . . . absorbs," says Saussure and thereby "elaborates *post hoc* a defined value" (*WGL* 2006, 60; *ELG* 2002, 88). Here both history and the future are positioned as functions of the necessities that signification requires. Absorption is the past; elaboration post hoc is what is to come. This is true for *langue* because it is true for *parole*, a dialectic of community and speaker every bit as real and exact as the dialectic between signifier and signified that actualizes them both in the daily life of the speaking subject. Saussure's "radical historicity," in Jonathan Culler's words, is "manifest" (1976, 28).

John E. Joseph maintains in his new biography of Saussure (in press) that reading Victor Egger's *La parole intérieure* in 1881 was what had solved the problem for Saussure, "all at once," as Joseph puts it (279). Egger, whose fame is lost to us now, had come very close indeed, particularly with his distinction between "*images-signes*" and "*des images constitutives de l'idée*" (1881, 241ff.). This was the route, in style if not in stance, to the distinction between signifier and signified. But Egger could not find the mechanism to connect them. The problem, writes Saussure in his reading notebook, is an "insufficient distinction between the passage from the *idea to the word* and the passage from the *word to the idea*" (quoted in Joseph in press). The problem, as it will be for Bergson and as it was for Hume, is what the factor is that allows the "passage" to occur.

Saussure's disappointment with Egger led him to his epochal conclusion. The factor, quite simply, is time. The "idea" is not qualitatively different from the "sensation." The "idea" is an earlier "sensation," one that had become a memory. "All the elements of language," says Joseph, "seem to qualify as memories" (in press). The "idea" was a past "sensation." The signified is not simply another signifier; it is a "retrospective" one (*WGL* 2006, 60; *ELG* 2002, 87). This also provided the dialectical edge lacking in empiricism. Because the hinge between "sensation" and "idea" is temporal, it is a dynamic and dialogical hinge that allows conversations between the past and the present—with others, with oneself, with culture—to unfold by necessity and at will. Freud called this "stream," to use William James's term (1890, 1:239), "free association." One intervenes in time through speech, gaining agency and recognition by participating in history and doing so with one's body.

This strenuous dialectic of speech and language, signifier and signified is what for Lacan is the dialectic of self and Other. How the subject knows and what the subject knows are one and the same thing. What the subject knows is the past. This is the temporal dissymmetry that Saussure's synchrony and diachrony present. They produce a series of familiar homologues. Hume's "resemblance" and "contiguity" become Saussure's "axis of simultaneities" and "axis of successions" (*CGL* 1959, 80; *CLG* 1972, 115), the "associative" and "syntagmatic" (*CGL* 1959, 122ff; *CLG* 1972, 170ff.), paradigm and syntagm. In 1956, they become Jakobson and Halle's metaphor and metonymy; in 1966, they become Genette's *récit* and *histoire*. The best novelistic example of their dialectical play is *Finnegans Wake* (1939), whose fundamental strategy is to highlight and exploit the axial structures that organize the flow of language; the novel's language moves items in each axis to the other and back again (see Heath 1972). Joyce even used Egger's term "*la parole intérieure*" to describe Édouard Dujardin's 1887 version of such a novelistic strategy when he inscribed the French translation of *Ulysses* to him (Ellmann 1959, 534n). Dujardin himself preferred the term "interior monologue," the revision of Egger's term by Paul Bourget in *Cosmopolis* (1893), although it had already been used by Dumas *père* almost fifty years earlier (1849, 132). Dujardin used it to title a book of his own on fictional technique in 1931 (see Santone 1999, 2009).

Saussure's *langue* and *parole* are complementary principles of being. Hardly dualities, they are difference as such. Their dialectic is the engine of both organic life and psychological desire. The subject lives this rift, or, rather, this tension between the axes of synchrony and diachrony, paradigm and syntagm, metaphor and metonymy, is what lives the subject. It testifies to the subject's life in time. Saussurean speech is, as both fact and metaphor, a sign of individual survival. Saussurean language is a sign of species survival.

Saussurean signification is also an environmental site. The subject's reaction to the environment produces, at one and the same time, whether embryologically or in infant development, both the internal world into which the subject flees and the external world that requires this flight. This is what Harold Bloom calls Freud's "catastrophe theory" of the psyche (1978). External and internal are produced in the reaction of the one to the other. Alan Bass translates Freud's *Bahnung* as "breaching" in order to stress, as James Strachey's milder "facilitation" does not, how mutual the production of inside and outside are in Freud's chiasmatic representation of time (see Derrida 1967b). Freud's "breaching" is Saussure's double articulation. Like speech and language or signifier and signified, inside and outside are created in a single, recursive gesture. Saussure's very authentic relation to Darwin resembles Freud's own. Saussure regards language development in the same way that Darwin regards the different development of the same species in different environments: "A language transported to a far-off locality," says Saussure in the *Écrits*, "will develop differently in two places" (*WGL* 2006, 204; *ELG* 2002, 291). This is because the response to the localities is different; language, like ecology, is interactive.

Freud's term for double articulation is deferred action. Later events, as he says in his "From the History of an Infantile Neurosis" (1918), give a new meaning to earlier ones, changing past and present in the process. This anamorphic posture gives the subject a heightened sense of its relation to time and grants the subject a greater, and ironic, sense of originality. It also leads inevitably to a stringent and new kind of historicism and to a negative historiography rather than to a positivist one. One recalls Saussure's description of the effect that a given occurrence in a signifying system has on the whole system. It is how T. S. Eliot describes the effect that the production of a new work of art has on prior artistic history in "Tradition and the Individual Talent":

> No poet, no artist of any art, has his complete meaning alone. His significance, his appreciation is the appreciation of his relation to the dead poets and artists. You cannot value him alone; you must set him, for contrast and comparison, among the dead. I mean this as a principle of aesthetic, not merely historical, criticism. The necessity that he shall conform, that he shall cohere, is not onesided; what happens when a new work of art is created is something that happens simultaneously to all the works of art which preceded it. The existing monuments form an ideal order among themselves, which is modified by the introduction of the new (the really new) work of art among them.
>
> (1919, 15)

This, of course, is also Foucault talking. New Historicism, with Foucault as its putative authorization, misses this key and enabling dimension of both Foucault's own recursive thought and his Saussurean procedures as a historian. They are negative because they are differential. What comes later puts what comes before in place. One sees the past by virtue of what one knows in the future. Thomas Laqueur (2003), for example, makes the mistake of assuming that Freud's essay on narcissism is simply one in a series of masturbation pamphlets whose history begins long before it, when in fact it is Freud's narcissism essay in 1914 that calls our attention only belatedly to the importance of autoeroticism and its literature as a historical topic. Indeed, primary or infantile narcissism is, for Freud in 1914, only a year after Saussure's death, an exemplary Saussurean *topos.* Here the child joins an image to what was hitherto an autonomic activity and converts autoerotism into autoeroticism. By finding an object, the child also finds itself as a subject. Lawrence Buell's remark that Darwin's "metaphor of selection . . . carries a different force in our time than in his" (1995, 284) is a far better example than Laqueur's of newer historicist and environmental thinking. It takes deferred action into account as the agent of historical process because it is its arbiter.

By the rule of double articulation, signifier and signified construct each other in a mutuality that produces different psychical worlds for different cultures. By the rule of colonialism, this difference is reduced to a minimum. "Speakers of different languages," in Harris's words, "will thus see things differently" (2001, 208). Frantz Fanon, who attended Lacan's lectures as a medical student in Paris, gives this link its clearest expression in his classic meditation on the colonial subject awash in the competing sign systems of oppressed and oppressor (1952). As Paul Gilroy points out (2004), the postcolonial subject is an exacerbated instance of the normative subject, its terms more plainly political, its identifications and objects of desire disconcerting.

If Saussure's temporality structures the reaction of subjects to their cultures, it also structures the reaction of cultures to their environment. The temporality of signification installs history in the subject, although the subject also changes history by reacting to the history that he confronts. Species and environment mutually condition each other because species react to the conditions that environments impose. The history of these adaptations is called genetics. Its "memory-traces" form the subject's phylogenetic heritage. Its study is called histology and neurology. The history of the subject's psychological adaptation to culture is called sociology. Saussure's theory of signification combines them all.

TRANSLATOR'S INTRODUCTION

Few other figures in the history of the science of language have commanded such lasting respect and inspired such varied accomplishments as Ferdinand de Saussure. Leonard Bloomfield justly credited the eminent Swiss professor with providing "a theoretic foundation to the newer trend in linguistics study," and European scholars have seldom failed to consider his views when dealing with any theoretical problem. But the full implications of his teachings, for both static and evolutionary studies, have still to be elaborated.

De Saussure succeeded in impressing his individual stamp on almost everything within his reach. At the age of twenty, while still a student at Leipzig, he published his monumental treatise on the Proto-Indo-European vocalic system. This treatise, though based on theories and facts that were common property in his day, is still recognized as the most inspired and exhaustive treatment of the Proto-Indo-European vocalism. He studied under Curtius, Hüschmann, Leskien, and Windisch, but his attempt to frame a coherent science of linguistics owes more to William Dwight Whitney's concept of the arbitrary nature of the sign than to the comparative studies of the neogrammarians. Despite the paucity of his publications (some 600 pages during his lifetime), De Saussure's influence has been far-reaching. In Paris, where he taught first Germanic languages and then comparative grammar, and also served as secretary of the Linguistic Society of Paris (1881–1891), his influence on the development of linguistics was decisive. His first-hand studies of Phrygian inscriptions and Lithuanian dialects may have been responsible for some of the qualities that subsequently endeared him to his students at the University of Geneva, where he taught comparative grammar, Sanskrit

(1891–1907), and later general linguistics (1907–1911). His unique insight into the phenomenon of language brought to fruition the best of contemporary thinking and long years of patient investigation and penetrating thought.

The dominant philosophical system of each age makes its imprint on each step in the evolution of linguistic science. The nineteenth century had a fragmentary approach to reality which prevented scholars from getting beyond the immediate facts in matters of speech. To those investigators, language was simply an inventory or mechanical sum of the units used in speaking. Piecemeal studies precluded the development of an insight into the structure (*Gestalteinheit*, pattern, or whole) into which the fragmentary facts fit. The atomistic conception of speech, reflected in the historical studies of the comparative philologists, had to give way to the functional and structural conception of language. De Saussure was among the first to see that language is a self-contained system whose interdependent parts function and acquire value through their relationship to the whole.

By focusing attention on the distinctly human side of speech, i.e. the system of language, De Saussure gave unity and direction to his science. Until the publication of his work (later translated into German, Japanese, Russian, and Spanish), only those who enjoyed the privilege of close association with De Saussure had access to his theories. By making available an English translation of his *Course,* I hope to contribute toward the realization of his goal: the study of language in and for itself.

To all those who have given generously of their time and talents in the preparation of this translation, I offer heartfelt thanks: to Gerald Dykstra, Daniel Girard, Lennox Grey, Aileen Kitchin, and André Martinet of Columbia University; to Charles Bazell of Istanbul University; to Henri Frei, Robert Godel, and Edmond Sollberger of the University of Geneva; to Dwight Bolinger of Harvard University; to Rulon Wells of Yale University; and to my good friends Kenneth Jimenez, Paul Swart, and Hugh Whittemore. In making minor revisions for the reprinting of the *Course,* I have been guided by the remarks of M. Godel,

Professor Leger Brosnahan of the University of Maryland, and Professor Ralph Paul deGorog, who reviewed the *Course* in *The Modern Language Journal.*

Wade Baskin
Southeastern State College

PREFACE TO THE FIRST EDITION

We have often heard Ferdinand de Saussure lament the dearth of principles and methods that marked linguistics during his developmental period. Throughout his lifetime, he stubbornly continued to search out the laws that would give direction to his thought amid the chaos. Not until 1906, when he took the place of Joseph Wertheimer at the University of Geneva, was he able to make known the ideas that he had nurtured through so many years. Although he taught three courses in general linguistics—in 1906–1907, 1908–1909, and 1910–1911—his schedule forced him to devote half of each course to the history and description of the Indo-European languages, with the result that the basic part of his subject received considerably less attention than it merited.

All those who had the privilege of participating in his richly rewarding instruction regretted that no book had resulted from it. After his death, we hoped to find in his manuscripts, obligingly made available to us by Mme. de Saussure, a faithful or at least an adequate outline of his inspiring lectures. At first we thought that we might simply collate F. de Saussure's personal notes and the notes of his students. We were grossly misled. We found nothing—or almost nothing—that resembled his students' notebooks. As soon as they had served their purpose, F. de Saussure destroyed the rough drafts of the outlines used for his lectures. In the drawers of his secretary we found only older outlines which, although certainly not worthless, could not be integrated into the material of the three courses.

Our discovery was all the more disappointing since professorial duties had made it impossible for us to attend F. de Saussure's last lectures—and these mark just as brilliant a step in his career as the much earlier one that had witnessed the appearance of his treatise on the vocalic system of Proto-Indo-European.

We had to fall back on the notes collected by students during the course of his three series of lectures. Very complete notebooks were placed at our disposal: for the first two courses, by Messrs. Louis Caille, Léopold Gautier, Paul Regard, and Albert Riedlinger; for the third—the most important—by Mme. Albert Sechehaye and by Messrs. George Dégallier and Francis Joseph. We are indebted to M. Louis Brütsch for notes on one special point. All these contributors deserve our sincere thanks. We also wish to express our profound gratitude to M. Jules Ronjat, the eminent Romance scholar, who was kind enough to review the manuscript before printing, and whose suggestions were invaluable.

What were we to do with our materials? First, the task of criticism. For each course and for each detail of the course, we had to compare all versions and reconstruct F. de Saussure's thought from faint, sometimes conflicting, hints. For the first two courses we were able to enlist the services of M. Riedlinger, one of the students who have followed the thought of the master with the greatest interest; his work was most valuable. For the third course one of us, A. Sechehaye, performed the same detailed task of collating and synthesizing the material.

But after that? Oral delivery, which is often contradictory in form to written exposition, posed the greatest difficulties. Besides, F. de Saussure was one of those men who never stand still; his thought evolved in all directions without ever contradicting itself as a result. To publish everything in the original form was impossible; the repetitions—inevitable in free oral presentation—overlappings, and variant formulations would lend a motley appearance to such a publication. To limit the book to a single course—and which one?—was to deprive the reader of the rich and varied content of the other two courses; by itself the third, the most definitive of the three courses, would not give a complete accounting of the theories and methods of F. de Saussure.

One suggestion was that we publish certain particularly original passages without change. This idea was appealing at first, but soon it became obvious that we would be distorting the thought of our master if we presented but fragments of a plan whose value stands out only in its totality.

We reached a bolder but also, we think, a more rational solution: to attempt a reconstruction, a synthesis, by using the third course as a starting point and by using all other materials at our disposal, including the personal notes of F. de Saussure, as supplementary sources. The problem of re-creating F. de Saussure's thought was all the more difficult because the re-creation had to be wholly objective. At each point we had to get to the crux of each particular thought by trying to see its definitive form in the light of the whole system. We had first to weed out variations and irregularities characteristic of oral delivery, then to fit the thought into its natural framework and present each part of it in the order intended by the author even when his intention, not always apparent, had to be surmised.

From this work of assimilation and reconstruction was born the book that we offer, not without apprehension, to the enlightened public and to all friends of linguistics.

Our aim was to draw together an organic whole by omitting nothing that might contribute to the overall impression. But for that very reason, we shall probably be criticized on two counts.

First, critics will say that this "whole" is incomplete. In his teaching the master never pretended to examine all parts of linguistics or to devote the same attention to each of those examined; materially, he could not. Besides, his main concern was not that. Guided by some fundamental and personal principles which are found everywhere in his work—and which form the woof of this fabric which is as solid as it is varied—he tried to penetrate; only where these principles find particularly striking applications or where they apparently conflict with some theory did he try to encompass.

That is why certain disciplines, such as semantics, are hardly touched upon. We do not feel that these lacunae detract from the overall architecture. The absence of a "linguistics of speaking" is regrettable. This study, which had been promised to the students of the third course, would doubtlessly have had a place of honor; why his promise could not be kept is too well known. All we could do was to collect the fleeting impressions from the rough outlines of this project and put them into their natural place.

Conversely, critics may say that we have reproduced facts bearing on points developed by F. de Saussure's predecessors. Not everything in such an extensive treatise can be new. But if known principles are necessary for the understanding of a whole, shall we be condemned for not having omitted them? The chapter on phonetic changes, for example, includes things that have been said before, and perhaps more definitively; but, aside from the fact that this part contains many valuable and original details, even a superficial reading will show to what extent its omission would detract from an understanding of the principles upon which F. de Saussure erects his system of static linguistics.

We are aware of our responsibility to our critics. We are also aware of our responsibility to the author, who probably would not have authorized the publication of these pages.

This responsibility we accept wholly, and we would willingly bear it alone. Will the critics be able to distinguish between the teacher and his interpreters? We would be grateful to them if they would direct toward us the blows which it would be unjust to heap upon one whose memory is dear to us.

Geneva, July 1915. Charles Bally, Albert Sechehaye

PREFACE TO THE SECOND EDITION

The second edition is essentially the same as the first. The editors have made some slight changes designed to facilitate reading and clarify certain points. Ch. B. Alb. S.

PREFACE TO THE THIRD EDITION

With the exception of a few minute corrections, this edition is the same as the preceding. Ch. B. Alb. S.

Course in General Linguistics

INTRODUCTION

Chapter I

A GLANCE AT THE HISTORY OF LINGUISTICS

The science that has been developed around the facts of language passed through three stages before finding its true and unique object.

First something called "grammar" was studied. This study, initiated by the Greeks and continued mainly by the French, was based on logic. It lacked a scientific approach and was detached from language itself. Its only aim was to give rules for distinguishing between correct and incorrect forms; it was a normative discipline, far removed from actual observation, and its scope was limited.

Next appeared philology. A "philological" school had existed much earlier in Alexandria, but this name is more often applied to the scientific movement which was started by Friedrich August Wolf in 1777 and which continues to this day. Language is not its sole object. The early philologists sought especially to correct, interpret and comment upon written texts. Their studies also led to an interest in literary history, customs, institutions, etc.[1] They applied the methods of criticism for their own purposes. When they dealt with linguistic questions, it was for the express purpose of comparing texts of different periods, determining the language peculiar to each author, or deciphering and explaining inscriptions made in an archaic or obscure language. Doubtless these investigations broke the ground for historical linguistics. Ritschl's studies of Plautus are actually linguistic. But philological criticism is still deficient on one point: it follows the written language too slavishly

[1] At the risk of offending some readers, certain stylistic characteristics of the original French are retained. [Tr.] (The bracketed abbreviations *S.*, *Ed.* and *Tr.* indicate whether footnotes are to be attributed to De Saussure, to the editors of the *Cours de linguistique générale*, or to the translator.)

and neglects the living language. Moreover, it is concerned with little except Greek and Latin antiquity.

The third stage began when scholars discovered that languages can be compared with one another. This discovery was the origin of "comparative philology." In 1816, in a work entitled *Über das Conjugationssystem der Sanskritsprache*, Franz Bopp compared Sanskrit with German, Greek, Latin, etc. Bopp was not the first to record their similarities and state that all these languages belong to a single family. That had been done before him, notably by the English orientalist W. Jones (died in 1794); but Jones' few isolated statements do not prove that the significance and importance of comparison had been generally understood before 1816. While Bopp cannot be credited with the discovery that Sanskrit is related to certain languages of Europe and Asia, he did realize that the comparison of related languages could become the subject matter of an independent science. To illuminate one language by means of another, to explain the forms of one through the forms of the other, that is what no one had done before him.

Whether Bopp could have created his science—so quickly at least—without the prior discovery of Sanskrit is doubtful. With Sanskrit as a third witness beside Latin and Greek, Bopp had a larger and firmer basis for his studies. Fortunately, Sanskrit was exceptionally well-fitted to the role of illuminating the comparison.

For example, a comparison of the paradigms of Latin *genus* (*genus, generis, genere, genera, generum,* etc.) and Greek (*génos, géneos, génei, génea, genéōn,* etc.) reveals nothing. But the picture changes as soon as we add the corresponding Sanskrit series (*ǵanas, ǵanasas, ǵanasi, ǵanasu, ǵanasām,* etc.). A glance reveals the similarity between the Greek forms and the Latin forms. If we accept tentatively the hypothesis that *ǵanas* represents the primitive state—and this step facilitates explanation—then we conclude that *s* must have fallen in Greek forms wherever it occurred between two vowels. Next we conclude that *s* became *r* in Latin under the same conditions. Grammatically, then, the Sanskrit paradigm exemplifies the concept of radical, a unit (*ǵanas*) that is quite definite and stable. Latin and Greek had the same forms as Sanskrit only in their earlier stages. Here Sanskrit is instructive precisely because it has preserved all the Indo-European *s*'s. Of course

Sanskrit failed in other respects to preserve the features of the prototype; for instance, it had completely revolutionized the vocalic system. But in general the original elements that Sanskrit has preserved are remarkably helpful in research—and fate decreed that it was to clarify many points in the study of other languages.

Other distinguished linguists soon added to the contribution of Bopp: Jacob Grimm, the founder of Germanic studies (his *Deutsche Grammatik* was published from 1822 to 1836); Pott, whose etymological studies made a considerable amount of material available to linguists; Kuhn, whose works dealt with both linguistics and comparative mythology; the Indic scholars Benfey and Aufrecht, etc.

Finally, among the last representatives of the school, Max Müller, G. Curtius, and August Schleicher deserve special attention. In different ways, all three did much to advance comparative studies. Max Müller popularized them in his brilliant discussions (*Lessons in the Science of Language*, 1861); but his failing was a certain lack of conscientiousness. Curtius, a distinguished philologist known especially for his *Grundzüge der griechischen Etymologie* (1879), was one of the first to reconcile comparative philology with classical philology. The latter had watched the progress of the new science suspiciously, and each school had mistrusted the other. Schleicher was the first to try to codify the results of piecemeal investigations. His *Compendium der vergleichenden Grammatik der indogermanischen Sprachen* (1861–62) is more or less a systemization of the science founded by Bopp. His book, with its long record of service, recalls better than any other the broad outlines of the comparative school, which is the first chapter in the history of Indo-European linguistics.

But the comparative school, which had the indisputable merit of opening up a new and fruitful field, did not succeed in setting up the true science of linguistics. It failed to seek out the nature of its object of study. Obviously, without this elementary step, no science can develop a method.

The first mistake of the comparative philologists was also the source of all their other mistakes. In their investigations (which embraced only the Indo-European languages), they never asked themselves the meaning of their comparisons or the significance of the relations that they discovered. Their method was exclusively comparative, not historical. Of course comparison is required for any historical reconstruction, but by itself it cannot be conclusive. And the conclusion was all the more elusive whenever the comparative philologists looked upon the development of two languages as a naturalist might look upon the growth of two plants. For example Schleicher, who always invites us to start from Proto-Indo-European and thus seems in a sense to be a confirmed historian, has no hesitancy in saying that Greek *e* and *o* are two grades (*Stufen*) of the vocalic system. This is because Sanskrit has a system of vocalic alternations that suggests the notion of grades. Schleicher supposed that each language has to pass through those grades separately and in exactly the same way, just as plants of the same species pass through the same developmental stages independently of one another, and saw a reinforced grade of *e* in Greek *o* and a reinforced grade of *ă* in Sanskrit *ā*. The fact is that a Proto-Indo-European alternation was reflected differently in Greek and in Sanskrit without there being any necessary equivalence between the grammatical effects produced in either language (see pp. 158 ff.).

The exclusively comparative method brought in a set of false notions. Having no basis in reality, these notions simply could not reflect the facts of speech. Language was considered a specific sphere, a fourth natural kingdom; this led to methods of reasoning which would have caused astonishment in other sciences. Today one cannot read a dozen lines written at that time without being struck by absurdities of reasoning and by the terminology used to justify these absurdities.

But from the viewpoint of methodology, the mistakes of the comparative philologists are not without value; the mistakes of an infant science give a magnified picture of those made by anyone in the first stages of scientific research, and I shall have occasion to point out several of them in the course of this exposition.

Not until around 1870 did scholars begin to seek out the principles that govern the life of languages. Then they began to see that similarities between languages are only one side of the linguistic phenomenon, that comparison is only a means or method of reconstructing the facts.

Linguistics proper, which puts comparative studies in their

proper place, owes its origin to the study of the Romance and Germanic languages. Romance studies, begun by Diez—his *Grammatik der romanischen Sprachen* dates from 1836–38—were instrumental in bringing linguistics nearer to its true object. For Romance scholars enjoyed privileged conditions that were unknown to Indo-European scholars. They had direct access to Latin, the prototype of the Romance languages, and an abundance of texts allowed them to trace in detail the evolution of the different dialects; these two circumstances narrowed the field of conjecture and provided a remarkably solid frame for all their research. Germanic scholars were in a similar situation. Though they could not study the prototype directly, numerous texts enabled them to trace the history of the languages derived from Proto-Germanic through the course of many centuries. The Germanic scholars, coming to closer grips with reality than had the first Indo-European scholars, reached different conclusions.

A first impetus was given by the American scholar Whitney, the author of *Life and Growth of Language* (1875). Shortly afterwards a new school was formed by the neogrammarians (*Junggrammatiker*), whose leaders were all Germans: K. Brugmann and H. Osthoff; the Germanic scholars W. Braune, E. Sievers, H. Paul; the Slavic scholar Leskien, etc. Their contribution was in placing the results of comparative studies in their historical perspective and thus linking the facts in their natural order. Thanks to them, language is no longer looked upon as an organism that develops independently but as a product of the collective mind of linguistic groups. At the same time scholars realized how erroneous and insufficient were the notions of philology and comparative philology.[2] Still, in spite of the services that they rendered, the neogrammarians did not illuminate the whole question, and the fundamental problems of general linguistics still await solution.

[2] The new school, using a more realistic approach than had its predecessor, fought the terminology of the comparative school, and especially the illogical metaphors that it used. One no longer dared to say, "Language does this or that," or "life of language," etc. since language is not an entity and exists only within speakers. One must not go too far, however, and a compromise is in order. Certain metaphors are indispensable. To require that only words that correspond to the facts of speech be used is to pretend that these facts no longer perplex us. This is by no means true, and in some instances I shall not hesitate to use one of the expressions condemned at that time. [S.]

Chapter II

SUBJECT MATTER AND SCOPE OF LINGUISTICS; ITS RELATIONS WITH OTHER SCIENCES

The subject matter of linguistics comprises all manifestations of human speech, whether that of savages or civilized nations, or of archaic, classical or decadent periods. In each period the linguist must consider not only correct speech and flowery language, but all other forms of expression as well. And that is not all: since he is often unable to observe speech directly, he must consider written texts, for only through them can he reach idioms that are remote in time or space.

The scope of linguistics should be:

a) to describe and trace the history of all observable languages, which amounts to tracing the history of families of languages and reconstructing as far as possible the mother language of each family;

b) to determine the forces that are permanently and universally at work in all languages, and to deduce the general laws to which all specific historical phenomena can be reduced; and

c) to delimit and define itself.

Linguistics is very closely related to other sciences that sometimes borrow from its data, sometimes supply it with data. The lines of demarcation do not always show up clearly. For instance, linguistics must be carefully distinguished from ethnography and prehistory, where language is used merely to document. It must also be set apart from anthropology, which studies man solely from the viewpoint of his species, for language is a social fact. But must linguistics then be combined with sociology? What are the relationships between linguistics and social psychology? Everything in language is basically psychological, including its material and mechanical manifestations, such as sound changes; and since linguistics provides social psychology with such valuable data, is it not part and parcel of this discipline? Here I shall raise many similar questions; later I shall treat them at greater length.

The ties between linguistics and the physiology of sounds are less difficult to untangle. The relation is unilateral in the sense that the study of languages exacts clarifications from the science of the physiology of sounds but furnishes none in return. In any event, the two disciplines cannot be confused. The thing that constitutes language is, as I shall show later, unrelated to the phonic character of the linguistic sign.

As for philology, we have already drawn the line: it is distinct from linguistics despite points of contact between the two sciences and mutual services that they render.

Finally, of what use is linguistics? Very few people have clear ideas on this point, and this is not the place to specify them. But it is evident, for instance, that linguistic questions interest all who work with texts—historians, philologists, etc. Still more obvious is the importance of linguistics to general culture: in the lives of individuals and societies, speech is more important than anything else. That linguistics should continue to be the prerogative of a few specialists would be unthinkable—everyone is concerned with it in one way or another. But—and this is a paradoxical consequence of the interest that is fixed on linguistics—there is no other field in which so many absurd notions, prejudices, mirages, and fictions have sprung up. From the psychological viewpoint these errors are of interest, but the task of the linguist is, above all else, to condemn them and to dispel them as best he can.

Chapter III

THE OBJECT OF LINGUISTICS

1. *Definition of Language*

What is both the integral and concrete object of linguistics? The question is especially difficult; later we shall see why; here I wish merely to point up the difficulty.

Other sciences work with objects that are given in advance and that can then be considered from different viewpoints; but not linguistics. Someone pronounces the French word *nu* 'bare': a superficial observer would be tempted to call the word a concrete linguistic object; but a more careful examination would reveal successively three or four quite different things, depending on whether the word is considered as a sound, as the expression of an idea, as the equivalent of Latin *nudum*, etc. Far from it being the object that antedates the viewpoint, it would seem that it is the viewpoint that creates the object; besides, nothing tells us in advance that one way of considering the fact in question takes precedence over the others or is in any way superior to them.

Moreover, regardless of the viewpoint that we adopt, the linguistic phenomenon always has two related sides, each deriving its values from the other. For example:

1) Articulated syllables are acoustical impressions perceived by the ear, but the sounds would not exist without the vocal organs; an *n*, for example, exists only by virtue of the relation between the two sides. We simply cannot reduce language to sound or detach sound from oral articulation; reciprocally, we cannot define the movements of the vocal organs without taking into account the acoustical impression (see pp. 38 ff.).

2) But suppose that sound were a simple thing: would it constitute speech? No, it is only the instrument of thought; by itself, it has no existence. At this point a new and redoubtable relationship arises: a sound, a complex acoustical-vocal unit, combines in turn with an idea to form a complex physiological-psychological unit. But that is still not the complete picture.

3) Speech has both an individual and a social side, and we cannot conceive of one without the other. Besides:

4) Speech always implies both an established system and an evolution; at every moment it is an existing institution and a product of the past. To distinguish between the system and its history, between what it is and what it was, seems very simple at first glance; actually the two things are so closely related that we can scarcely keep them apart. Would we simplify the question by studying the linguistic phenomenon in its earliest stages—if we

began, for example, by studying the speech of children? No, for in dealing with speech, it is completely misleading to assume that the problem of early characteristics differs from the problem of permanent characteristics. We are left inside the vicious circle.

From whatever direction we approach the question, nowhere do we find the integral object of linguistics. Everywhere we are confronted with a dilemma: if we fix our attention on only one side of each problem, we run the risk of failing to perceive the dualities pointed out above; on the other hand, if we study speech from several viewpoints simultaneously, the object of linguistics appears to us as a confused mass of heterogeneous and unrelated things. Either procedure opens the door to several sciences—psychology, anthropology, normative grammar, philology, etc.—which are distinct from linguistics, but which might claim speech, in view of the faulty method of linguistics, as one of their objects.

As I see it there is only one solution to all the foregoing difficulties: *from the very outset we must put both feet on the ground of language and use language as the norm of all other manifestations of speech.* Actually, among so many dualities, language alone seems to lend itself to independent definition and provide a fulcrum that satisfies the mind.

But what is language [*langue*]? It is not to be confused with human speech [*langage*], of which it is only a definite part, though certainly an essential one. It is both a social product of the faculty of speech and a collection of necessary conventions that have been adopted by a social body to permit individuals to exercise that faculty. Taken as a whole, speech is many-sided and heterogeneous; straddling several areas simultaneously—physical, physiological, and psychological—it belongs both to the individual and to society; we cannot put it into any category of human facts, for we cannot discover its unity.

Language, on the contrary, is a self-contained whole and a principle of classification. As soon as we give language first place among the facts of speech, we introduce a natural order into a mass that lends itself to no other classification.

One might object to that principle of classification on the ground that since the use of speech is based on a natural faculty whereas language is something acquired and conventional, language should not take first place but should be subordinated to the natural instinct.

That objection is easily refuted.

First, no one has proved that speech, as it manifests itself when we speak, is entirely natural, i.e. that our vocal apparatus was designed for speaking just as our legs were designed for walking. Linguists are far from agreement on this point. For instance Whitney, to whom language is one of several social institutions, thinks that we use the vocal apparatus as the instrument of language purely through luck, for the sake of convenience: men might just as well have chosen gestures and used visual symbols instead of acoustical symbols. Doubtless his thesis is too dogmatic; language is not similar in all respects to other social institutions (see p. 73 f. and p. 75 f.); moreover, Whitney goes too far in saying that our choice happened to fall on the vocal organs; the choice was more or less imposed by nature. But on the essential point the American linguist is right: language is a convention, and the nature of the sign that is agreed upon does not matter. The question of the vocal apparatus obviously takes a secondary place in the problem of speech.

One definition of *articulated speech* might confirm that conclusion. In Latin, *articulus* means a member, part, or subdivision of a sequence; applied to speech, articulation designates either the subdivision of a spoken chain into syllables or the subdivision of the chain of meanings into significant units; *gegliederte Sprache* is used in the second sense in German. Using the second definition, we can say that what is natural to mankind is not oral speech but the faculty of constructing a language, i.e. a system of distinct signs corresponding to distinct ideas.

Broca discovered that the faculty of speech is localized in the third left frontal convolution; his discovery has been used to substantiate the attribution of a natural quality to speech. But we know that the same part of the brain is the center of *everything* that has to do with speech, including writing. The preceding statements, together with observations that have been made in different cases of aphasia resulting from lesion of the centers of localization, seem to indicate: (1) that the various disorders of oral speech are bound up in a hundred ways with those of written speech; and (2) that what is lost in all cases of aphasia or agraphia is less the faculty of producing a given sound or writing a given sign than the ability to evoke by means of an instrument, regardless of what it is, the signs of a regular system of speech. The obvious implication is that beyond the functioning of the various organs there exists a more general faculty which governs signs and which would be the linguistic faculty proper. And this brings us to the same conclusion as above.

To give language first place in the study of speech, we can advance a final argument: the faculty of articulating words—whether it is natural or not—is exercised only with the help of the instrument created by a collectivity and provided for its use; therefore, to say that language gives unity to speech is not fanciful.

2. *Place of Language in the Facts of Speech*

In order to separate from the whole of speech the part that belongs to language, we must examine the individual act from which the speaking-circuit can be reconstructed. The act requires the presence of at least two persons; that is the minimum number necessary to complete the circuit. Suppose that two people, A and B, are conversing with each other:

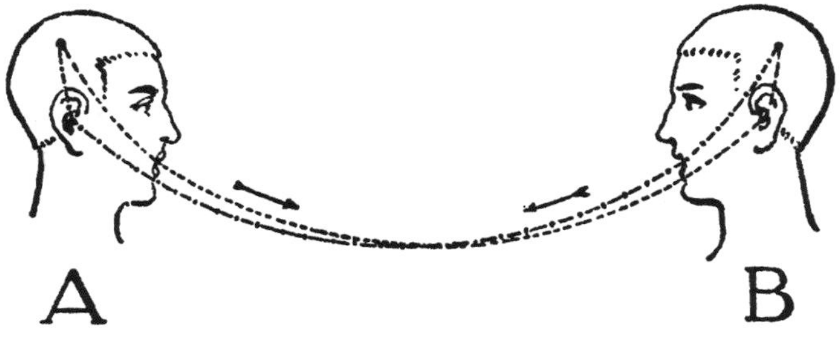

Suppose that the opening of the circuit is in A's brain, where mental facts (concepts) are associated with representations of the linguistic sounds (sound-images) that are used for their expression. A given concept unlocks a corresponding sound-image in the brain; this purely *psychological* phenomenon is followed in turn by a *physiological* process: the brain transmits an impulse corresponding to the image to the organs used in producing sounds. Then the sound waves travel from the mouth of A to the ear of B: a purely *physical* process. Next, the circuit continues in B, but the order is reversed: from the ear to the brain, the physiological transmission of the sound-image; in the brain, the psychological association of the image with the corresponding concept. If B then speaks, the new act will follow—from his brain to A's—exactly the same course as the first act and pass through the same successive phases, which I shall diagram as follows:

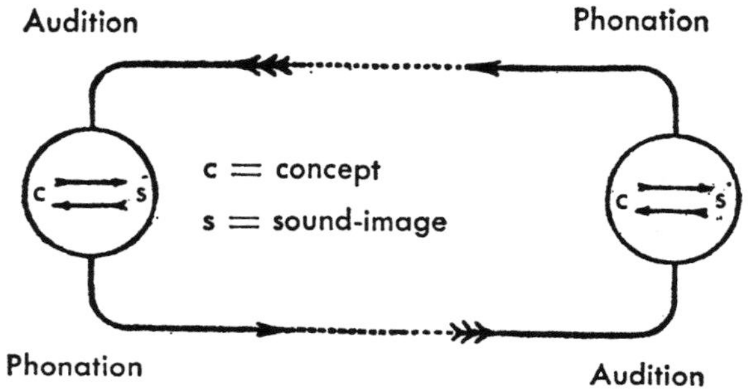

The preceding analysis does not purport to be complete. We might also single out the pure acoustical sensation, the identification of that sensation with the latent sound-image, the muscular image of phonation, etc. I have included only the elements thought to be essential, but the drawing brings out at a glance the distinction between the physical (sound waves), physiological (phonation and audition), and psychological parts (word-images and concepts). Indeed, we should not fail to note that the word-image stands apart from the sound itself and that it is just as psychological as the concept which is associated with it.

The circuit that I have outlined can be further divided into:

a) an outer part that includes the vibrations of the sounds which travel from the mouth to the ear, and an inner part that includes everything else;

b) a psychological and a nonpsychological part, the second including the physiological productions of the vocal organs as well as the physical facts that are outside the individual;

c) an active and a passive part: everything that goes from the associative center of the speaker to the ear of the listener is active, and everything that goes from the ear of the listener to his associative center is passive;

d) finally, everything that is active in the psychological part of the circuit is executive ($c \rightarrow s$), and everything that is passive is receptive ($s \rightarrow c$).

We should also add the associative and co-ordinating faculty that we find as soon as we leave isolated signs; this faculty plays the dominant role in the organization of language as a system (see pp. 122 ff.).

But to understand clearly the role of the associative and co-ordinating faculty, we must leave the individual act, which is only the embryo of speech, and approach the social fact.

Among all the individuals that are linked together by speech, some sort of average will be set up: all will reproduce—not exactly of course, but approximately—the same signs united with the same concepts.

How does the social crystallization of language come about? Which parts of the circuit are involved? For all parts probably do not participate equally in it.

The nonpsychological part can be rejected from the outset. When we hear people speaking a language that we do not know, we perceive the sounds but remain outside the social fact because we do not understand them.

Neither is the psychological part of the circuit wholly responsible: the executive side is missing, for execution is never carried out by the collectivity. Execution is always individual, and the individual is always its master: I shall call the executive side *speaking* [*parole*].

Through the functioning of the receptive and co-ordinating faculties, impressions that are perceptibly the same for all are made on the minds of speakers. How can that social product be pictured in such a way that language will stand apart from everything else? If we could embrace the sum of word-images stored in the minds of all individuals, we could identify the social bond that constitutes language. It is a storehouse filled by the members of a given community through their active use of speaking, a grammatical system that has a potential existence in each brain, or, more specifically, in the brains of a group of individuals. For language is not complete in any speaker; it exists perfectly only within a collectivity.

In separating language from speaking we are at the same time separating: (1) what is social from what is individual; and (2) what is essential from what is accessory and more or less accidental.

Language is not a function of the speaker; it is a product that is passively assimilated by the individual. It never requires premeditation, and reflection enters in only for the purpose of classification, which we shall take up later (pp. 122 ff.).

Speaking, on the contrary, is an individual act. It is wilful and intellectual. Within the act, we should distinguish between: (1) the combinations by which the speaker uses the language code for expressing his own thought; and (2) the psychophysical mechanism that allows him to exteriorize those combinations.

Note that I have defined things rather than words; these definitions are not endangered by certain ambiguous words that do not have identical meanings in different languages. For instance, German *Sprache* means both "language" and "speech"; *Rede* almost corresponds to "speaking" but adds the special connotation of "discourse." Latin *sermo* designates both "speech" and "speaking," while *lingua* means "language," etc. No word corresponds exactly to any of the notions specified above; that is why all definitions of words are made in vain; starting from words in defining things is a bad procedure.

To summarize, these are the characteristics of language:

1) Language is a well-defined object in the heterogeneous mass of speech facts. It can be localized in the limited segment of the speaking-circuit where an auditory image becomes associated with a concept. It is the social side of speech, outside the individual who can never create nor modify it by himself; it exists only by virtue of a sort of contract signed by the members of a community. Moreover, the individual must always serve an apprenticeship in order to learn the functioning of language; a child assimilates it only gradually. It is such a distinct thing that a man deprived of the use of speaking retains it provided that he understands the vocal signs that he hears.

2) Language, unlike speaking, is something that we can study separately. Although dead languages are no longer spoken, we can easily assimilate their linguistic organisms. We can dispense with the other elements of speech; indeed, the science of language is possible only if the other elements are excluded.

3) Whereas speech is heterogeneous, language, as defined, is homogeneous. It is a system of signs in which the only essential thing is the union of meanings and sound-images, and in which both parts of the sign are psychological.

4) Language is concrete, no less so than speaking; and this is a help in our study of it. Linguistic signs, though basically psychological, are not abstractions; associations which bear the stamp of collective approval—and which added together constitute language—are realities that have their seat in the brain. Besides, linguistic signs are tangible; it is possible to reduce them to conventional written symbols, whereas it would be impossible to provide detailed photographs of acts of speaking [*actes de parole*]; the pronunciation of even the smallest word represents an infinite number of muscular movements that could be identified and put into graphic form only with great difficulty. In language, on the contrary, there is only the sound-image, and the latter can be translated into a fixed visual image. For if we disregard the vast number of movements necessary for the realization of sound-images in speaking, we see that each sound-image is nothing more than the sum of a limited number of elements or phonemes that can in turn be called up by a corresponding number of written symbols (see pp. 61 ff.). The very possibility of putting the things that relate to language into graphic form allows dictionaries and grammars to represent it accurately, for language is a storehouse of sound-images, and writing is the tangible form of those images.

3. *Place of Language in Human Facts: Semiology*

The foregoing characteristics of language reveal an even more important characteristic. Language, once its boundaries have been marked off within the speech data, can be classified among human phenomena, whereas speech cannot.

We have just seen that language is a social institution; but several features set it apart from other political, legal, etc. institutions.

We must call in a new type of facts in order to illuminate the special nature of language.

Language is a system of signs that express ideas, and is therefore comparable to a system of writing, the alphabet of deaf-mutes, symbolic rites, polite formulas, military signals, etc. But it is the most important of all these systems.

A science that studies the life of signs within society is conceivable; it would be a part of social psychology and consequently of general psychology; I shall call it *semiology*[3] (from Greek *sēmeîon* 'sign'). Semiology would show what constitutes signs, what laws govern them. Since the science does not yet exist, no one can say what it would be; but it has a right to existence, a place staked out in advance. Linguistics is only a part of the general science of semiology; the laws discovered by semiology will be applicable to linguistics, and the latter will circumscribe a well-defined area within the mass of anthropological facts.

To determine the exact place of semiology is the task of the psychologist.[4] The task of the linguist is to find out what makes language a special system within the mass of semiological data. This issue will be taken up again later; here I wish merely to call attention to one thing: if I have succeeded in assigning linguistics a place among the sciences, it is because I have related it to semiology.

Why has semiology not yet been recognized as an independent science with its own object like all the other sciences? Linguists have been going around in circles: language, better than anything else, offers a basis for understanding the semiological problem; but language must, to put it correctly, be studied in itself; heretofore language has almost always been studied in connection with something else, from other viewpoints.

There is first of all the superficial notion of the general public: people see nothing more than a name-giving system in language (see p. 65), thereby prohibiting any research into its true nature.

[3] *Semiology* should not be confused with *semantics*, which studies changes in meaning, and which De Saussure did not treat methodically; the fundamental principle of semantics is formulated on page 75. [Ed.]

[4] Cf. A. Naville, *Classification des Sciences*, (2nd. ed.), p. 104. [Ed.] The scope of semiology (or semiotics) is treated at length in Charles Morris' *Signs, Language and Behavior* (New York: Prentice-Hall, 1946). [Tr.]

Then there is the viewpoint of the psychologist, who studies the sign-mechanism in the individual; this is the easiest method, but it does not lead beyond individual execution and does not reach the sign, which is social.

Or even when signs are studied from a social viewpoint, only the traits that attach language to the other social institutions—those that are more or less voluntary—are emphasized; as a result, the goal is by-passed and the specific characteristics of semiological systems in general and of language in particular are completely ignored. For the distinguishing characteristic of the sign—but the one that is least apparent at first sight—is that in some way it always eludes the individual or social will.

In short, the characteristic that distinguishes semiological systems from all other institutions shows up clearly only in language where it manifests itself in the things which are studied least, and the necessity or specific value of a semiological science is therefore not clearly recognized. But to me the language problem is mainly semiological, and all developments derive their significance from that important fact. If we are to discover the true nature of language we must learn what it has in common with all other semiological systems; linguistic forces that seem very important at first glance (e.g., the role of the vocal apparatus) will receive only secondary consideration if they serve only to set language apart from the other systems. This procedure will do more than to clarify the linguistic problem. By studying rites, customs, etc. as signs, I believe that we shall throw new light on the facts and point up the need for including them in a science of semiology and explaining them by its laws.

Chapter IV

LINGUISTICS OF LANGUAGE AND LINGUISTICS OF SPEAKING

In setting up the science of language within the overall study of speech, I have also outlined the whole of linguistics. All other elements of speech—those that constitute speaking—freely subordinate themselves to the first science, and it is by virtue of this subordination that the parts of linguistics find their natural place.

Consider, for example, the production of sounds necessary for speaking. The vocal organs are as external to language as are the electrical devices used in transmitting the Morse code to the code itself; and phonation, i.e., the execution of sound-images, in no way affects the system itself. Language is comparable to a symphony in that what the symphony actually is stands completely apart from how it is performed; the mistakes that musicians make in playing the symphony do not compromise this fact.

An argument against separating phonation from language might be phonetic changes, the alterations of the sounds which occur in speaking and which exert such a profound influence on the future of language itself. Do we really have the right to pretend that language exists independently of phonetic changes? Yes, for they affect only the material substance of words. If they attack language as a system of signs, it is only indirectly, through subsequent changes of interpretation; there is nothing phonetic in the phenomenon (see p. 84). Determining the causes of phonetic changes may be of interest, and the study of sounds will be helpful on this point; but none of this is essential: in the science of language, all we need do is to observe the transformations of sounds and to calculate their effects.

What I have said about phonation applies to all other parts of speaking. The activity of the speaker should be studied in a number of disciplines which have no place in linguistics except through their relation to language.

The study of speech is then twofold: its basic part—having as its object language, which is purely social and independent of the individual—is exclusively psychological; its secondary part—which has as its object the individual side of speech, i.e. speaking, including phonation—is psychophysical.

Doubtless the two objects are closely connected, each depending on the other: language is necessary if speaking is to be intelligible and produce all its effects; but speaking is necessary for the establishment of language, and historically its actuality always comes first. How would a speaker take it upon himself to associate an idea with a word-image if he had not first come across the association in an act of speaking? Moreover, we learn our mother language by listening to others; only after countless experiences is it deposited in our brain. Finally, speaking is what causes language to evolve: impressions gathered from listening to others modify our linguistic habits. Language and speaking are then interdependent; the former is both the instrument and the product of the latter. But their interdependence does not prevent their being two absolutely distinct things.

Language exists in the form of a sum of impressions deposited in the brain of each member of a community, almost like a dictionary of which identical copies have been distributed to each individual (see p. 13). Language exists in each individual, yet is common to all. Nor is it affected by the will of the depositaries. Its mode of existence is expressed by the formula:

$$1 + 1 + 1 + 1 \ldots = \text{I (collective pattern)}$$

What part does speaking play in the same community? It is the sum of what people say and includes: (a) individual combinations that depend on the will of speakers, and (b) equally wilful phonational acts that are necessary for the execution of these combinations.

Speaking is thus not a collective instrument; its manifestations are individual and momentary. In speaking there is only the sum of particular acts, as in the formula:

$$(1 + 1' + 1'' + 1''' \ldots)$$

For all the foregoing reasons, to consider language and speaking from the same viewpoint would be fanciful. Taken as a whole, speech cannot be studied, for it is not homogeneous; but the distinction and subordination proposed here clarify the whole issue.

Such is the first bifurcation that we find in trying to formulate the theory of speech. We must choose between two routes that cannot be followed simultaneously; they must be followed separately.

One might if really necessary apply the term linguistics to each of the two disciplines and speak of a linguistics of speaking. But that science must not be confused with linguistics proper, whose sole object is language.

I shall deal only with linguistics of language, and if I subsequently use material belonging to speaking to illustrate a point, I shall try never to erase the boundaries that separate the two domains.

Chapter V

INTERNAL AND EXTERNAL ELEMENTS OF LANGUAGE

My definition of language presupposes the exclusion of everything that is outside its organism or system—in a word, of everything known as "external linguistics." But external linguistics deals with many important things—the very ones that we think of when we begin the study of speech.

First and foremost come all the points where linguistics borders on ethnology, all the relations that link the history of a language and the history of a race or civilization. The close interaction of language and ethnography brings to mind the bonds that join linguistic phenomena proper (see pp. 7 f.). The culture of a nation exerts an influence on its language, and the language, on the other hand, is largely responsible for the nation.

Second come the relations between language and political history. Great historical events like the Roman conquest have an incalculable influence on a host of linguistic facts. Colonization, which is only one form that conquest may take, brings about changes in an idiom by transporting it into different surroundings. All kinds of facts could be cited as substantiating evidence. For instance, Norway adopted Danish when she united politically with Denmark; the Norwegians are trying today to throw off that linguistic influence. The internal politics of states is no less important to the life of languages; certain governments (like the Swiss) allow the coexistence of several idioms; others (like the French) strive for linguistic unity. An advanced state of civilization favors the development of special languages (juridical language, scientific terminology, etc.).

Here we come to a third point: the relations between language and all sorts of institutions (the Church, the school, etc.). All these institutions in turn are closely tied to the literary development of a language, a general phenomenon that is all the more inseparable from political history. At every point the literary language oversteps the boundaries that literature apparently marks off; we need only consider the influence of *salons*, the court, and national academies. Moreover, the literary language raises the important question of conflicts between it and local dialects (see pp. 195 ff.); the linguist must also examine the reciprocal relations of book language and the vernacular; for every literary language, being the product of the culture, finally breaks away from its natural sphere, the spoken language.

Finally, everything that relates to the geographical spreading of languages and dialectal splitting belongs to external linguistics. Doubtless the distinction between internal and external linguistics seems most paradoxical here, since the geographical phenomenon is so closely linked to the existence of any language; but geographical spreading and dialectal splitting do not actually affect the inner organism of an idiom.

Some have maintained that the foregoing issues simply cannot be separated from the study of language proper. The viewpoint has been prevalent especially since the placing of so much emphasis on "Realia."[5] Just as the inner organism of a plant is modified by alien forces (terrain, climate, etc.) does not the grammatical organism depend constantly on the external forces of linguistic change? It seems that we can scarcely give a satisfactory explanation of the technical terms and loan-words that abound in language without considering their development. Is it possible to distinguish the natural, organic growth of an idiom from its artificial forms, such as the literary language, which are due to external, and therefore inorganic forces? Common languages are always developing alongside local dialects.

[5] *Realien* is used in German to refer to all material facts of life, the shape, dimensions, and the like of objects, things, etc. Cf. the numerous works in German entitled Reallexicon. [Tr.]

I believe that the study of external linguistic phenomena is most fruitful; but to say that we cannot understand the internal linguistic organism without studying external phenomena is wrong. Take as an example the borrowing of foreign words. We observe from the outset that borrowing is not a constant force in the life of a language. In certain isolated valleys there are dialects that have never taken a single artificial term from the outside. Should we say that such idioms are outside the conditions of normal speech and that they require "teratological"[6] study inasmuch as they have never suffered admixture? More important still, a loan-word no longer counts as such whenever it is studied within a system; it exists only through its relation with, and opposition to, words associated with it, just like any other genuine sign. Knowledge of the circumstances that contributed to the development of a language, generally speaking, is never indispensable. For certain languages—e.g. Zend and Old Slavic—even the identity of the original speakers is unknown, but lack of such information in no way hinders us in studying these languages internally and learning about the transformations that they have undergone. In any case, separation of the two viewpoints is mandatory, and the more rigidly they are kept apart, the better it will be.

The best proof of the need for separating the two viewpoints is that each creates a distinct method. External linguistics can add detail to detail without being caught in the vise of a system. Each writer, for instance, will group as he sees fit facts about the spreading of a language beyond its territory. If he looks for the forces that created a literary language beside local dialects, he can always use simple enumeration. If he arranges the facts more or less systematically, he will do this solely for the sake of clarity.

In internal linguistics the picture differs completely. Just any arrangement will not do. Language is a system that has its own arrangement. Comparison with chess will bring out the point. In chess, what is external can be separated relatively easily from what is internal. The fact that the game passed from Persia to Europe is external; against that, everything having to do with its system and rules is internal. If I use ivory chessmen instead of wooden ones, the change has no effect on the system, but if I decrease or

[6] 'Pertaining to the study of monsters,' see p. 54, footnote. [Tr.]

increase the number of chessmen, this change has a profound effect on the "grammar" of the game. One must always distinguish between what is internal and what is external. In each instance one can determine the nature of the phenomenon by applying this rule: everything that changes the system in any way is internal.

Chapter VI

GRAPHIC REPRESENTATION OF LANGUAGE

1. *Need for Studying the Subject*

The concrete object of linguistic science is the social product deposited in the brain of each individual, i.e. language. But the product differs with linguistic groups: we have to work with languages. The linguist is obliged to acquaint himself with the greatest possible number of languages in order to determine what is universal in them by observing and comparing them.

But we generally learn about languages only through writing. Even in studying our native language, we constantly make use of written texts. The necessity of using written evidence increases when dealing with remote idioms, and all the more when studying idioms that no longer exist. We would have direct texts at our disposal in every instance only if people had always done what is now being done in Paris and Vienna. There, samples of all languages are being recorded. Even so, recorded specimens could be made available to others only through writing.

Writing, though unrelated to its inner system, is used continually to represent language. We cannot simply disregard it. We must be acquainted with its usefulness, shortcomings, and dangers.

2. *Influence of Writing; Reasons for Its Ascendance over the Spoken Form*

Language and writing are two distinct systems of signs; the second exists for the sole purpose of representing the first. The linguistic object is not both the written and the spoken forms of words; the spoken forms alone constitute the object. But the spoken word is so intimately bound to its written image that the latter manages to usurp the main role. People attach even more importance to the written image of a vocal sign than to the sign itself. A similar mistake would be in thinking that more can be learned about someone by looking at his photograph than by viewing him directly.

This illusion, which has always existed, is reflected in many of the notions that are currently bandied about on the subject of language. Take the notion that an idiom changes more rapidly when writing does not exist. Nothing could be further from the truth. Writing may retard the process of change under certain conditions, but its absence in no way jeopardizes the preservation of language. The oldest written texts of Lithuanian, which is still spoken in eastern Prussia and in a part of Russia, date from 1540; but the language of even that late period offers a more faithful picture of Proto-Indo-European than does Latin of 300 B.C. This one example is enough to show the extent to which languages are independent of writing.

Certain very slight linguistic facts have been preserved without the help of any notation. During the whole Old High German period, people wrote *tōten, fuolen, stōzen;* near the end of the twelfth century the forms *töten, füelen* appeared, but *stōzen* subsisted. How did the difference originate? Wherever the umlaut occurred, there was a *y* in the following syllable. Proto-Germanic had **daupyan*, **folyan*, but **stautan*. At the very beginning of the literary period (about 800) the *y* became so weak that no trace of it appears in writing for three centuries; still, a slight trace had remained in the spoken form; that is how it miraculously reappeared as an umlaut around 1180! Without the help of writing, a slight difference in pronunciation was accurately transmitted.

Thus language does have a definite and stable oral tradition that is independent of writing, but the influence of the written form prevents our seeing this. The first linguists confused language and writing, just as the humanists had done before them. Even Bopp failed to distinguish clearly between letters and sounds. His works give the impression that a language and its alphabet are inseparable. His immediate successors fell into the same trap; the transcription *th* (for the fricative þ) caused Grimm to think not only that *th* was a double sound but also that it was an aspirated occlusive, and he accordingly assigned it a specific place in his law of consonantal mutation or *Lautverschiebung* (see p. 144). Still today intelligent men confuse language and writing. To take but one example, Gaston Deschamps credited Berthelot with "preserving French from ruin" because he had opposed spelling reform.

But how is the influence of writing to be explained?

1) First, the graphic form of words strikes us as being something permanent and stable, better suited than sound to account for the unity of language throughout time. Though it creates a purely fictitious unity, the superficial bond of writing is much easier to grasp than the only true bond, the bond of sound.

2) Most people pay more attention to visual impressions simply because these are sharper and more lasting than aural impressions; that is why they show a preference for the former. The graphic form manages to force itself upon them at the expense of sound.

3) The literary language adds to the undeserved importance of writing. It has its dictionaries and grammars; in school, children are taught from and by means of books; language is apparently governed by a code; the code itself consists of a written set of strict rules of usage, orthography; and that is why writing acquires primary importance. The result is that people forget that they learn to speak before they learn to write, and the natural sequence is reversed.

4) Finally, when there is a disagreement between language and orthography, settlement of the dispute is difficult for everyone except the linguist; and since he is given no voice in the matter, the written form almost inevitably wins out, for any solution supported by it is easier; thus writing assumes undeserved importance.

3. *Systems of Writing*

There are only two systems of writing:

1) In an ideographic system each word is represented by a single sign that is unrelated to the sounds of the word itself. Each written

sign stands for a whole word and, consequently, for the idea expressed by the word. The classic example of an ideographic system of writing is Chinese.

2) The system commonly known as "phonetic" tries to reproduce the succession of sounds that make up a word. Phonetic systems are sometimes syllabic, sometimes alphabetic, i.e., based on the irreducible elements used in speaking.

Moreover, ideographic systems freely become mixtures when certain ideograms lose their original value and become symbols of isolated sounds.

The statement that the written word tends to replace the spoken one in our minds is true of both systems of writing, but the tendency is stronger in the ideographic system. To a Chinese, an ideogram and a spoken word are both symbols of an idea; to him writing is a second language, and if two words that have the same sound are used in conversation, he may resort to writing in order to express his thought. But in Chinese the mental substitution of the written word for the spoken word does not have the annoying consequences that it has in a phonetic system, for the substitution is absolute; the same graphic symbol can stand for words from different Chinese dialects.

I shall limit discussion to the phonetic system, and especially to the one used today, the system that stems from the Greek alphabet.[7]

[7] The correspondence between De Saussure's system of transcription and that recommended by the International Phonetic Association is roughly as follows:

DE SAUSSURE	IPA		DE SAUSSURE	IPA	
p	[p]	*p*in	l	[l]	*l*et
b	[b]	*b*in	r	[r]	*r*un
m	[m]	*m*an	i	[i]	r*e*peat
t	[t]	*t*en	u	[u]	b*oo*t
d	[d]	*d*ig	ü	[y]	French p*u*r
n	[n]	*n*ot	ę, è	[ε]	p*e*t
k	[k]	*c*at	ẹ, é	[e]	ch*a*otic
g	[g]	*g*et	ẽ	[ε̃]	French *vin*
ṅ	[η]	thi*ng*	ǫ	[ɔ]	*ou*ght
f	[f]	*f*ox	ọ	[o]	n*o*tation
v	[v]	*v*ixen	õ	[ɔ̃]	French *bon*
þ	[θ]	*th*in	ǫ̈	[œ]	French s*eu*l
ð	[ð]	*th*en	ọ̈	[ϕ]	French cr*eu*se
ʂ	[s]	*s*ing	ö̃	[œ̃]	French *un*

When first devised a phonetic alphabet—unless borrowed and already marked by inconsistencies—gives a fairly rational representation of language. With respect to logic, Greek is especially noteworthy (see p. 64). But the harmonious relation between writing and pronunciation does not last. Why? This question must be examined.

4. *Reasons for the Discrepancy between Writing and Pronunciation*

Of the numerous causes of lack of agreement between writing and pronunciation, I shall recall only the more important ones.

First, language is constantly evolving, whereas writing tends to remain stable. The result is that a point is reached where writing no longer corresponds to what it is supposed to record. A transcription that is accurate at a particular moment will be absurd a century later. For a time people may change their graphic symbols to conform with changes in pronunciation, then relinquish the effort. This happened in French in the case of *oi:*

	Pronunciation	Written Forms
Eleventh Century	1 *rei, lei*	*rei, lei*
Thirteenth Century	2 *roi, loi*	*roi, loi*
Fourteenth Century	3 *roè, loè*	*roi, loi*
Nineteenth Century	4 *rwa, lwa*	*roi, loi*

Up until period 2 changes in pronunciation were recorded; each step in the history of the language was matched by a corresponding step in the history of writing. But after the fourteenth century the written form of the words remained unchanged while the evolution of the language continued; from that moment the discrepancy between the language and its orthography increased progressively. Finally, the practice of joining discordant terms had its repercussion on the graphic system itself: the combination *oi* acquired a value that was unrelated to either *o* or *i*.

---

z	[z]	*z*ero	ɑ	[ɑ]	f*a*ther
š	[ʃ]	*s*ure	ã	[ɑ̃]	French bl*an*c
ž	[ʒ]	a*z*ure	w	[w]	*w*ait
x′	[ç]	German i*ch*	y	[j]	*y*es
x	[x]	German do*ch*	ə	[ə]	*a*bove

See especially pages 46–49. [Tr.]

Such examples could be multiplied indefinitely. For instance, why should the French write *mais* 'but' and *fait* 'fact' when the words are pronounced *mè* and *fè*? Why does *c* often have the value of *s*? The answer is that French has retained outmoded spellings.

Spelling always lags behind pronunciation. The *l* in French is today changing to *y;* speakers say *éveyer*, *mouyer*, just as they say *essuyer* 'wipe,' *nettoyer* 'clean'; but the written forms of these words are still *éveiller* 'awaken,' *mouiller* 'soak.'

Another reason for discrepancy between spelling and pronunciation is this: if an alphabet is borrowed from another language, its resources may not be appropriate for their new function; expedients will have to be found (e.g. the use of two letters to designate a single sound). Take the voiceless dental fricative þ of the Germanic languages. Since Latin had no sign for this sound, *th* was used. The Merovingian king Chilperic tried to add a special symbol for this sound to the Latin alphabet, but his attempt was unsuccessful and *th* won acceptance. During the Middle Ages English had a closed *e* (e.g. *sed*) and an open *e* (e.g. *led*); since the alphabet failed to provide distinct symbols for the two sounds, the spellings *seed* and *lead* were devised. French uses the double symbol *ch* to stand for hushing *š*, etc.

The influence of etymology also helps to widen the gap between spelling and pronunciation. It has been especially strong during certain periods (e.g. the Renaissance). Even a false etymology often forces itself into the spelling of a word: *d* was inserted in French *poids* 'weight' as if the word were derived from Latin *pondus; poids* actually comes from *pensum*.[8] Whether the application of the principle is correct matters little; the fallacy is in spelling words according to their etymology.

Other reasons for the discrepancy are not so obvious; some absurdities cannot be excused even on etymological grounds. Why was *thun* used instead of *tun* in German? The *h* was said to represent the aspiration that followed the initial consonant; but it would have to be inserted wherever aspiration occurs, and many similar words were never written with *h* (*Tugend*, *Tisch*, etc.).

[8] Cf. English *island*, derived from *ig* 'island' and *land* 'land' but influenced by *isle*, and *doubt*, derived from Old French *douter* but later changed to conform with Latin *dubitare*. [Tr.]

5. *Results of the Discrepancy*

To classify the inconsistencies of writing would take too long. One salient disadvantage is the multiplicity of symbols that stand for the same sound. For *ž* French uses *j, g, ge* (*joli* 'pretty,' *geler* 'freeze,' *geai* 'jay'); for *z*, both *z* and *s;* for *s, c, ç* and *t* (*nation* 'nation'), *sc* (*acquiescer* 'acquiesce'), *sç* (*acquiesçant* 'acquiescent'), *x* (*dix* 'ten'); and for *k* it uses *c, qu, k, ch, cc, cqu* (*acquérir* 'acquire'). Conversely, a single symbol stands for several values: *t* stands for *t* or *s*, *g* for *g* or *ž*, etc.[9]

"Indirect spellings" also merit our attention. There is no double consonant in *Zettel, Teller*, etc.; German uses *tt, ll*, etc. for the sole purpose of indicating that the preceding vowel is open and short. Through a similar aberration English adds a final silent *e* to lengthen the preceding vowel: *mad, made.* The *e*, which actually affects only the preceding syllable, creates a second syllable for the eye.

These irrational spellings still stand for something in language; but others have neither rime nor reason. French has no double consonants except the old futures *mourrai* '(I) shall die,' *courrai* '(I) shall run,' etc.; yet illegitimate double consonants abound in the orthography of the language (*bourru* 'surly,' *sottise* 'foolishness,' *souffrir* 'suffer,' etc.).

Being unstable and striving always for regularity, writing may vacillate at times; the result is fluctuating orthographies that stem from efforts to record sounds at different periods. Take *ertha, erdha, erda*, or *thrī, dhrī, drī* in Old High German: *th, dh, d* stand for the same phonic element. But which element? Writing does not provide the answer. The complication that arises is this: confronted with two spellings for the same word, we cannot always decide whether two pronunciations are actually represented. Suppose that texts of neighboring dialects show the spelling *asca* for a word in one of the dialects and *ascha* for the same word in the other; if the sound is the same, the transcriptions point to an orthographic fluctuation; if not, the difference is phonological and dialectal, as in the Greek forms *paízō, paízdō, paíddō*. Or two successive periods may be

[9] The discrepancy between spelling and pronunciation is of course more striking in English than in French: two perfectly riming sounds are written *fight* and *bite; c* stands for the same sound as both *s* and *k;* etc. [Tr.]

involved. The English forms *hwat, hweel,* etc. were later replaced by *what, wheel,* etc. Does this point to a graphic change or to a phonetic change?

The preceding discussion boils down to this: writing obscures language; it is not a guise for language but a disguise. That fact is clearly illustrated by the spelling of French *oiseau* 'bird.' Not one spoken sound (*wazǫ*) is indicated by its own symbol. Here writing fails to record any part of the picture of language.

Another result is that the less writing represents what it is supposed to represent, the stronger the tendency to use it as a basis becomes. Grammarians never fail to draw attention to the written form. Psychologically, the tendency is easily explained, but its consequences are annoying. Free use of the words "pronounce" and "pronunciation" sanctions the abuse and reverses the real, legitimate relationship between writing and language. Whoever says that a certain letter must be pronounced a certain way is mistaking the written image of a sound for the sound itself. For French *oi* to be pronounced *wa,* this spelling would have to exist independently; actually *wa* is written *oi.* To attribute the oddity to an exceptional pronunciation of *o* and *i* is also misleading, for this implies that language depends on its written form and that certain liberties may be taken in writing, as if the graphic symbols were the norm.

False notions about the relationship between sound and graphic symbols appear even in grammatical rules, as in the case of French *h.* Some words that begin with an unaspirated vowel are written with *h* through remembrance of their Latin forms: *homme* 'man' (formerly *ome*) because of Latin *homo.* But in words of Germanic origin, initial *h* was actually pronounced: *hache* 'hatchet,' *hareng* 'herring,' *honte* 'shame,' etc. As long as aspiration was used, words of Germanic origin obeyed the laws governing initial consonants: speakers said *deu haches* 'two hatchets,' *le hereng* 'the herring'; other words obeyed the laws governing initial vowels; speakers said *deu̯-z-ommes* 'two men,' *l'omme* 'the man.' For that period the rule, "Liaison and elision do not occur before aspirated *h,*" was correct. But nowadays the formula is meaningless. Aspirated *h* no longer exists unless the label is applied to something which is not a sound but which prevents liaison and elision. Again we are involved in a vicious circle, and *h* is but a fictitious offspring of writing.

The pronunciation of a word is determined, not by its spelling, but by its history. The form of a word at a particular moment stands for a moment in its enforced evolution. Precise laws govern its evolution. Each step is determined by the preceding step. The only thing to consider is the one most often forgotten: the evolution of the word, its etymology.

The name of the town of *Auch* is *ǫš* in phonetic transcription. That is the only French word in which final *ch* stands for *š*. But we explain nothing by saying, "Final *ch* is pronounced *š* only in *Auch*." The only question that concerns us is this: How could Latin *Auscii* have changed to *ǫš*? Orthography is unimportant.

Should French *gageure* 'wager' be pronounced with *ö* or *ü*? Some speakers say: *gažör*, for *heure* 'hour' is pronounced *ör*. Others say: No, it is *gažür*, for *ge* is equivalent *ž*, as in *geôle* 'jail.' The argument is pointless. The real issue is etymological: *gageure* was formed from *gager* 'earn' just as *tournure* 'figure' was formed from *tourner* 'turn'; only *gažür* is justifiable; *gažör* is due solely to the equivocal nature of writing.

But the tyranny of writing goes even further. By imposing itself upon the masses, spelling influences and modifies language. This happens only in highly literate languages where written texts play an important role. Then visual images lead to wrong pronunciations; such mistakes are really pathological.[10] Spelling practices cause mistakes in the pronunciation of many French words. For instance, there were two spellings for the surname Lefèvre (from Latin *faber*), one popular and simple, the other learned and etymological: *Lefèvre* and *Lefèbvre*. Because *v* and *u* were not kept apart in the old system of writing, *Lefèbvre* was read as *Lefèbure*, with a *b* that had never really existed and a *u* that was the result of ambiguity. Now, the latter form is actually pronounced.

Mispronunciations due to spelling will probably appear more frequently as time goes on, and the number of letters pronounced

[10] *Pathology* was given currency in French by Littré. It was used subsequently by Gilliéron and Darmesteter as well as by De Saussure. See note 6. [Tr.]

by speakers will probably increase. Some Parisians already pronounce the *t* in *sept femmes* 'seven women';[11] Darmesteter foresees the day when even the last two letters of *vingt* 'twenty' will be pronounced—truly an orthographic monstrosity.

Such phonic deformations belong to language but do not stem from its natural functioning. They are due to an external influence. Linguistics should put them into a special compartment for observation: they are teratological cases.[12]

Chapter VII

PHONOLOGY[13]

1. *Definition*

Whoever consciously deprives himself of the perceptible image of the written word runs the risk of perceiving only a shapeless and unmanageable mass. Taking away the written form is like depriving a beginning swimmer of his life belt.

To substitute immediately what is natural for what is artificial would be desirable; but this is impossible without first studying the sounds of language; apart from their graphic symbols, sounds are only vague notions, and the prop provided by writing, though deceptive, is still preferable. The first linguists, who knew nothing about the physiology of articulated sounds, were constantly falling into a trap; to me, it means a first step in the direction of truth, for the study of sounds themselves furnishes the desired prop. Modern

[11] The pronunciation [sɛ] is now obsolescent. Cf. the trend toward pronouncing the *t* in *often*. [Tr.]

[12] De Saussure's terminology is reminiscent of the biological parlance of Gilliéron (e.g. in *Pathologie et thérapeutique verbales,* Paris, 1921). [Tr.]

[13] De Saussure later modifies and expands his definition of phonology (see especially pp. 34, 42 ff., 117 ff. and 131). Only M. Grammont has followed De Saussure's practice. English and American linguists often use phonology to indicate the historical study of sounds or the study of the functioning of sounds in a particular language, phonetics for the study of the modalities of sounds used in speaking, and phonemics (corresponding to French *phonologie* and German *Phonologie*) for the study of the distinctive sounds of language. [Tr.]

linguists have finally seen the light; pursuing for their own ends investigations started by others (physiologists, theoreticians of singing, etc.), they have given linguists an auxiliary science that has freed it from the written word.

The physiology of sounds (German *Laut-* or *Sprachphysiologie*) is often called phonetics (French *phonétique*, German *Phonetik*). To me this name seems inappropriate. Instead, I shall use *phonology*. For phonetics first designated—and should continue to designate—the study of the evolutions of sounds. Two absolutely distinct disciplines should not be lumped together under the same name. Phonetics is a historical science; it analyses events and changes, and moves through time. Phonology is outside time, for the articulatory mechanism never changes.

The two studies are distinct but not opposites. Phonetics is a basic part of the science of language; phonology—this bears repeating—is only an auxiliary discipline and belongs exclusively to speaking (see pp. 17 ff.). Just what phonational movements could accomplish if language did not exist is not clear; but they do not constitute language, and even after we have explained all the movements of the vocal apparatus necessary for the production of each auditory impression, we have in no way illuminated the problem of language. It is a system based on the mental opposition of auditory impressions, just as a tapestry is a work of art produced by the visual oppositions of threads of different colors; the important thing in analysis is the role of the oppositions, not the process through which the colors were obtained.

An outline of the phonological system is given in the Appendix; here I am trying merely to determine the extent to which phonology can help linguistics to escape the delusions of writing.

2. *Phonological Writing*

The linguist needs above all else a means of transcribing articulated sounds that will rule out all ambiguity. Actually, countless graphic systems have been proposed.

What are the requirements for a truly phonological system of writing? First, there should be one symbol for each element of the spoken chain. This requirement is not always considered. Thus English phonologists, concerned with classification rather than analysis, have two- and three-letter symbols for certain sounds. Second, there should be some means for making a rigid distinction between implosive and explosive sounds (see pp. 49 ff.).

Are there grounds for substituting a phonological alphabet for a system already in use? Here I can only broach this interesting subject. I think that phonological writing should be for the use of linguists only. First, how would it be possible to make the English, Germans, French, etc. adopt a uniform system! Next, an alphabet applicable to all languages would probably be weighed down by diacritical marks; and—to say nothing of the distressing appearance of a page of phonological writing—attempts to gain precision would obviously confuse the reader by obscuring what the writing was designed to express. The advantages would not be sufficient to compensate for the inconveniences. Phonological exactitude is not very desirable outside science.

Reading is another issue. We read in two ways: a new or unknown word is spelled out letter by letter; but a common, ordinary word is embraced by a single glance, independently of its letters, so that the image of the whole word acquires an ideographic value. Here traditional orthography takes revenge. It is useful to distinguish between French *tant* 'so much' and *temps* 'weather'; *et* 'and,' *est* 'is,' and *ait* 'have'; *du* 'of the' and *dû* 'had to'; *il devait* 'he owed' and *ils devaient* 'they owed,' etc.[14] Let us hope only that the most flagrant absurdities of writing will be eliminated. Although a phonological alphabet is helpful in the teaching of languages, its use should not be generalized.

3. *Validity of Evidence Furnished by Writing*

One must not think that spelling reform should immediately follow the realization that writing is deceptive. The genuine contribution of phonology is in providing precautionary measures for dealing with the written form through which we must pass in order to reach language. Evidence furnished by writing is valid only when interpreted. We must draw up for each language studied a *phonological system*, i.e. a description of the sounds with which it functions; for each language operates on a fixed number of well-differentiated phonemes. This system is the only set of facts that

[14] Cf. English *sow* and *sew; to, too,* and *two; due* and *dew,* etc. [Tr.]

interests the linguist. Graphic symbols bear but a faint resemblance to it; the difficulty of determining the accuracy of the resemblance varies according to the idiom and circumstances.

The linguist who deals with a language of the past has only indirect data at his disposal. What resources can he use in setting up its phonological system?

1) First and foremost is *external evidence*, especially contemporary descriptions of the sounds and pronunciations of the period. French grammarians of the sixteenth and seventeenth centuries, especially those interested in teaching foreigners, left us many interesting observations. But the information contained in the writings of contemporaries is often vague, for the authors have no phonological method. The terminology of their descriptions is whimsical and lacks scientific precision. The result is that their evidence must in turn be interpreted. Names given to sounds, for instance, are often misleading: Greek grammarians called voiced *b, d, g*, etc. "middle" consonants (*mésai*), and voiceless *p, t, k*, etc. *psīlai*, which Latin grammarians translated by *tenues*.

2) More accurate information will result from combining external data with internal evidence, which I shall class under two headings.

a) The first class comprises evidence based on the *regularity of phonetic evolutions*. Knowing what sound a letter stood for during another period is important in determining the value of that letter. Its present value is the result of an evolution that allows us to cast aside certain hypotheses from the outset. For instance, the exact value of Sanskrit *ç* is unknown, but the fact that it replaced palatal Proto-Indo-European *k* clearly limits the field of conjecture.

If the linguist knows both the point of departure and the parallel evolution of similar sounds of a particular language during the same period, he can use analogical reasoning and set up a proportion.

The problem is naturally easier if the object is to determine an intermediate pronunciation when both the starting point and the end result are known. French *au* (e.g. in *sauter* 'jump') must have been a diphthong during the Middle Ages, for it is half-way between older *al* and modern *o*. And if we learn by some other means that the diphthong still existed at a particular moment, we are safe in assuming that it also existed during the preceding period. We do not know exactly what *z* stands for in a word like Old High German *wazer;* but our guideposts are the older form *water* on the one hand and Modern German *Wasser* on the other. The *z* must be a sound half-way between *t* and *s;* we can reject any hypothesis that fails to consider both *t* and *s;* to hold that *z* stands for a palatal sound, for example, would be impossible, for only a dental articulation can logically come between two other dental articulations.

b) There are several types of *contemporary evidence*. Spelling differences furnish one of many types. During one period we find that Old High German has *wazer*, *zehan*, *ezan* but never *wacer*, *cehan*, etc. When we find the forms *esan* and *essan*, *waser* and *wasser*, etc., however, we easily conclude that the sound of *z* was close to *s* but different from the sound that *c* stood for during the same period. The subsequent appearance of such forms as *wacer* proves that the two originally distinct phonemes became somewhat mingled.

Poetic texts are invaluable documents in the study of pronunciation. They furnish many types of information, depending on whether the system of versification is based on the number of syllables, quantity, or similarity of sounds (alliteration, assonance, and rime). Greek indicated certain long vowels in writing (e.g. *ō*, transcribed *ω*) but not others. We must consult the poets in order to find out about the quantity of *a*, *i*, and *u*. Thus rime allows us to determine until what period the final consonants of Old French *gras* and *faz* (Latin *faciō* 'I do') were different and from what moment they were brought together and merged. Rime and assonance also show that *e* derived from Latin *a* (e.g. *père* 'father' from *patrem*, *tel* 'such' from *talem*, *mer* 'sea' from *mare*) was not pronounced like other *e*'s. These words never appear in rime or assonance with *elle* 'she' (from *illa*), *vert* 'green' (from *viridem*), *belle* 'beautiful' (from *bella*), etc.

Finally there is the evidence furnished by the spelling of loanwords, puns, cock-and-bull stories, etc. In Gothic, for example, *kawtsjo* reveals information about the pronunciation of *cautio* in Vulgar Latin. That French *roi* 'king' was pronounced *rwè* at the end of the eighteenth century is attested by the following story cited by Nyrop (*Grammaire historique de la langue française*,

p. 178): A woman who had been brought before the revolutionary tribunal was asked whether she had not said in the presence of witnesses that a king (*roi*) was needed; she replied "that she was not speaking of a king like Capet or the others at all, but of a *rouet maître* 'spinning wheel.' "

All the foregoing procedures help us to acquire some knowledge of the phonological system of a period as well as to interpret and use profitably the evidence furnished by writing.

In dealing with a living language, the only rational method consists of (a) setting up the system of sounds as revealed by direct observation, and (b) observing the system of signs used to represent—imperfectly—these sounds. Many grammarians still hold to the old method that I have criticized and simply tell how each letter is pronounced in the language they wish to describe. By using the older method, however, they cannot present clearly the phonological system of an idiom.

Nevertheless, great strides in the right direction have already been taken, and phonologists have made an important contribution toward reforming our ideas about writing and spelling.

APPENDIX

Principles of Phonology

Chapter I

PHONOLOGICAL SPECIES

1. *Definition of the Phoneme*

[For this part we were able to use a stenographic reproduction of three lectures given by Saussure in 1897, "Théorie de la syllabe," in which he also touches upon the general principles discussed in Chapter I; moreover, much of the material in his personal notes deals with phonology; on many points, the notes illuminate and complete the data furnished by Courses I and III. (Editors' note.)]

Many phonologists limit themselves almost exclusively to the phonational act, i.e. the production of sound by the vocal organs (larynx, mouth, etc.) and neglect the auditory side. Their method is wrong. Not only does the auditory impression come to us just as directly as the image of the moving vocal organs, but it is also the basis of any theory. Auditory impressions exist unconsciously before phonological units are studied; our ear tells us what *b*, *t*, etc. are. Even if all the movements made by the mouth and larynx in pronouncing a chain of sounds could be photographed, the observer would still be unable to single out the subdivisions in the series of articulatory movements; he would not know where one sound began and the next one ended. Without the auditory impression, how can we say that in *fal*, for instance, there are three units rather than two or four? But when we hear a sound in a spoken chain, we can identify it immediately; as long as there is an impression of homogeneity, the sound is unique. What matters is not the length of the sound (cf. *fāl* and *făl*) but the quality of the impression. The sound-chain is not divided into equal beats but into homogeneous ones; each beat is characterized by unity of impression, and that is the natural point of departure for phonology.

Here the early Greek alphabet is noteworthy. Each simple sound is represented in Greek by a single graphic sign, and each sign always stands for the same simple sound. The Greek alphabet was an ingenious discovery that was later handed down to the Romans. In the transcription of *bárbaros* 'barbarian,' each letter corresponds to a homogeneous beat:

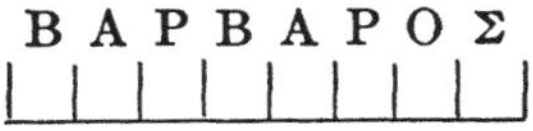

In the drawing above, the horizontal line stands for the phonetic chain, and the short vertical bars indicate passage from one sound to another. In the early Greek alphabet there are no complex graphs like English *š* for *s*, no interchangeable letters for single sounds like *c* and *s* for *s*, no single signs for double sounds like *x* for *ks*. A one-to-one ratio between sounds and graphs—the necessary and sufficient basis for a good phonological system of writing—was realized almost completely by the Greeks.[1]

Other nations did not grasp this principle, and their alphabets do not analyze the spoken chain according to its homogeneous auditory beats. The Cypriots, for example, stopped at more complex units like *pa, ti, do,* etc. Such notation is called syllabic, but this name is hardly accurate since there are still other types of syllables (e.g. *pak, tra,* etc.). The Semites indicated only the consonants. They would have transcribed a word like *bárbaros* as BRBRS.

Delimitation of the sounds of the spoken chain can be based only on auditory impressions; but description of these sounds is an entirely different process. Description can be carried out only on

[1] To be sure, they wrote Χ, φ, Θ for *kh, th, ph;* φΕΡΟ stands for *phéro;* but this is a later innovation; archaic inscriptions read ΚΗΑΡΙΣ and not ΧΑΡΙΣ. The same inscriptions have two signs for *k, kappa* and *koppa,* but the situation is different: two real differences in pronunciation were involved, *k* being sometimes palatal and sometimes velar; besides, *koppa* later disappeared. Finally—and this is a more subtle point—in early Greek and Latin inscriptions a double consonant is often indicated by a simple letter (e.g. Latin *fuisse,* written FUISE); this is an infraction of the principle since the double *s* lasts two beats—beats that are not homogeneous, as we shall see later, and that make distinct impressions; but the mistake is excusable since the two sounds have a common characteristic even though they are distinct (cf. pp. 51 ff.). [S.]

the basis of the articulatory act, for it is impossible to analyze the units of sound in their own chain. We must go back to the movements involved in phonation; there, a given sound obviously corresponds to a given act: *b* (auditory beat) = *b′* (articulatory beat). The first units obtained by cutting the spoken chain are made up of *b* and *b′*; they are phonemes; a phoneme is the sum of the auditory impressions and articulatory movements, the unit heard and the unit spoken, each conditioning the other: thus it is a complex unit with a foot in each chain.

The elements first obtained through analysis of the spoken chain are like the links of this chain: they are irreducible moments that cannot be studied outside the time that they occupy. A grouping like *ta*, for instance, will always be one moment plus another, one fragment of a certain length plus another. Against this, the irreducible *t*, taken separately, can be studied in the abstract, outside time. We can speak of *t* in general as the *T* species (I use capitals to indicate species), of *i* in general as the *I* species, etc. if we consider only the distinctive character of a sound and neglect everything that depends on succession in time. Similarly, a musical series *do, re, mi* can be treated only as a concrete series in time, but if I select one of its irreducible elements, I can study it in the abstract.

Having analyzed a sufficient number of spoken chains from different languages, the phonologist can identify and classify the elements with which each language operates. Then, if he ignores acoustically unimportant variations, he will find that the number of species is not indefinite. Special works list these species and describe them in detail.[2] Here I wish merely to show the simple, invariable principles upon which any such classification is based.

But first let me say a few words about the vocal apparatus, the possible functioning of the different organs, and the role of these same organs as producers of sound.

[2] Cf. Sievers, *Grundzüge der Phonetik*, fifth ed., 1902; Jespersen, *Lehrbuch der Phonetik*, second ed., 1913; Roudet, *Eléments de phonétique générale*, 1910. [Ed.]

2. *The Vocal Apparatus and Its Functioning*[3]

1) I limit description of the vocal apparatus to a schematic drawing in which *A* designates the nasal cavity, *B* the oral cavity, and *C* the larynx (with the glottis ε between the two vocal cords).

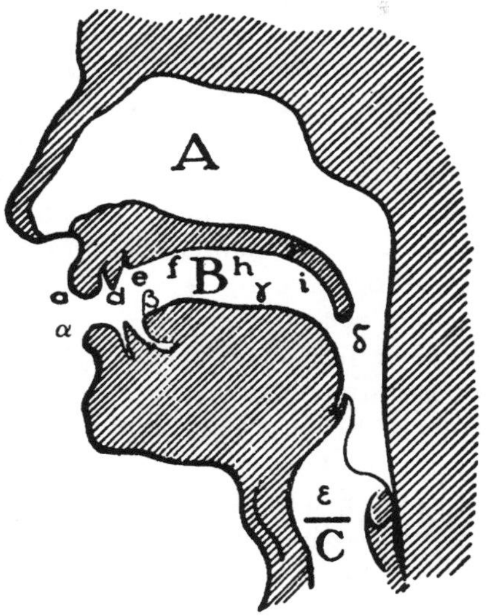

In the mouth, the parts of the vocal apparatus that should be singled out are these: the lips *α* and *a;* the tongue *β*—*γ* (*β* designating the point and *γ* the rest); the upper teeth *d;* the palate, made up of the bony hard palate *f-h* in the front and the movable membrane or soft palate *i* in the back; and, finally, the uvula *δ*.

The Greek letters indicate organs that are active during articulation; the Latin letters identify the passive parts.

The glottis ε, made up of two parallel muscles or vocal cords, opens when the cords are drawn apart and closes when they come together. Complete closure does not occur in speech; the opening is sometimes wide, sometimes narrow. When the opening is wide, allowing

[3] De Saussure's brief description has been supplemented by material based on Jespersen's *Lehrbuch der Phonetik,* from which we have also borrowed the principle used in setting up the table of phonemes below (see pp. 44 ff.). But we are merely carrying out De Saussure's intent, and the reader may be assured that these additions do not alter his thought in any way. [Ed.]

the air to pass freely, no vibration is heard; voicing occurs when air passes through a narrow opening, causing the cords to vibrate. There is no other alternative in the normal emission of sounds.

The nasal cavity is a completely immobile organ; the stream of air can be stopped only by raising the uvula δ; it is an open or a closed door.

The oral cavity offers a wide range of possibilities; the lips can be used to increase the length of the channel, the jaws can be puffed out or drawn in, and a great variety of movements of the lips and tongue can be used to contract or even to close the cavity.

The role played by the same organs in producing sounds is directly proportional to their mobility; uniformity in the functioning of the larynx and nasal cavity is matched by diversity in the functioning of the oral cavity.

Air that is expelled from the lungs first passes through the glottis. It is possible to produce a laryngeal sound by tightening the vocal cords, but the larynx cannot produce phonological varieties that allow us to separate and classify the sounds of language; in this respect, the laryngeal sound is uniform. Perceived directly as it emitted by the glottis the sound seems to have an almost invariable quality.

The nasal channel serves as nothing more than a resonator for the vocal vibrations that pass through it. It does not function as a producer of sound.

The oral cavity, on the contrary, functions both as a producer of sound and as a resonator. When the glottis is wide-open, there is no laryngeal vibration; the sound that is heard originates in the oral cavity (I leave to the physicist the task of deciding whether it is a sound or merely a noise). But when tightening of the vocal cords causes the glottis to vibrate, the mouth serves mainly to modify the laryngeal sound.

In short, the factors involved in the production of sound are expiration, oral articulation, vibration of the larynx, and nasal resonance.

But simple enumeration does not identify the differential properties of phonemes. In classifying phonemes, what constitutes them is of much less importance than what distinguishes them from each other. A negative force can be more important in classifying a phoneme than a positive one. Thus expiration, a positive element that is part of every phonational act, has no differentiating value; but nasal resonance may characterize phonemes by its absence, a negative force, just as well as by its presence. The important thing is that two of the elements enumerated above are constant, and that they are necessary and sufficient for the production of sound:

a) expiration
b) oral articulation;

whereas the other two may be either absent or superimposed on the first two:

c) vibration of the larynx
d) nasal resonance.

Moreover, we know that while *a*, *c*, and *d* are uniform, *b* makes possible the production of many varieties of sounds.

We should also bear in mind that a phoneme is identified when its phonational act is determined, and that all species of phonemes will be determined when all phonational acts are identified. The foregoing classification of forces involved in the production of sound shows that phonational acts are differentiated only by *b*, *c*, and *d*. For each phoneme we must determine its oral articulation, whether a laryngeal sound is present (~) or absent ([ ]), and whether nasal resonance is present (. . . .) or absent ([ ]). When one of these three is unknown, the identification of a sound is incomplete. But as soon as all three are known, their different combinations determine all the basic species of phonational acts.

The following table gives the possible variations:

	I	II	III	IV
a	Expiration	Expiration	Expiration	Expiration
b	Oral Articulation	Oral Articulation	Oral Articulation	Oral Articulation
c	[ ]	~	[ ]	~
d	[ ]	[ ]	. . . .	. . . .

Column I designates voiceless sounds, II voiced sounds, III voiceless nasalized sounds, and IV voiced nasalized sounds.

But one unknown remains: the nature of the oral articulation;

therefore, the most important thing is to determine the possible varieties of oral articulation.

3. *Classification of Sounds According to Their Oral Articulation*

Sounds are generally classed according to the place of their articulation. My point of departure will be different. Regardless of where articulation takes place, there is always a certain *aperture*, i.e., a certain degree of opening that ranges between two extremes, complete closure and maximum opening. On that basis, and proceeding from minimum to maximum aperture, sounds will fall into seven categories that I shall designate by the numbers 0, 1, 2, 3, 4, 5, 6. Only within each category shall I distribute phonemes into different types according to their place of articulation.

I shall conform to current terminology even though it is imperfect or incorrect at many points: words like guttural, palatal, dental, liquid, etc. are all more or less illogical. A more rational plan would be to divide the palate into a certain number of areas. Then by focusing attention on lingual articulation, it would always be possible to specify the main point of contact. In devising a formula, I shall draw upon this notion and use the letters of the sketch of the vocal apparatus (see p. 41): the number of the aperture is placed between a Greek letter (indicating an active organ) and a Latin letter (indicating a passive organ). Thus *β0e* means that complete closure is maintained while the tip of the tongue is placed against the upper alveolar ridge.

Finally, within each articulation the different species of phonemes are marked by concomitant features—laryngeal sound and nasal resonance—which differentiate by their absence as well as by their presence.

The two accompanying features and the formula provide a simple, rational means of classifying phonemes. Of course, one should not expect to find here phonemes that have a complex or special character, regardless of their practical importance (e.g. the aspirates *ph*, *dh*, etc.; the affricates *tš*, *dž*, *pf*, etc.; palatalized consonants; weak vowels like ə or mute *e*, etc.). Nor should one expect to find simple phonemes that have no practical importance and that are not considered differentiated sounds.

A. *Zero Aperture: Occlusives*

Occlusives include all phonemes produced by complete closure, the airtight but brief sealing of the oral cavity. This is not the place to discuss whether a sound is produced when closure or release occurs; actually it may be produced in either way (see pp. 51 ff.).

The three main types of occlusives are named according to their places of articulation: labials (*p*, *b*, *m*); dentals (*t*, *d*, *n*); and gutturals (*k*, *g*, *ṅ*).

The first type is articulated with the lips; for the second, the tip of the tongue is placed against the front of the palate; for the third, the back of the tongue makes contact with the back part of the palate.

Many languages, notably the Indo-European, make a distinction between two guttural articulations, one palatal (in the *f-h* area) and the other velar (in the *i* area), but elsewhere (e.g. in English) the difference goes unnoticed and the ear likens a back *k* (such as the sound of *c* in *cart*) to a front *k* (as in *king*).

The following table gives the formulas for the various occlusive phonemes:

LABIALS			DENTALS			GUTTURALS		
p	b	(m)	t	d	(n)	k	g	(ṅ)
αOa	αOa	αOa	βOe	βOe	βOe	γOh	γOh	γOh
[ ]	~	~	[ ]	~	~	[ ]	~	~
[ ]	[ ]	....	[ ]	[ ]	....	[ ]	[ ]	....

Nasal *m*, *n*, and *ṅ* are really voiced nasalized occlusives; in pronouncing *amba*, one raises the uvula to close the nasal fossae in shifting from *m* to *b*.

In theory, each type has a voiceless nasal—a nasal sound unaccompanied by glottal vibration; thus voiceless *m* occurs after a voiceless sound in the Scandinavian languages; French also has voiceless nasals, but speakers do not look upon them as differential elements.

Nasals are put inside parentheses in the table; although the mouth is completely closed during their articulation, the opening of the nasal channel gives them wider aperture (see Class C).

B. *Aperture 1: Fricatives or Spirants*

The phonemes of Class B are characterized by incomplete closure which allows the air to pass through the oral cavity. The name spirant is all too general; while the word fricative tells nothing about the degree of closure, it does suggest friction resulting from the expulsion of air (Latin *fricāre*).

The phonemes of Class B, unlike those of Class A, do not fall into three types. First, labials proper (corresponding to *p* and *b*) are rarely used; I shall disregard them; they are ordinarily replaced by labiodentals, which are produced by contact between the lower lip and upper teeth (*f* and *v*). Dentals are divided into several varieties, depending on the shape which the tip of the tongue takes on making contact; without going into detail, I shall use β, β′, and β″ to designate the different shapes of the tip of the tongue. Among the sounds that involve the palate, the ear generally singles out a front articulation (palatal) and a back articulation (velar).[4]

LABIO-DENTALS		DENTALS					
f	v	þ	ð	s	z	š	ž
αId [ ] [ ]	αId ~ [ ]	βId [ ] [ ]	βId ~ [ ]	β′Id [ ] [ ]	β′Id ~ [ ]	β″Id [ ] [ ]	β″Id ~ [ ]

PALATALS		GUTTURALS	
χ′	γ′	χ	γ
γIf [ ] [ ]	γIf ~ [ ]	γIi [ ] [ ]	γIi ~ [ ]

þ = English *th* in *thing*
ð = " *th* in *then*
s = " *s* in *say*
z = " *s* in *rose*
š = " *sh* in *show*
ž = " *g* in *rouge*
χ′ = German *ch* in *ich*
γ′ = North German *g* in *liegen*
χ = German *ch* in *Bach*
γ = North German *g* in *Tage*

[4] Faithful to his method, De Saussure did not think it necessary to make the same distinction, for Class A, in spite of the importance of the two series K_1 and K_2 in Proto-Indo-European. The omission is deliberate. [Ed.]

Is there a sound among the fricatives to match *n*, *m*, *ṅ*, etc. among the occlusives—i.e. a nasal *v*, *z*, etc.? It is easy to imagine that there is; for instance, a nasal *v* is heard in French *inventer* 'invent'; but in most languages the nasal fricative is not a distinctive sound.[5]

C. *Aperture 2: Nasals* (see above, p. 45)

D. *Aperture 3: Liquids*

Two kinds of articulation are classed as liquids.

(1) In lateral articulation (indicated by *l̦* in the formulas below) the tongue rests against the front palate but leaves an opening on both sides. It is possible to single out, according to the place of articulation, dental *l*, palatal *l'*, and guttural of velar *ł*. In most languages lateral phonemes are voiced in the same way as *b*, *z*, etc. Still, a voiceless lateral is not impossible; it exists even in French, where an *l* that follows a voiceless phoneme may be pronounced without the laryngeal sound (e.g. the *l* of *pluie* 'rain' against the *l* of *bleu* 'blue'); but speakers are not conscious of the difference.

There is no point in discussing nasal *l*, which is very rare and nondifferentiating, although it does occur, especially after a nasal sound (e.g. the *l* in French *branlant* 'shaking').

(2) In vibrant articulation (indicated by *r̦* in the formula below) the tongue is held farther from the palate than for *l*, but a variable number of contacts between the tongue and palate makes the aperture for vibrants equivalent to the aperture for laterals. Vibration is produced in two ways: with the tip of the tongue thrust forward against the alveolar ridge (trilled *r*), or with the back of the tongue in contact with the palate (a dorsal *r* or burr). What was said about voiced or nasal laterals is also applicable to vibrants.

l̦	l'	ł	r	
β'3e	γ'3f-h	γ'3i	β▾3e	$\gamma 3i^{v}_{\wedge}$
～	～	～	～	～
[ ]	[ ]	[ ]	[ ]	[ ]

[5] The French reads, "mais en générale la fricative nasale n'est pas un son dont la langue ait conscience." [Tr.]

Beyond aperture 3, we enter into a new field; from *consonants* we pass to *vowels*. Up to this point, I have not brought up the distinction between the two for a very simple reason: the phonational mechanism is the same for both. The formula for a vowel is comparable in every way to the formula for a voiced consonant. From the viewpoint of oral articulation, no distinction need be made. Only the acoustical effect is different. Beyond a certain degree of aperture, the mouth functions mainly as a resonator: the timbre of the laryngeal sound stands out, and oral noise decreases. How much of the laryngeal sound is cut out depends on how tightly the mouth is closed; the wider the mouth is opened, the more noise lessens; thus sound predominates in vowels through a purely mechanical process.

E. *Aperture 4: i, u, ü*

The vowels of Class E require much more closure than the other vowels—almost as much as consonants. Certain consequences that will appear later justify the name semi-vowels, which is generally given to phonemes of Class E.

The phoneme *i* is pronounced with retracted lips (—) and front articulation, *u* with rounded lips (○) and back articulation, and *ü* with the lip position of *u* and the articulation of *i*.

Like all other vowels, *i*, *u*, and *ü* have nasalized forms. Here we can disregard them since they are rare. It is worth noting, however, that the sounds written *in* and *un* in French are really not nasalized *i* and *u* (see below).

Is there a voiceless *i*, i.e. articulated without a laryngeal sound? The same question arises for *u* and *ü*, and for all vowels. Such phonemes, corresponding to voiceless consonants, exist but are not to be confused with whispered vowels, i.e., vowels articulated with the glottis relaxed. Voiceless vowels are like the aspirated *h*'s that are pronounced before them: in *hi*, an *i* with no vibration is first heard, then a normal *i*.

i	u	ü
— 4f	○ 4i	○ 4f
~	~	~
[ ]	[ ]	[ ]

F. *Aperture 5: e, o, ö*

The articulation of the phonemes of Class F corresponds exactly to the articulation of *i*, *u*, *ü*. Nasalized vowels occur frequently (e.g. French *ẽ*, *õ*, *ö̃* as in *pin* 'pine,' *pont* 'bridge,' *brun* 'brown'). Voiceless forms are the aspirated *h* of *he*, *ho*, *hö*.

N. B. Many languages single out several degrees of aperture within Class F; French, for instance, has at least two series, one closed (*ẹ*, *ọ*, *ọ̈* as in *dé* 'thimble,' *dos* 'back,' *deux* 'two') and the other open (*ę*, *ǫ*, *ǫ̈* as in *mer* 'sea,' *mort* 'death,' *meurtre* 'murder').

e	o	ö	ẽ	õ	ö̃
—5f	○5i	○5f	—5f	○5i	○5f
~	~	~	~	~	~
[ ]	[ ]	[ ]	....	....	....

a	ã
—6i	—6i
~	~
[ ]	....

G. *Aperture 6: a*

The *a* has maximum aperture. This vowel has a nasalized form, *ã*—slightly more contracted, to be sure—and a voiceless form, the *h* of *ha*.

Chapter II

PHONEMES IN THE SPOKEN CHAIN

1. *Need for Studying Sounds in the Spoken Chain*

Detailed analyses of speech sounds can be found in special treatises, especially in the works of English phoneticians.

Do detailed analyses alone fulfill the auxiliary role of phonology in the science of linguistics? Such a mass of details has no value in itself; only synthesis matters. The linguist does not need to be a consummate phonologist; he asks only to be given certain data that are necessary for the study of language.

The method of phonology is particularly faulty at one point: phonologists too often forget that language is made up not only of sounds but also of expanses of spoken sounds; they still do not devote enough attention to the reciprocal relations of sounds. These relations are not immediately discernible; syllables are easier to identify than their sounds. We have seen (pp. 25 ff.) that some primitive systems of writing noted syllabic units; only later was the alphabetic system devised.

Besides, it is never a simple unit that proves embarrassing in linguistics. If at a particular moment every *a* became *o* in a particular language, nothing would result from the change; the linguist may simply record the phenomenon without trying to explain it phonologically. The science of sounds becomes invaluable only when two or more elements are involved in a relationship based upon their inner dependence, for the variations of each element are limited by the variations of the other element or elements; the single fact that there are two elements calls for a relationship and a rule—and this is quite different from a simple statement. In trying to find a phonological principle, this science is then contradicting itself by showing partiality to isolated sounds. Two phonemes are enough to lead to bewilderment. In Old High German, for instance, *hagl, balg, wagn, lang, donr, dorn* later became *hagal, balg, wagan, lang, donnar, dorn;* the result differs according to the nature and the order of the phonemes involved; sometimes a vowel occurs between the original consonants, sometimes the combination is left intact. But how can the law be formulated? Where did the difference originate? Doubtless in the combinations of the consonants (*gl, lg, gn*, etc.) contained in the words. Each combination obviously contains an occlusive that is either preceded or followed by a liquid or a nasal. But what does that prove? As long as we look upon *g* and *n* as homogeneous quantities, we cannot understand why the mere order of contact in *g-n* and *n-g* should affect the results.

Beside the phonology of species, there is then room for a completely different science that uses binary combinations and sequences of phonemes as a point of departure, and this is something else entirely. In the study of isolated sounds, to note the position of the vocal organs is sufficient; the acoustical quality of a phoneme is not an issue, for it is determined by the ear; as for articulation, the speaker has unlimited freedom. But when we come to the pronunciation of two sounds that are joined, the problem is not so simple; we must bear in mind the possible discrepancy between the effect desired and the effect produced. We do not always have the ability to pronounce what we intend. Freedom in linking phonological species is checked by the possibility of linking articulatory movements. To give an account of what takes place within groups, there should be a science of sound that would treat articulatory movements like algebraic equations: a binary combination implies a certain number of mechanical and acoustical elements that mutually condition each other; the variation of one has a necessary and calculable repercussion on the others. In a phonational act, the one thing which has a universal character that places it above all the local differences of its phonemes is the mechanical regularity of the articulatory movements. The importance of combinatory phonology in general linguistics is obvious. Whereas traditional phonology generally gives rules for articulating all sounds—variable and accidental elements of languages—and stops there, combinatory phonology limits the possibilities and defines the constant relations of interdependent phonemes. The case of *hagl, balg,* etc. (see p. 50) brings up the much discussed question of Proto-Indo-European sonants; now combinatory phonology is most helpful in resolving the question, for the syllabic grouping of phonemes is its sole concern from start to finish. Though that is not the only problem to be solved by the same method, one fact is certain; we simply cannot discuss the question of sonants unless we give full consideration to the laws that govern the combining of phonemes.

2. *Implosion and Explosion*

I shall start from a basic observation: there is a perceptible difference in the pronunciation of the two *p*'s of *appa*. The first *p* results from closure, the second from release. The two impressions are so similar that phoneticians used a single *p* to transcribe the sequence *pp* (see p. 41, note). But we can use special signs (><) to indicate this difference between the two *p*'s of *appa* (*ap͐p᷾a*) and to identify them when they do not follow each other (cf. *ap͐ta, atp᷾a*).

This distinction holds for all other occlusives and for fricatives (*affa*), nasals (*amma*), liquids (*alla*), and for all phonemes in general, including all vowels except *a*(*adda*).

Closure has been termed *implosion* and release *explosion*. A *p* is either implosive (*p*) or explosive (*p*). We may speak in the same sense of *closing* and *opening* sounds.

Doubtless we can single out, besides implosion and explosion, an interval during which occlusion is prolonged at will; and if a phoneme has wider aperture (cf. the *l* of *alla*) the emission of the sound itself continues while the vocal organs remain motionless. Generally, all spoken chains contain intermediate stretches that I shall call *holds* or *sistants*. But they are like implosive articulations, for their effect is the same. In the following pages I am going to consider only implosions and explosions.[6]

The method I have outlined would be unacceptable in a comprehensive treatment of phonology, but it is justifiable in a sketch designed to reduce the essentials of syllabication to as simple a plan as possible. I do not pretend to resolve thereby all the difficulties brought about by dividing the spoken chain into syllables, but simply to provide a rational basis for studying the problem.

One further remark. Opening and closing movements necessary for the emission of sounds must not be confused with the different apertures of the sounds themselves. Any given phoneme can be both implosive and explosive, but aperture does not influence implosion and explosion in the sense that the two movements become less distinct as aperture increases. In *i, u, ü* the difference is still quite apparent; in *aiia* we can detect a closing *i* and an opening *i*: similarly, in *auua*, *aüüa* the implosive sound and the following explosive sound differ so sharply that writing sometimes breaks its regular pattern and records the difference; English *w*, German *j*,

[6] De Saussure's treatment of holds is one of the most debatable points in his theory. To prevent certain objections one should note that any sistant (e.g. that in the articulation of *f*) is the result of two forces: (1) the pressure of air against the opposing organs and (2) the resistance of the organs as they tighten to equalize the pressure. A hold is thus only continued implosion. That is why the effect is the same throughout whenever a hold and an implosive sound of the same species are uttered in sequence. Accordingly, to unite the two types of articulation in one mechanical and acoustical entity is not illogical. Explosion, on the contrary, is opposed to both: by definition it is a release. See also Section 6. [Ed.]

and often French *y* (in *yeux* 'eyes,' etc.) stand for opening sounds in opposition to *u* and *i*, which are used for $\overset{>}{u}$ and $\overset{<}{i}$. But when the aperture is wider (e.g. *e* and *o*) it is hardly possible to distinguish between implosion and explosion in practice, although a difference is theoretically conceivable (cf. $a\overset{>}{e}\overset{<}{e}a$, $a\overset{>}{o}\overset{<}{o}a$). Finally, as we have already seen, maximum aperture wipes out all difference; *a* has neither implosion nor explosion.

Each phoneme except *a* must therefore be split, yielding the following list of irreducible units:

$\overset{>}{p}$ $\overset{<}{p}$, etc.
$\overset{>}{f}$ $\overset{<}{f}$, etc.
$\overset{>}{m}$ $\overset{<}{m}$, etc.
$\overset{>}{r}$ $\overset{<}{r}$, etc.
$\overset{>}{i}$ $\overset{<}{y}$, etc.
$\overset{>}{e}$ $\overset{<}{e}$, etc.
a.

Far from discarding the distinctions sanctioned by spelling ($\overset{<}{u}$, $\overset{<}{i}$), I shall carefully preserve them (*w*, *y*); justification for my viewpoint will be found below (see Section 7).

For the first time we have broken away from abstraction. Now for the first time we have found the concrete, irreducible units that occupy a place and correspond to a beat in the spoken chain: *p* was nothing except an abstract unit linking the common characters of $\overset{>}{p}$ and $\overset{<}{p}$, the only units that actually exist. In the same way, the still higher abstraction of "labiality" links together *P B M*. We may speak of *P* as if it were a zoological species; there are male and female representatives of the species, but there is no ideal specimen. Before, we had been singling out and classifying the abstractions; but we had to go beyond the abstract to reach the concrete.

Phonology made a great mistake in considering abstractions real units without examining more carefully the definition of the unit. The Greek alphabet was successful in singling out the abstract elements—an accomplishment that presupposes a most remarkable analysis (see p. 39); still, the analysis of the Greeks was incomplete, for it was not carried out fully.

Exactly what is an unqualified *p*? Considered in time as part of the spoken chain, it is neither specifically $\overset{<}{p}$ nor $\overset{>}{p}$, and still less $\overset{>}{p}\overset{<}{p}$, this combination being clearly decomposable; and if we consider it outside the spoken chain, it is a thing which has no independent existence and with which we can do nothing. By itself, what does a combination like *l* + *g* mean? Two abstractions cannot form a moment in time. But to talk about *lk*, *lk*, *lk*, *lk*, and thus to draw together the genuine elements of speaking is quite different. Then we see why two elements suffice to embarrass traditional phonology, and the impossibility of working with abstract phonological units—as it did—is demonstrated.

One theory states that in any simple phoneme considered in the chain (e.g., *p* in *pa* or *apa*), implosion and explosion (*apa*) occur successively. Doubtless any release must be preceded by closure. To take still another example, in pronouncing *rp* I must first establish closure for *r*, then articulate an opening *r* while closure for *p* is being formed by the lips. But I need only specify my viewpoint in order to answer that objection. In analyzing a phonational act, I shall consider only the differential elements that make a distinct impression on the ear, allowing delimitation of the acoustical units of the spoken chain. Only the acoustic-motor units are to be considered; hence the articulation of explosive *r* along with implosive *p* is nonexistent to me, for it produces no perceptible sound, or at least is not important in the chain of phonemes. One must appreciate this basic point fully in order to understand the developments that follow.

3. *Different Combinations of Explosions and Implosions in the Chain*

Consider now what may result from each sequence of the four combinations of implosives and explosives that are theoretically possible: (1) <>, (2) ><, (3) <<, (4) >>.

1) *Explosive-Implosive Combination* (<>). Without breaking the spoken chain, we can always join explosive and implosive phonemes: *kr*, *pi*, *ym*, etc. (e.g. Sanskrit *krta-*, English *pity*, Proto-Indo-European **ymto-*, etc.). Of course, some combinations like *kt*, etc. have no practical acoustical effect, but the fact remains that the articulating of an opening *k* leaves the vocal organs in the right position for making closure at any given point. The two phonational movements do not interfere with each other.

2) *Implosive-Explosive Combination* (><). Under the same con-

ditions—and with the same reservations—it is always possible to join implosive and explosive phonemes: i͐m᷾, k͐l᷾, etc. (e.g. Greek *haîma*, English *active*, etc.).

Of course the successive articulatory moments do not follow each other so naturally as they do in the reverse order of combination 1. The difference between initial implosions and explosions is this: explosion, which tends to neutralize the vocal organs, does not engage the following moment; but implosion sets up a definite position that cannot be the point of departure for just any explosion. For that reason one must always resort to some facilitating movement to put the organs necessary for articulating the second phoneme into the right position. While executing *s* in s͐p᷾, for instance, the lips must close to prepare for opening *p*. But experience shows that the facilitating movement has no appreciable effect. It produces only a furtive sound that in no way interferes with the succession of the chain.

3) *Implosive Link* (<<). Two consecutive explosions can be produced, but if the second belongs to a phoneme of less or of equal aperture, the impression of acoustical unity that results in the opposite case or in the sequences of combinations 1 and 2 will be missing: p᷾k᷾ can be pronounced (p᷾k᷾a), but these sounds do not form a chain, for the *P* and *K* species have the same aperture. This rather unnatural pronunciation would result from stopping after the first *a* of *cha-p᷾k᷾a*.[7] On the contrary, p᷾r᷾ gives the impression of continuity (cf. *price*); nor does r᷾y᷾ cause difficulty (cf. French *rien* 'nothing'). Why? Because at the very instant the first explosion occurs, the vocal organs have already assumed the right position for executing the second explosion without interfering with the acoustical effect of the first; thus the organs are already in position for the *r* of *price* while *p* is being pronounced. But it is impossible to pronounce the reverse series *rp*, not because this is mechanically impossible (we can prepare for p᷾ while articulating opening r᷾), but because the movement of the r᷾, coming against the smaller aperture of p᷾, would be imperceptible. Two separate movements would

[7] To be sure combinations of explosive phonemes having the same aperture are very common in some languages (e.g. initial *kt* in Greek; cf. *kteíno*); although these combinations are easy to pronounce, they lack acoustical unity. (See the following note.)

be required to make r̆p̆ audible, and the emission would be interrupted.

A continuous explosive link may include more than two elements provided that each successive aperture is wider than the preceding one (e.g. *k̂r̂ŵa*). Aside from a few special cases which I cannot discuss in detail,[8] the natural limit of the possible number of explosions is the number of degrees of aperture distinguishable in practice.

4) *Implosive Link* (>>). The reverse law governs the implosive link: whenever a particular phoneme is more open than the following one, the impression of continuity persists (e.g. *ĭr̆*, *r̆l̆*); if this condition is not met—if the following phoneme is more open or has the same aperture—pronunciation is still possible, but the impression of continuity is lacking: *s̆r̆* in *ăs̆r̆ta* is basically the same as *p̆k̆* in *cha-pka* (see p. 55). This phenomenon parallels the one analyzed in the explosive link in every way: in *r̆l̆* the *l̆*, by virtue of its narrower aperture, exempts *r* from explosion; in a link like *r̆m̆*, made up of phonemes with different points of articulation, *m̆* does not exempt *r̆* from exploding but brings about the same result by covering its explosion completely. Otherwise, as in the reverse order *m̆r̆*, the furtive, mechanically indispensable explosion breaks the spoken chain.

An implosive link, like an explosive one, obviously can include more than two elements if each has wider aperture than the following one (cf. *ăr̆s̆t̆*).

Leaving aside the breaking of links, we turn now to the normal continuous chain—one that might be termed physiological—as rep-

[8] Through deliberate over-simplification, De Saussure considers here only the degree of aperture of the phoneme, not the place and specific nature of its articulation (whether voiceless or voiced, vibrant or lateral, etc.). Conclusions drawn from the principle of aperture alone are not applicable without exception to all actual cases. In a sequence like *trya*, for instance, only with difficulty can the first three elements be pronounced without breaking the chain: *t̂r̂y̆ă* (unless *y̆* palatalizes the *r̂* and merges with it); but the three elements in *try* make a perfect explosive link (cf. also p. 63 concerning *meurtrier*, etc.); *trwa*, on the contrary, offers no difficulty. Links like *pmla*, etc., where it is difficult to avoid pronouncing the nasal implosively (*p̂m̆l̂ă*), should also be cited. The aberrant cases show up especially in explosion, an instantaneous act that tolerates absolutely no hindrances. [Ed.]

resented by French *particulièrement:* p̌ ǎ ř ľ ǐ ǩ ǔ ľ y̌ ě ř m̌ ǎ.[9] The chain is characterized by a succession of graduated links corresponding to a succession of releases and closures of the vocal organs.

The normal chain thus defined makes possible the following observations which are of capital importance.

4. *Syllabic Boundary and Vocalic Peak*

Passing from an implosion to an explosion in a chain of sounds produces a peculiar effect that marks the syllabic boundary (e.g. the ǐǩ of *particulièrement*). The regular coincidence of a mechanical principle and a definite acoustical effect assures the implosive-explosive combination of a right to existence in phonology. Its character persists regardless of the species that compose it. It constitutes a type that contains as many species as there are possible combinations.

The syllabic boundary sometimes occurs at different points in the same series of phonemes, depending on the speed of passage from implosion to explosion. In *ardra*, for instance, neither the division ǎřďřǎ nor the division ǎřďřǎ breaks the chain, for both the implosive link ǎřď and the explosive link ďř are graduated. The same would apply to ǔľy̌ě of *particulièrement* (ǔľy̌ě or ǔľy̌ě).

Next, we notice that in passing from silence to initial implosion (>)—e.g. *art* in *artist*—or from explosion to implosion (<>) e.g. *part* in *particulièrement*—the sound where the initial implosion occurs is distinguished from neighboring sounds by its own vocalic effect. In no way does the vocalic effect depend on the wider aperture of the sound *a*, for in p̌řt, *r* produces the same effect; it is inherent in initial implosions regardless of their phonological species, i.e., their degree of aperture; whether the implosion comes after a silence or after an explosion matters little. A sound that makes a vocalic impression is a *vocalic peak.*

Vocalic peaks have also been called *sonants,* and all other sounds in the same syllable *con-sonants* [*consonantes*]. Vowels and consonants [*consonnes*] designate different species (see p. 48); sonants

[9] Note the difference in the syllabication of English *particularly* [p̌ǎř ťǐǩ ǐǔ ľǎř ľǐ]. [Tr.]

and con-sonants, on the other hand, designate functions within syllables. The dual system of terminology clears up the confusion that has existed for a long time. Thus the *I* species is the same in French *fidèle* 'faithful' and *pied* 'foot'; it is a vowel;[10] but it is a sonant in *fidèle* and a *con-sonant* in *pied*. Analysis shows that sonants are always implosive while non-sonants may be either implosive (e.g. $\overset{>}{\imath}$ in English *bo*$\overset{>}{\imath}$, written *boy*) or explosive (e.g. $\overset{<}{y}$ in French $\overset{<}{p}\overset{<}{y}\overset{>}{e}$, written *pied*). Analysis only confirms the distinction set up between the two classes. Regularly, *e, o, a* are sonants, but this is merely a coincidence: having wider aperture than any of the other sounds, they are always at the beginning of an implosive chain. Conversely occlusives, which have minimum aperture, are always con-sonants. In practice phonemes of apertures 2, 3, and 4 (nasals, liquids, and semivowels) play either role, depending on contiguous sounds and the nature of their articulation.

5. *Criticism of Theories of Syllabication*

The ear perceives syllabic division in every spoken chain; it also perceives a sonant in every syllable. One can accept both facts and still wonder why they should hold true. Different explanations have been offered.

1) Noticing that some phonemes are more sonorous than others, some scholars have tried to base syllables on the sonority of phonemes. But how is it that sonorous phonemes like *i* and *u* do not necessarily form syllables? Besides, where does sonority stop since fricatives like *s* are syllabic (e.g. *pst*)? If only the relative sonority of sounds in contact is at stake, how can one explain such combinations as *wl* (e.g. Proto-Indo-European **wlkos* 'wolf'), where the least sonorous element is syllabic?

2) E. Sievers was the first to show that a sound classed as a vowel does not necessarily make a vocalic impression (e.g. we saw above, p. 52 f., that *y* and *w* are nothing except *i* and *u*); but one who asks why a sound should have a dual function—or a dual acoustical effect, for "function" means just that—is given this reply: the function of a given sound depends on whether the sound receives the "syllabic accent."

This is a vicious circle. If I am free under all circumstances to

[10] Cf. English *fee* [fij] and *few* [fju]. [Tr.]

place the syllabic accent that creates sonants wherever I choose, then the accent might as well be called sonantic. But if syllabic means anything, its meaning must derive from the laws of the syllable. Not only are such laws lacking, but the sonantic quality is described as *silbenbildend*, as if the formation of syllables depended on syllabic accent.

The difference between our method and (1) and (2) above is obvious: by analyzing syllables as they occur in the chain, we found the irreducible units, opening and closing sounds; then by combining these units, we were able to define the syllabic boundary and vocalic peak. Now we know the physiological conditions under which the acoustical effects must occur. The theories criticized above follow the opposite course: from isolated phonological species, the proponents of the theories pretend to deduce the boundary of the syllable and the position of the sonant. In a given series of phonemes, one pronunciation may be more natural and easier than another; but by and large the possibility of choosing between opening and closing articulations persists, and syllabication depends on the choice rather than directly on phonological species.

Doubtless my theory neither exhausts nor resolves all questions. Hiatus, for example, which occurs very frequently, is simply a *broken implosive link*, deliberate or unintentional: e.g. $\overset{>}{i}$-$\overset{<}{a}$ (in French *il cria* 'he shouted') and $\overset{>}{a}$-$\overset{<}{i}$ (in French *ébahi* 'amazed').[11] It occurs more easily when the phonological species have wide aperture.

There are also broken explosive links which, though ungraduated, fall into a phonetic chain just as do normal groups. I mentioned one example earlier, *kteíno* (see p. 55, note). Or take the sequence *pzta:* normally it can be pronounced only $\overset{>}{p}\overset{>}{z}\overset{<}{t}\overset{<}{a}$; it should comprise two syllables, and it does have two if the laryngeal sound of *z* is pronounced distinctly; but if *z* is muffled, the opposition between it and *a* is insufficient since *z* is one of the phonemes that require least aperture; the result is that only one syllable is perceived and something like $\overset{>}{p}\overset{>}{z}\overset{<}{t}\overset{<}{a}$ is heard.

In all broken explosive links, when will and intention interfere, to some extent it will be possible to eschew physiological neces-

[11] Cf. English *rearm* ($\overset{>}{i}$-$\overset{<}{a}$) and *Aïda* ($\overset{>}{a}$-$\overset{<}{i}$). [Tr.]

sities. Determining what is wilful and what is physiological is often difficult. But phonation depends on a succession of implosions and explosions, and this is basic in syllabication.

6. *Length of Implosion and Explosion*

Our explanation of syllables in terms of the functioning of explosions and implosions leads to an important observation that is simply a generalization of a metrical fact. We can separate two types of long vowels in Latin and Greek: those long by nature (*māter*) and those long by position (*fāctus*). Why is *fac* counted long in *factus?* because of the *ct* combination? No, for if the combination alone determined length, every syllable beginning with two consonants would also be long; but this is not true (cf. *clĭens*, etc.).

The real reason is that explosion and implosion are basically different with respect to length. The first is always so rapid that it cannot be measured by the ear; for that reason also, it never makes a vocalic impression. Only implosion is measurable; hence we feel that we dwell longer on the vowel where implosion begins.

Besides, we know that vowels which occur before a combination of an occlusive or fricative and a liquid are treated in two ways: the *a* in *patron* may be either long or short; the principle is the same in either instance. Actually $\overset{<}{l}\overset{<}{r}$ and $\overset{>}{l}\overset{<}{r}$ are pronounced with equal ease; the first method of articulation allows *a* to remain short; the second creates a long syllable. The same dual treatment of *a* is not possible in a word like *factus;* $\overset{>}{c}\overset{<}{t}$ can be pronounced, but $\overset{<}{c}\overset{<}{t}$ cannot.

7. *Phonemes of Aperture 4; Diphthongs; Questions about Transcription*

Finally, the phonemes of aperture 4 call for some additional remarks. We have seen that, contrary to what happens with other sounds, usage has sanctioned a double set of graphs ($w = \overset{<}{u}$, $u = \overset{>}{u}$; $y = \overset{<}{i}$, $i = \overset{>}{i}$) for the phonemes of aperture 4 (see p. 52). The reason is simple: in groups like *aiya, auwa* the distinction between release and closure is more striking than elsewhere; $\overset{>}{i}$ and $\overset{>}{u}$ make a clear vocalic impression, $\overset{<}{i}$ and $\overset{<}{u}$ a consonantal impression.[12] Without

[12] The *i* of aperture 4 must not be confused with the soft palatal fricative (e.g. the *g* in North German *liegen*), a phonological species that has all the characteristics of a consonant. [S.]

pretending to explain the fact, I wish to point out that consonantal *i* is never accompanied by closure: the *ĭ* in *ai* never has the same effect as the *y* in *aiya* (cf. English *boy* and French *pied*); through position, then, *y* is a consonant and *i* a vowel, for these variations of the *I* species do not occur indifferently. The same remarks apply to *u* and *w*, *ü* and *ẅ*.

The preceding discussion clarifies the question of the diphthong. It is only a special kind of implosive link; *ărta* and *ăŭta* are absolutely parallel; only the aperture of the second element is different. A diphthong is an implosive link in which the second phoneme is relatively open, making a specific acoustical impression. We might say that the sonant continues in the second element of the combination. Conversely, a combination like *l̆y̆a* is distinguished from a combination like *l̆r̆a* only by the degree of aperture of the last explosive. This means that what phonologists call ascending diphthongs are not really diphthongs but explosive-implosive combinations in which the first element does not produce a specific acoustical effect even though it is relatively open (*l̆y̆ă*). Combinations like *ŭo*, *ĭa*, with the accent on *ŭ* and *ĭ* (e.g. *buob*, *liab* in certain German dialects), are also false diphthongs that fail to make the impression of unity produced by *ŏŭ*, *ăĭ*, etc.; we cannot pronounce *ŭŏ* as implosive + implosive and avoid breaking the link without calling in some device to impose an artificial unity on the combination.

Our definition of the diphthong—which relates it to the general principle of implosive links—shows that it is not, as one might think, an incongruous something not to be classed among phonological phenomena; there is no need for putting it into a special category. The uniqueness of the diphthong is really of no interest or importance; the important thing is to determine, not the end of the sonant, but its beginning.

E. Sievers and many other linguists make a distinction in writing between *i*, *u*, *ü*, *r̥*, *n̥*, etc. and *i̯*, *u̯*, *ü̯*, *r*, *n*, etc. (*i̯* = *unsilbisches i*, *i* = *silbisches i*); they write *mirta*, *mai̯rta*, *mi̯arta* while I write *mirta*, *mairta*, *myarta*. Having noticed that *i* and *y* belong to the same phonological species, they wanted especially to have a single generic sign for both (still clinging to the notion that a chain of sound is composed of species in juxtaposition). Their transcription, though based on oral evidence, is illogical and eliminates the very distinction that should be made: (1) opening *i*, *u* (= *y*, *w*) are confused with closing *i*, *u* (e.g. they cannot distinguish between *newo* and *neuo*); conversely, closing *i*, *u* are sliced in two (cf. *mirta* and *mairta*). Here are some examples of difficulties that result from using Siever's system. First, Old Greek *dwís* and *duís* against *rhéwō* and *rheûma*. The two oppositions occur under exactly the same phonological conditions and are usually indicated by the same graphic symbols. The *u* is either opening (*w*) or closing (*u*) depending upon whether the following phoneme is more open or more closed. But the transcription *du̯is*, *duis*, *rheu̯o*, *rheu̯ma* wipes out completely these oppositions. Similarly, in Proto-Indo-European the two series *māter*, *mātrai*, *māteres*, *mātrsu* and *sūneu*, *sūnewai*, *sūnewes*, *sūnusu* are strictly parallel in their dual treatment of both *r* and *u*. In the second series at least, the opposition between implosives and explosives is crystal clear in writing. But the transcription that I have criticized (*sūneu̯*, *sūneu̯ai*, *sūneu̯es*, *sūnusu*) obscures the opposition. Existing distinctions between opening and closing sounds (*u*, *w*, etc.) should not only be preserved but extended to cover the whole system. Thus we should write *māter*, *mātρai*, *māteρes*, *mātrsu;* then the functioning of syllabication would stand out; vocalic peaks and syllabic boundaries would be revealed.

Editor's Note. The theories discussed above throw light on several problems, some of which Saussure touched upon in his lectures. We shall give a few examples.

1) Sievers cites *beritṇnṇn* (German *berittenen*) as a typical example to show that a single sound may alternately function twice as a sonant and twice as a non-sonant (actually *n* functions only once as a con-sonant, and the word should be transcribed *beritṇnṇ*, but that matters little). No example would show more clearly that "sound" and "species" are not synonymous. For if we dwell on the *n*, i.e. implosion and sistant articulation, the result is only a long syllable. To create an alternation of sonantic and con-sonantic *n*'s, we would have to pass from implosion (first *n*) to explosion (second *n*) and back to implosion (third *n*). Since the two implosions are preceded by no other implosion, both are sonantic.

2) In French words like *meurtrier* 'murderer,' *ouvrier* 'worker,'

etc., final *–trier*, *–vrier* formed only one syllable regardless of how they were actually pronounced (cf. p. 56, note). Later, speakers began to pronounce them in two syllables (*meur-tri-er*, with or without hiatus, i.e. *–t̂r̆ìĕ* or *t̂r̆ìy̆ĕ*). The change was brought about, not by placing a "syllabic accent" on the *i* element, but by changing its explosive articulation to implosive.

The vulgar pronunciation of *ouvrier* is *ouvérier*.[13] This change is similar to the dividing of *–vrier* into two syllables, but here the second element (*r*) rather than the third changed its articulation and became a sonant: *uvr̆y̆ĕ* → *uvr̂y̆ĕ*. An *e* subsequently developed in front of sonantic *r*.

3) We might also cite the well-known case of prosthetic vowels in front of *s* followed by a consonant in French: Latin *scūtum* → *iscūtum* → French *escu*, *écu* 'shield.' Here *sk* is a broken link (see p. 55); *ŝk̆* is more natural. But implosive *s* serves as a vocalic peak when at the beginning of the sentence or when the preceding word ends in a consonant with weak aperture. Prosthetic *i* and *e* only exaggerate the sonantic quality of *s:* any perceptible phonological characteristic tends to become more pronounced whenever speakers try to preserve it. The same phenomenon is responsible for *esclandre* 'scandal' and the vulgar pronunciations *esquelette*, *estatue* (Standard French *squelette* 'skeleton,' *statue* 'statue'); it also shows up in the vulgar pronunciation of the preposition *de* 'of,' transcribed *ed: un oeil ed tanche* 'a tench's eye.' Through syncope *de tanche* became *d'tanche;* but to be perceptible in this position *d* must be implosive (*d̂tanche*); the result was again the development of a prosthetic vowel.

4) It is scarcely necessary to come back to Indo-European sonants and to ask, for example, why Old High German *hagl* changed to *hagal* while *balg* remained intact. Here the *l*, the second element of an implosive link (*bâl̂ĝ*), functioned as a con-sonant and had no reason to change its function. But the *l* of *hagl*, also implosive, was a vocalic peak. Being sonantic, it developed a more open prosthetic vowel (an *a* if we accept spelling as evidence). The vowel became less distinct with the passage of time, however, and today *Hagel* is

[13] Cf. English *burglar*. [Tr.]

again pronounced *hằg̑l̀*. The quality of the *l* is responsible for the difference between the pronunciation of the German word and French *aigle* 'eagle': *Hagel* has a closing *l* while the French word has an opening *l* followed by a mute *e* (*ẻg̑ĺə*).

PART ONE
General Principles

Chapter I

NATURE OF THE LINGUISTIC SIGN

1. *Sign, Signified, Signifier*

Some people regard language, when reduced to its elements, as a naming-process only—a list of words, each corresponding to the thing that it names. For example:

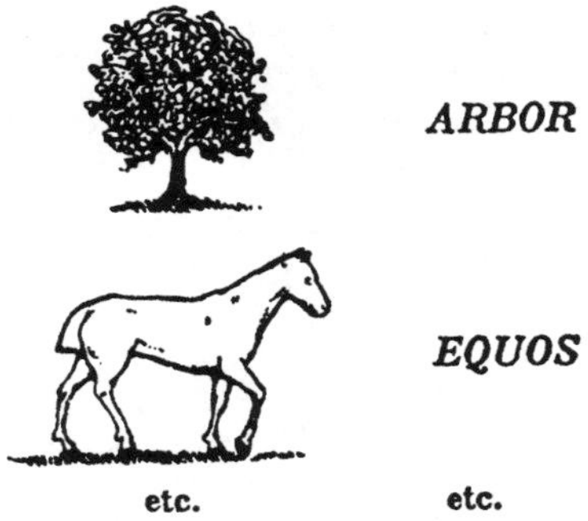

This conception is open to criticism at several points. It assumes that ready-made ideas exist before words (on this point, see below, p. 111); it does not tell us whether a name is vocal or psychological in nature (*arbor,* for instance, can be considered from either viewpoint); finally, it lets us assume that the linking of a name and a thing is a very simple operation—an assumption that is anything but true. But this rather naive approach can bring us near the truth by showing us that the linguistic unit is a double entity, one formed by the associating of two terms.

We have seen in considering the speaking-circuit (p. 11) that both terms involved in the linguistic sign are psychological and are united in the brain by an associative bond. This point must be emphasized.

The linguistic sign unites, not a thing and a name, but a concept and a sound-image.[1] The latter is not the material sound, a purely physical thing, but the psychological imprint of the sound, the impression that it makes on our senses. The sound-image is sensory, and if I happen to call it "material," it is only in that sense, and by way of opposing it to the other term of the association, the concept, which is generally more abstract.

The psychological character of our sound-images becomes apparent when we observe our own speech. Without moving our lips or tongue, we can talk to ourselves or recite mentally a selection of verse. Because we regard the words of our language as sound-images, we must avoid speaking of the "phonemes" that make up the words. This term, which suggests vocal activity, is applicable to the spoken word only, to the realization of the inner image in discourse. We can avoid that misunderstanding by speaking of the *sounds* and *syllables* of a word provided we remember that the names refer to the sound-image.

The linguistic sign is then a two-sided psychological entity that can be represented by the drawing:

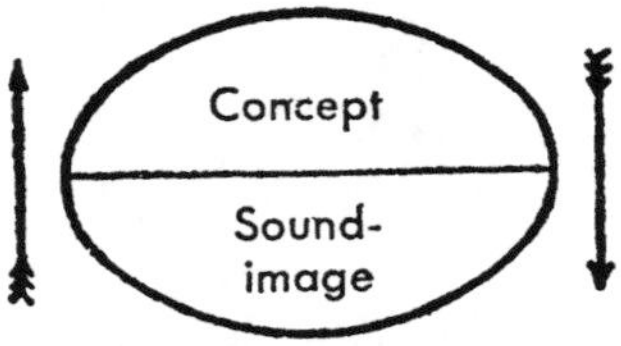

The two elements are intimately united, and each recalls the other. Whether we try to find the meaning of the Latin word *arbor* or the word that Latin uses to designate the concept "tree," it is

[1] The term sound-image may seem to be too restricted inasmuch as beside the representation of the sounds of a word there is also that of its articulation, the muscular image of the phonational act. But for F. de Saussure language is essentially a depository, a thing received from without (see p. 13). The sound-image is par excellence the natural representation of the word as a fact of potential language, outside any actual use of it in speaking. The motor side is thus implied or, in any event, occupies only a subordinate role with respect to the sound-image. [Ed.]

clear that only the associations sanctioned by that language appear to us to conform to reality, and we disregard whatever others might be imagined.

Our definition of the linguistic sign poses an important question of terminology. I call the combination of a concept and a sound-image a *sign*, but in current usage the term generally designates only a sound-image, a word, for example (*arbor*, etc.). One tends to forget that *arbor* is called a sign only because it carries the concept "tree," with the result that the idea of the sensory part implies the idea of the whole.

Ambiguity would disappear if the three notions involved here were designated by three names, each suggesting and opposing the others. I propose to retain the word *sign* [*signe*] to designate the whole and to replace *concept* and *sound-image* respectively by *signified* [*signifié*] and *signifier* [*signifiant*]; the last two terms have the advantage of indicating the opposition that separates them from each other and from the whole of which they are parts. As regards *sign*, if I am satisfied with it, this is simply because I do not know of any word to replace it, the ordinary language suggesting no other.

The linguistic sign, as defined, has two primordial characteristics. In enunciating them I am also positing the basic principles of any study of this type.

2. *Principle I: The Arbitrary Nature of the Sign*

The bond between the signifier and the signified is arbitrary. Since I mean by sign the whole that results from the associating of the signifier with the signified, I can simply say: *the linguistic sign is arbitrary.*

The idea of "sister" is not linked by any inner relationship to the succession of sounds *s-ö-r* which serves as its signifier in French;

that it could be represented equally by just any other sequence is proved by differences among languages and by the very existence of different languages: the signified "ox" has as its signifier *b-ö-f* on one side of the border and *o-k-s* (*Ochs*) on the other.

No one disputes the principle of the arbitrary nature of the sign, but it is often easier to discover a truth than to assign to it its proper place. Principle I dominates all the linguistics of language; its consequences are numberless. It is true that not all of them are equally obvious at first glance; only after many detours does one discover them, and with them the primordial importance of the principle.

One remark in passing: when semiology becomes organized as a science, the question will arise whether or not it properly includes modes of expression based on completely natural signs, such as pantomime. Supposing that the new science welcomes them, its main concern will still be the whole group of systems grounded on the arbitrariness of the sign. In fact, every means of expression used in society is based, in principle, on collective behavior or—what amounts to the same thing—on convention. Polite formulas, for instance, though often imbued with a certain natural expressiveness (as in the case of a Chinese who greets his emperor by bowing down to the ground nine times), are nonetheless fixed by rule; it is this rule and not the intrinsic value of the gestures that obliges one to use them. Signs that are wholly arbitrary realize better than the others the ideal of the semiological process; that is why language, the most complex and universal of all systems of expression, is also the most characteristic; in this sense linguistics can become the master-pattern for all branches of semiology although language is only one particular semiological system.

The word *symbol* has been used to designate the linguistic sign, or more specifically, what is here called the signifier. Principle I in particular weighs against the use of this term. One characteristic of the symbol is that it is never wholly arbitrary; it is not empty, for there is the rudiment of a natural bond between the signifier and the signified. The symbol of justice, a pair of scales, could not be replaced by just any other symbol, such as a chariot.

The word *arbitrary* also calls for comment. The term should not imply that the choice of the signifier is left entirely to the speaker (we shall see below that the individual does not have the power to change a sign in any way once it has become established in the linguistic community); I mean that it is unmotivated, i.e. arbitrary in that it actually has no natural connection with the signified.

In concluding let us consider two objections that might be raised to the establishment of Principle I:

1) *Onomatopoeia* might be used to prove that the choice of the signifier is not always arbitrary. But onomatopoeic formations are never organic elements of a linguistic system. Besides, their number is much smaller than is generally supposed. Words like French *fouet* 'whip' or *glas* 'knell' may strike certain ears with suggestive sonority, but to see that they have not always had this property we need only examine their Latin forms (*fouet* is derived from *fāgus* 'beech-tree,' *glas* from *classicum* 'sound of a trumpet'). The quality of their present sounds, or rather the quality that is attributed to them, is a fortuitous result of phonetic evolution.

As for authentic onomatopoeic words (e.g. *glug-glug, tick-tock,* etc.), not only are they limited in number, but also they are chosen somewhat arbitrarily, for they are only approximate and more or less conventional imitations of certain sounds (cf. English *bow-bow* and French *ouaoua*). In addition, once these words have been introduced into the language, they are to a certain extent subjected to the same evolution—phonetic, morphological, etc.—that other words undergo (cf. *pigeon,* ultimately from Vulgar Latin *pīpiō,* derived in turn from an onomatopoeic formation): obvious proof that they lose something of their original character in order to assume that of the linguistic sign in general, which is unmotivated.

2) *Interjections,* closely related to onomatopoeia, can be attacked on the same grounds and come no closer to refuting our thesis. One is tempted to see in them spontaneous expressions of reality dictated, so to speak, by natural forces. But for most interjections we can show that there is no fixed bond between their signified and their signifier. We need only compare two languages on this point to see how much such expressions differ from one language to the next (e.g. the English equivalent of French *aïe!* is *ouch!*). We know, moreover, that many interjections were once

words with specific meanings (cf. French *diable!* 'darn!' *mordieu!* 'golly!' from *mort Dieu* 'God's death,' etc.).[2]

Onomatopoeic formations and interjections are of secondary importance, and their symbolic origin is in part open to dispute.

3. *Principle II: The Linear Nature of the Signifier*

The signifier, being auditory, is unfolded solely in time from which it gets the following characteristics: (a) it represents a span, and (b) the span is measurable in a single dimension; it is a line.

While Principle II is obvious, apparently linguists have always neglected to state it, doubtless because they found it too simple; nevertheless, it is fundamental, and its consequences are incalculable. Its importance equals that of Principle I; the whole mechanism of language depends upon it (see p. 122 f.). In contrast to visual signifiers (nautical signals, etc.) which can offer simultaneous groupings in several dimensions, auditory signifiers have at their command only the dimension of time. Their elements are presented in succession; they form a chain. This feature becomes readily apparent when they are represented in writing and the spatial line of graphic marks is substituted for succession in time.

Sometimes the linear nature of the signifier is not obvious. When I accent a syllable, for instance, it seems that I am concentrating more than one significant element on the same point. But this is an illusion; the syllable and its accent constitute only one phonational act. There is no duality within the act but only different oppositions to what precedes and what follows (on this subject, see p. 131).

[2] Cf. English *goodness!* and *zounds!* (from *God's wounds*). [Tr.]

Chapter II

IMMUTABILITY AND MUTABILITY OF THE SIGN

1. *Immutability*

The signifier, though to all appearances freely chosen with respect to the idea that it represents, is fixed, not free, with respect to the linguistic community that uses it. The masses have no voice in the matter, and the signifier chosen by language could be replaced by no other. This fact, which seems to embody a contradiction, might be called colloquially "the stacked deck." We say to language: "Choose!" but we add: "It must be this sign and no other." No individual, even if he willed it, could modify in any way at all the choice that has been made; and what is more, the community itself cannot control so much as a single word; it is bound to the existing language.

No longer can language be identified with a contract pure and simple, and it is precisely from this viewpoint that the linguistic sign is a particularly interesting object of study; for language furnishes the best proof that a law accepted by a community is a thing that is tolerated and not a rule to which all freely consent.

Let us first see why we cannot control the linguistic sign and then draw together the important consequences that issue from the phenomenon.

No matter what period we choose or how far back we go, language always appears as a heritage of the preceding period. We might conceive of an act by which, at a given moment, names were assigned to things and a contract was formed between concepts and sound-images; but such an act has never been recorded. The notion that things might have happened like that was prompted by our acute awareness of the arbitrary nature of the sign.

No society, in fact, knows or has ever known language other than as a product inherited from preceding generations, and one to be accepted as such. That is why the question of the origin of speech is not so important as it is generally assumed to be. The question is not even worth asking; the only real object of linguistics is the normal, regular life of an existing idiom. A particular language-state is always the product of historical forces, and these forces explain why the sign is unchangeable, i.e. why it resists any arbitrary substitution.

Nothing is explained by saying that language is something inherited and leaving it at that. Can not existing and inherited laws be modified from one moment to the next?

To meet that objection, we must put language into its social setting and frame the question just as we would for any other social institution. How are other social institutions transmitted? This more general question includes the question of immutability. We must first determine the greater or lesser amounts of freedom that the other institutions enjoy; in each instance it will be seen that a different proportion exists between fixed tradition and the free action of society. The next step is to discover why in a given category, the forces of the first type carry more weight or less weight than those of the second. Finally, coming back to language, we must ask why the historical factor of transmission dominates it entirely and prohibits any sudden widespread change.

There are many possible answers to the question. For example, one might point to the fact that succeeding generations are not superimposed on one another like the drawers of a piece of furniture, but fuse and interpenetrate, each generation embracing individuals of all ages—with the result that modifications of language are not tied to the succession of generations. One might also recall the sum of the efforts required for learning the mother language and conclude that a general change would be impossible. Again, it might be added that reflection does not enter into the active use of an idiom—speakers are largely unconscious of the laws of language; and if they are unaware of them, how could they modify them? Even if they were aware of these laws, we may be sure that their awareness would seldom lead to criticism, for people are generally satisfied with the language they have received.

The foregoing considerations are important but not topical. The following are more basic and direct, and all the others depend on them.

1) *The arbitrary nature of the sign.* Above, we had to accept the theoretical possibility of change; further reflection suggests that the arbitrary nature of the sign is really what protects language from any attempt to modify it. Even if people were more conscious of language than they are, they would still not know how to discuss it. The reason is simply that any subject in order to be discussed must have a reasonable basis. It is possible, for instance, to discuss whether the monogamous form of marriage is more reasonable than the polygamous form and to advance arguments to support either side. One could also argue about a system of symbols, for the symbol has a rational relationship with the thing signified (see p. 68); but language is a system of arbitrary signs and lacks the necessary basis, the solid ground for discussion. There is no reason for preferring *soeur* to *sister*, *Ochs* to *boeuf*, etc.

2) *The multiplicity of signs necessary to form any language.* Another important deterrent to linguistic change is the great number of signs that must go into the making of any language. A system of writing comprising twenty to forty letters can in case of need be replaced by another system. The same would be true of language if it contained a limited number of elements; but linguistic signs are numberless.

3) *The over-complexity of the system.* A language constitutes a system. In this one respect (as we shall see later) language is not completely arbitrary but is ruled to some extent by logic; it is here also, however, that the inability of the masses to transform it becomes apparent. The system is a complex mechanism that can be grasped only through reflection; the very ones who use it daily are ignorant of it. We can conceive of a change only through the intervention of specialists, grammarians, logicians, etc.; but experience shows us that all such meddlings have failed.

4) *Collective inertia toward innovation.* Language—and this consideration surpasses all the others—is at every moment everybody's concern; spread throughout society and manipulated by it, language is something used daily by all. Here we are unable to set up any comparison between it and other institutions. The prescriptions of codes, religious rites, nautical signals, etc., involve only a certain number of individuals simultaneously and then only

during a limited period of time; in language, on the contrary, everyone participates at all times, and that is why it is constantly being influenced by all. This capital fact suffices to show the impossibility of revolution. Of all social institutions, language is least amenable to initiative. It blends with the life of society, and the latter, inert by nature, is a prime conservative force.

But to say that language is a product of social forces does not suffice to show clearly that it is unfree; remembering that it is always the heritage of the preceding period, we must add that these social forces are linked with time. Language is checked not only by the weight of the collectivity but also by time. These two are inseparable. At every moment solidarity with the past checks freedom of choice. We say *man* and *dog*. This does not prevent the existence in the total phenomenon of a bond between the two antithetical forces—arbitrary convention by virtue of which choice is free and time which causes choice to be fixed. Because the sign is arbitrary, it follows no law other than that of tradition, and because it is based on tradition, it is arbitrary.

2. *Mutability*

Time, which insures the continuity of language, wields another influence apparently contradictory to the first: the more or less rapid change of linguistic signs. In a certain sense, therefore, we can speak of both the immutability and the mutability of the sign.[3]

In the last analysis, the two facts are interdependent: the sign is exposed to alteration because it perpetuates itself. What predominates in all change is the persistence of the old substance; disregard for the past is only relative. That is why the principle of change is based on the principle of continuity.

Change in time takes many forms, on any one of which an important chapter in linguistics might be written. Without entering into detail, let us see what things need to be delineated.

First, let there be no mistake about the meaning that we attach to the word change. One might think that it deals especially with

[3] It would be wrong to reproach F. de Saussure for being illogical or paradoxical in attributing two contradictory qualities to language. By opposing two striking terms, he wanted only to emphasize the fact that language changes in spite of the inability of speakers to change it. One can also say that it is intangible but not unchangeable. [Ed.]

phonetic changes undergone by the signifier, or perhaps changes in meaning which affect the signified concept. That view would be inadequate. Regardless of what the forces of change are, whether in isolation or in combination, they always result in *a shift in the relationship between the signified and the signifier.*

Here are some examples. Latin *necāre* 'kill' became *noyer* 'drown' in French. Both the sound-image and the concept changed; but it is useless to separate the two parts of the phenomenon; it is sufficient to state with respect to the whole that the bond between the idea and the sign was loosened, and that there was a shift in their relationship. If instead of comparing Classical Latin *necāre* with French *noyer*, we contrast the former term with *necare* of Vulgar Latin of the fourth or fifth century meaning 'drown' the case is a little different; but here again, although there is no appreciable change in the signifier, there is a shift in the relationship between the idea and the sign.[4]

Old German *dritteil* 'one-third' became *Drittel* in Modern German. Here, although the concept remained the same, the relationship was changed in two ways: the signifier was changed not only in its material aspect but also in its grammatical form; the idea of *Teil* 'part' is no longer implied; *Drittel* is a simple word. In one way or another there is always a shift in the relationship.

In Anglo-Saxon the preliterary form *fot* 'foot' remained while its plural **fōti* became *fēt* (Modern English *feet*). Regardless of the other changes that are implied, one thing is certain: there was a shift in their relationship; other correspondences between the phonetic substance and the idea emerged.

Language is radically powerless to defend itself against the forces which from one moment to the next are shifting the relationship between the signified and the signifier. This is one of the consequences of the arbitrary nature of the sign.

Unlike language, other human institutions—customs, laws, etc. —are all based in varying degrees on the natural relations of things; all have of necessity adapted the means employed to the ends pursued. Even fashion in dress is not entirely arbitrary; we can deviate only slightly from the conditions dictated by the human

[4] From May to July of 1911, De Saussure used interchangeably the old terminology (*idea* and *sign*) and the new (*signified* and *signifier*). [Tr.]

body. Language is limited by nothing in the choice of means, for apparently nothing would prevent the associating of any idea whatsoever with just any sequence of sounds.

To emphasize the fact that language is a genuine institution, Whitney quite justly insisted upon the arbitrary nature of signs; and by so doing, he placed linguistics on its true axis. But he did not follow through and see that the arbitrariness of language radically separates it from all other institutions. This is apparent from the way in which language evolves. Nothing could be more complex. As it is a product of both the social force and time, no one can change anything in it, and on the other hand, the arbitrariness of its signs theoretically entails the freedom of establishing just any relationship between phonetic substance and ideas. The result is that each of the two elements united in the sign maintains its own life to a degree unknown elsewhere, and that language changes, or rather evolves, under the influence of all the forces which can affect either sounds or meanings. The evolution is inevitable; there is no example of a single language that resists it. After a certain period of time, some obvious shifts can always be recorded.

Mutability is so inescapable that it even holds true for artificial languages. Whoever creates a language controls it only so long as it is not in circulation; from the moment when it fulfills its mission and becomes the property of everyone, control is lost. Take Esperanto as an example; if it succeeds, will it escape the inexorable law? Once launched, it is quite likely that Esperanto will enter upon a fully semiological life; it will be transmitted according to laws which have nothing in common with those of its logical creation, and there will be no turning backwards. A man proposing a fixed language that posterity would have to accept for what it is would be like a hen hatching a duck's egg: the language created by him would be borne along, willy-nilly, by the current that engulfs all languages.

Signs are governed by a principle of general semiology: continuity in time is coupled to change in time; this is confirmed by orthographic systems, the speech of deaf-mutes, etc.

But what supports the necessity for change? I might be reproached for not having been as explicit on this point as on the principle of immutability. This is because I failed to distinguish between the different forces of change. We must consider their great variety in order to understand the extent to which they are necessary.

The causes of continuity are *a priori* within the scope of the observer, but the causes of change in time are not. It is better not to attempt giving an exact account at this point, but to restrict discussion to the shifting of relationships in general. Time changes all things; there is no reason why language should escape this universal law.

Let us review the main points of our discussion and relate them to the principles set up in the Introduction.

1) Avoiding sterile word definitions, within the total phenomenon represented by speech we first singled out two parts: language and speaking. Language is speech less speaking. It is the whole set of linguistic habits which allow an individual to understand and to be understood.

2) But this definition still leaves language outside its social context; it makes language something artificial since it includes only the individual part of reality; for the realization of language, a community of speakers [*masse parlante*] is necessary. Contrary to all appearances, language never exists apart from the social fact, for it is a semiological phenomenon. Its social nature is one of its inner characteristics. Its complete definition confronts us with two inseparable entities, as shown in this drawing:

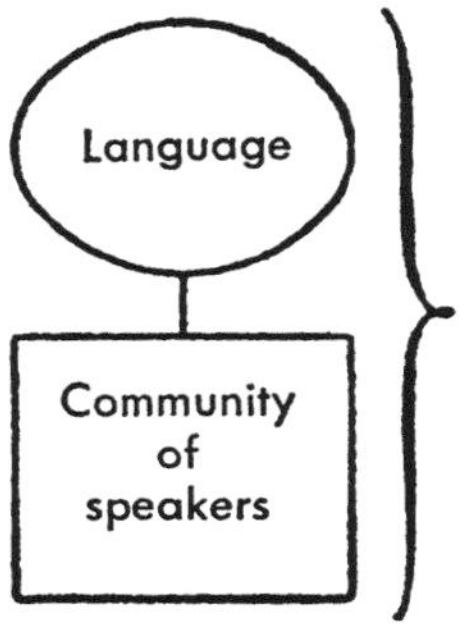

But under the conditions described language is not living—it has only potential life; we have considered only the social, not the historical, fact.

3) The linguistic sign is arbitrary; language, as defined, would therefore seem to be a system which, because it depends solely on a rational principle, is free and can be organized at will. Its social nature, considered independently, does not definitely rule out this viewpoint. Doubtless it is not on a purely logical basis that group psychology operates; one must consider everything that deflects reason in actual contacts between individuals. But the thing which keeps language from being a simple convention that can be modified at the whim of interested parties is not its social nature; it is rather the action of time combined with the social force. If time is left out, the linguistic facts are incomplete and no conclusion is possible.

If we considered language in time, without the community of speakers—imagine an isolated individual living for several centuries—we probably would notice no change; time would not influence language. Conversely, if we considered the community of speakers without considering time, we would not see the effect of the social forces that influence language. To represent the actual facts, we must then add to our first drawing a sign to indicate passage of time:

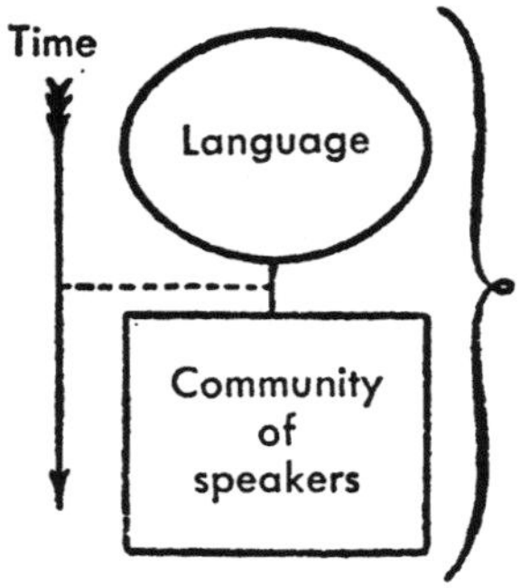

Language is no longer free, for time will allow the social forces at work on it to carry out their effects. This brings us back to the principle of continuity, which cancels freedom. But continuity necessarily implies change, varying degrees of shifts in the relationship between the signified and the signifier.

Chapter III

STATIC AND EVOLUTIONARY LINGUISTICS

1. *Inner Duality of All Sciences Concerned with Values*

Very few linguists suspect that the intervention of the factor of time creates difficulties peculiar to linguistics and opens to their science two completely divergent paths.

Most other sciences are unaffected by this radical duality; time produces no special effects in them. Astronomy has found that the stars undergo considerable changes but has not been obliged on this account to split itself into two disciplines. Geology is concerned with successions at almost every instant, but its study of strata does not thereby become a radically distinct discipline. Law has its descriptive science and its historical science; no one opposes one to the other. The political history of states is unfolded solely in time, but a historian depicting a particular period does not work apart from history. Conversely, the science of political institutions is essentially descriptive, but if the need arises it can easily deal with a historical question without disturbing its unity.

On the contrary, that duality is already forcing itself upon the economic sciences. Here, in contrast to the other sciences, political economy and economic history constitute two clearly separated disciplines within a single science; the works that have recently appeared on these subjects point up the distinction. Proceeding as they have, economists are—without being well aware of it—obeying an inner necessity. A similar necessity obliges us to divide linguistics into two parts, each with its own principle. Here as in political economy we are confronted with the notion of *value;* both sciences are concerned with *a system for equating things of different orders*—labor and wages in one and a signified and signifier in the other.

Certainly all sciences would profit by indicating more precisely the co-ordinates along which their subject matter is aligned. Everywhere distinctions should be made, according to the following illustration, between (1) *the axis of simultaneities* (AB), which stands for the relations of coexisting things and from which the intervention of time is excluded; and (2) *the axis of successions* (CD), on which only one thing can be considered at a time but upon which are located all the things on the first axis together with their changes.

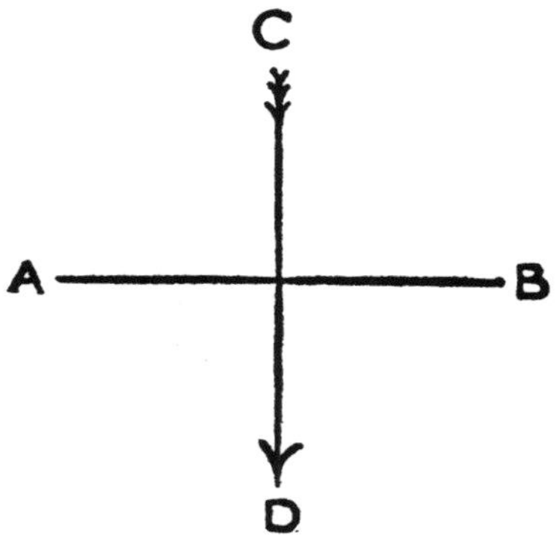

For a science concerned with values the distinction is a practical necessity and sometimes an absolute one. In these fields scholars cannot organize their research rigorously without considering both co-ordinates and making a distinction between the system of values per se and the same values as they relate to time.

This distinction has to be heeded by the linguist above all others, for language is a system of pure values which are determined by nothing except the momentary arrangement of its terms. A value —so long as it is somehow rooted in things and in their natural relations, as happens with economics (the value of a plot of ground, for instance, is related to its productivity)—can to some extent be traced in time if we remember that it depends at each moment upon a system of coexisting values. Its link with things gives it, perforce, a natural basis, and the judgments that we base on such values are therefore never completely arbitrary; their variability is limited. But we have just seen that natural data have no place in linguistics.

Again, the more complex and rigorously organized a system of values is, the more it is necessary, because of its very complexity, to study it according to both co-ordinates. No other system embodies this feature to the same extent as language. Nowhere else do we find such precise values at stake and such a great number and diversity of terms, all so rigidly interdependent. The multiplicity of signs, which we have already used to explain the continuity of language, makes it absolutely impossible to study simultaneously relations in time and relations within the system.

The reasons for distinguishing two sciences of language are clear. How should the sciences be designated? Available terms do not all bring out the distinction with equal sharpness. "Linguistic history" and "historical linguistics" are too vague. Since political history includes the description of different periods as well as the narration of events, the student might think that he is studying a language according to the axis of time when he describes its successive states, but this would require a separate study of the phenomena that make language pass from one state to another. *Evolution* and *evolutionary linguistics* are more precise, and I shall use these expressions often; in contrast, we can speak of the science of *language-states* [*états de langue*] or *static linguistics.*

But to indicate more clearly the opposition and crossing of two orders of phenomena that relate to the same object, I prefer to speak of *synchronic* and *diachronic* linguistics. Everything that relates to the static side of our science is synchronic; everything that has to do with evolution is diachronic. Similarly, *synchrony* and *diachrony* designate respectively a language-state and an evolutionary phase.

2. *Inner Duality and the History of Linguistics*

The first thing that strikes us when we study the facts of language is that their succession in time does not exist insofar as the speaker is concerned. He is confronted with a state. That is why the linguist who wishes to understand a state must discard all knowledge of everything that produced it and ignore diachrony. He can enter the mind of speakers only by completely suppressing the past. The intervention of history can only falsify his judgment. It would be absurd to attempt to sketch a panorama of the Alps by viewing them simultaneously from several peaks of the Jura; a panorama must be made from a single vantage point. The same applies to language; the linguist can neither describe it nor draw up standards of usage except by concentrating on one state. When he follows the evolution of the language, he resembles the moving observer who goes from one peak of the Jura to another in order to record the shifts in perspective.

Ever since modern linguistics came into existence, it has been completely absorbed in diachrony. Comparative Indo-European philology uses the materials at hand to reconstruct hypothetically an older type of language; comparison is but a means of reconstructing the past. The method is the same in the narrower study of subgroups (Romance languages, Germanic languages, etc.); states intervene only irregularly and piecemeal. Such is the tendency introduced by Bopp. His conception of language is therefore hybrid and hesitating.

Against this, what was the procedure of those who studied language before the beginning of modern linguistics, i.e. the "grammarians" inspired by traditional methods? It is curious to note that here their viewpoint was absolutely above reproach. Their works clearly show that they tried to describe language-states. Their program was strictly synchronic. The *Port Royal Grammar*, for example, attempts to describe the state of French under Louis XIV and to determine its values. For this, the language of the Middle Ages is not needed; the horizontal axis is followed faithfully (see p. 80), without digression. The method was then correct, but this does not mean that its application was perfect. Traditional grammar neglects whole parts of language, such as word formation; it is normative and assumes the role of prescribing rules, not of recording facts; it lacks overall perspective; often it is unable even to separate the written from the spoken word, etc.

Classical grammar has been criticized as unscientific; still, its basis is less open to criticism and its data are better defined than is true of the linguistics started by Bopp. The latter, occupying ill-defined ground, has no clear-cut objective. It straddles two areas because it is unable to make a sharp distinction between states and successions.

Linguistics, having accorded too large a place to history, will turn back to the static viewpoint of traditional grammar but in a new spirit and with other procedures, and the historical method will have contributed to this rejuvenation; the historical method will in turn give a better understanding of language-states. The old grammar saw only the synchronic fact; linguistics has revealed a new class of phenomena; but that is not enough; one must sense the opposition between the two classes of facts to draw out all its consequences.

3. *Inner Duality Illustrated by Examples*

The opposition between the two viewpoints, the synchronic and the diachronic, is absolute and allows no compromise. A few facts will show what the difference is and why it is irreducible.

Latin *crispus* 'crisp' provided French with the root *crép–* from which were formed the verbs *crépir* 'rough-cast' and *décrepir* 'remove mortar.' Against this, at a certain moment the word *dēcrepitus,* of unknown origin, was borrowed from Latin and became *décrépit* 'decrepit.' Certainly today the community of speakers sets up a relation between *un mur décrépi* 'a wall from which mortar is falling' and *un homme décrépit* 'a decrepit man,' although historically the two words have nothing in common; people often speak of the *façade décrépite* of a house. And this is static, for it concerns the relation between two coexisting forms of language. For its realization, the concurrence of certain evolutionary events was necessary. The pronunciation of *crisp–* had to become *crép–*, and at a particular moment a new word had to be borrowed from Latin. It is obvious that the diachronic facts are not related to the static facts which they produced. They belong to a different class.

Here is a more telling example. In Old High German the plural of *gast* 'guest' was first *gasti*, that of *hant* 'hand' was *hanti*, etc. Later the final *–i* produced an umlaut, i.e. it resulted in the changing of the *a* of the preceding syllable to *e: gasti → gesti; hanti → henti.* Then the final *–i* lost its timbre: *gesti → geste*, etc. The result is that today German has *Gast: Gäste, Hand: Hände*, and a whole group of words marked by the same difference between the singular and the plural. A very similar fact occurred in Anglo-Saxon: the earlier forms were *fōt: *fōti, tōþ: *tōþi, gōs: *gōsi*, etc. Through an initial phonetic change, umlaut, **fōti* became **fēti;* through a second, the fall of final *–i, fēti* became *fēt;* after that, *fōt* had as its plural *fēt; tōþ, tēþ; gōs, gēs,* etc. (Modern English *foot: feet, tooth: teeth, goose: geese.*)

Previously, when speakers used *gast: gasti, fōt: fōti,* the simple addition of an *i* marked the plural; *Gast: Gäste* and *fōt: fēt* show a new mechanism for indicating the plural. The mechanism is not the same in both instances; in Old English there is only opposition between vowels; in German there is in addition the presence or absence of final *–e;* but here this difference is unimportant.

The relation between a singular and its plural, whatever the forms may be, can be expressed at each moment by a horizontal axis:

·←——→· Period A
·←——→· Period B

Whatever facts have brought about passage from one form to another should be placed along a vertical axis, giving the overall picture:

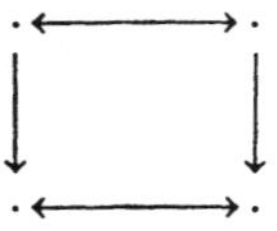
Period A
Period B

Our illustration suggests several pertinent remarks:

1) In no way do diachronic facts aim to signal a value by means of another sign; that *gasti* became *gesti, geste* (*Gäste*) has nothing to do with the plural of substantives; in *tragit* → *trägt,* the same umlaut occurs in verbal inflection, and so forth. A diachronic fact is an independent event; the particular synchronic consequences that may stem from it are wholly unrelated to it.

2) Diachronic facts are not even directed toward changing the system. Speakers did not wish to pass from one system of relations to another; modification does not affect the arrangement but rather its elements.

Here we again find the principle enunciated previously: never is the system modified directly. In itself it is unchangeable; only certain elements are altered without regard for the solidarity that binds them to the whole. It is as if one of the planets that revolve around the sun changed its dimensions and weight: this isolated event would entail general consequences and would throw the whole system out of equilibrium. The opposition of two terms is needed to express plurality: either *fōt: fōti* or *fōt: fēt;* both procedures are possible, but speakers passed from one to the other, so to speak, without having a hand in it. Neither was the whole replaced nor did one system engender another; one element in the first system was changed, and this change was enough to give rise to another system.

3) The foregoing observation points up the ever *fortuitous* nature of a state. In contrast to the false notion that we readily fashion for ourselves about it, language is not a mechanism created and arranged with a view to the concepts to be expressed. We see on the contrary that the state which resulted from the change was not destined to signal the meaning with which it was impregnated. In a fortuitous state (*fōt: fēt*), speakers took advantage of an existing difference and made it signal the distinction between singular and plural; *fōt: fēt* is no better for this purpose than *fōt: *fōti*. In each state the mind infiltrated a given substance and breathed life into it. This new perspective, inspired by historical linguistics, is unknown to traditional grammar, which could never acquire it by its own methods. Most philosophers of language are equally ignorant of it, and yet nothing is more important from the philosophical viewpoint.

4) Are facts of the diachronic series of the same class, at least, as facts of the synchronic series? By no means, for we have seen that changes are wholly unintentional while the synchronic fact is always significant. It always calls forth two simultaneous terms. Not *Gäste* alone but the opposition *Gast: Gäste* expresses the plural. The diachronic fact is just the opposite: only one term is involved, and for the new one to appear (*Gäste*), the old one (*gasti*) must first give way to it.

To try to unite such dissimilar facts in the same discipline would certainly be a fanciful undertaking. The diachronic perspective deals with phenomena that are unrelated to systems although they do condition them.

Here are some other examples to strengthen and complement the conclusions drawn from the first ones.

In French, the accent always falls on the last syllable unless this syllable contains a mute *e* (ə). This is a synchronic fact, a relation between the whole set of French words and accent. What is its source? A previous state. Latin had a different and more complicated system of accentuation: the accent was on the penultimate syllable when the latter was long; when short, the accent fell back on the antepenult (cf. *amī́cus, ánima*). The Latin law suggests relations that are in no way analogous to the French law. Doubtless the accent is the same in the sense that it remained in the same position; in French words it always falls on the syllable that had it in Latin: *amī́cum* → *amí, ánimum* → *âme*. But the two formulas are different for the two moments because the forms of the words changed. We know that everything after the accent either disappeared or was reduced to mute *e*. As a result of the alteration of the word, the position of the accent with respect to the whole was no longer the same; subsequently speakers, conscious of the new relation, instinctively put the accent on the last syllable, even in borrowed words introduced in their written forms (*facile, consul, ticket, burgrave*, etc.). Speakers obviously did not try to change systems, to apply a new formula, since in words like *amī́cum* → *amí* the accent always remained on the same syllable; but a diachronic fact was interposed: speakers changed the position of the accent without having a hand in it. A law of accentuation, like everything that pertains to the linguistic system, is an arrangement of terms, a fortuitous and involuntary result of evolution.

Here is an even more striking example. In Old Slavic, *slovo* 'word' has in the instrumental singular *slovem'ь*, in the nominative plural *slova*, in the genitive plural *slov'ь*, etc.; in the declension each case has its own ending. But today the weak vowels *ь* and *'ь*, Slavic representatives of Proto-Indo-European *ĭ* and *ŭ*, have disappeared. Czech, for example, has *slovo, slovem, slova, slov;* likewise *žena* 'woman': accusative singular *ženu*, nominative plural *ženy*, genitive plural *žen*. Here the genitive (*slov, žen*) has zero inflection. We see then that a material sign is not necessary for the expression of an idea; language is satisfied with the opposition between something and nothing. Czech speakers recognize *žen* as a genitive plural simply because it is neither *žena* nor *ženu* nor any of the other forms. It seems strange at first glance that such a particular notion as that of the genitive plural should have taken the zero sign, but this very fact proves that everything comes about through sheer accident. Language is a mechanism that continues to function in spite of the deteriorations to which it is subjected.

All this confirms the principles previously stated. To summarize:

Language is a system whose parts can and must all be considered in their synchronic solidarity.

Since changes never affect the system as a whole but rather one or another of its elements, they can be studied only outside the system. Each alteration doubtless has its countereffect on the system, but the initial fact affected only one point; there is no inner bond between the initial fact and the effect that it may subsequently produce on the whole system. The basic difference between successive terms and coexisting terms, between partial facts and facts that affect the system, precludes making both classes of fact the subject matter of a single science.

4. *The Difference between the Two Classes Illustrated by Comparisons*

To show both the autonomy and the interdependence of synchrony we can compare the first to the projection of an object on a plane surface. Any projection depends directly on the nature of the object projected, yet differs from it—the object itself is a thing apart. Otherwise there would not be a whole science of projections; considering the bodies themselves would suffice. In linguistics there is the same relationship between the historical facts and a language-state, which is like a projection of the facts at a particular moment. We do not learn about synchronic states by studying bodies, i.e. diachronic events, any more than we learn about geometric projections by studying, even carefully, the different types of bodies.

Similarly if the stem of a plant is cut transversely, a rather complicated design is formed by the cut surface; the design is simply one perspective of the longitudinal fibers, and we would be able to see them on making a second cut perpendicular to the first. Here again one perspective depends on the other; the longitudinal cut shows the fibers that constitute the plant, and the transversal cut shows their arrangement on a particular plane; but the second is distinct from the first because it brings out certain relations between the fibers—relations that we could never grasp by viewing the longitudinal plane.

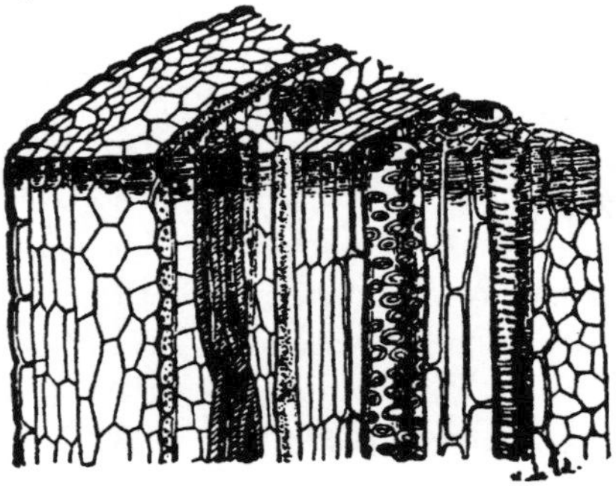

But of all comparisons that might be imagined, the most friutful is the one that might be drawn between the functioning of language and a game of chess. In both instances we are confronted with a system of values and their observable modifications. A game of chess is like an artificial realization of what language offers in a natural form.

Let us examine the matter more carefully.

First, a state of the set of chessmen corresponds closely to a state of language. The respective value of the pieces depends on their position on the chessboard just as each linguistic term derives its value from its opposition to all the other terms.

In the second place, the system is always momentary; it varies from one position to the next. It is also true that values depend above all else on an unchangeable convention, the set of rules that exists before a game begins and persists after each move. Rules that are agreed upon once and for all exist in language too; they are the constant principles of semiology.

Finally, to pass from one state of equilibrium to the next, or—according to our terminology—from one synchrony to the next, only one chesspiece has to be moved; there is no general rummage. Here we have the counterpart of the diachronic phenomenon with all its peculiarities. In fact:

(a) In each play only one chesspiece is moved; in the same way in language, changes affect only isolated elements.

(b) In spite of that, the move has a repercussion on the whole system; it is impossible for the player to foresee exactly the extent of the effect. Resulting changes of value will be, according to the circumstances, either nil, very serious, or of average importance. A certain move can revolutionize the whole game and even affect pieces that are not immediately involved. We have just seen that exactly the same holds for language.

(c) In chess, each move is absolutely distinct from the preceding and the subsequent equilibrium. The change effected belongs to neither state: only states matter.

In a game of chess any particular position has the unique characteristic of being freed from all antecedent positions; the route used in arriving there makes absolutely no difference; one who has followed the entire match has no advantage over the curious party who comes up at a critical moment to inspect the state of the game; to describe this arrangement, it is perfectly useless to recall what had just happened ten seconds previously. All this is equally applicable to language and sharpens the radical distinction between diachrony and synchrony. Speaking operates only on a language-state, and the changes that intervene between states have no place in either state.

At only one point is the comparison weak: the chessplayer *intends* to bring about a shift and thereby to exert an action on the system, whereas language premeditates nothing. The pieces of language are shifted—or rather modified—spontaneously and fortuitously. The umlaut of *Hände* for *hanti* and *Gäste* for *gasti* (see p. 83) produced a new system for forming the plural but also gave rise to verbal forms like *trägt* from *tragit*, etc. In order to make the game of chess seem at every point like the functioning of language, we would have to imagine an unconscious or unintelligent player. This sole difference, however, makes the comparison even more instructive by showing the absolute necessity of making a distinction between the two classes of phenomena in linguistics. For if diachronic facts cannot be reduced to the synchronic system which they condition when the change is intentional, all the more will they resist when they set a blind force against the organization of a system of signs.

5. *The Two Linguistics Contrasted According to Their Methods and Principles*

Everywhere the opposition between diachrony and synchrony stands out.

For instance—and to begin with the most apparent fact—they are not of equal importance. Here it is evident that the synchronic viewpoint predominates, for it is the true and only reality to the community of speakers (see p. 81). The same is true of the linguist: if he takes the diachronic perspective, he no longer observes language but rather a series of events that modify it. People often affirm that nothing is more important than understanding the genesis of a particular state; this is true in a certain sense: the forces that have shaped the state illuminate its true nature, and knowing them protects us against certain illusions (see pp. 84 ff.); but this only goes to prove clearly that diachronic linguistics is not an end in itself. What is said of journalism applies to diachrony: it leads everywhere if one departs from it.

The methods of diachrony and synchrony also differ, and in two ways.

(a) Synchrony has only one perspective, the speakers', and its whole method consists of gathering evidence from speakers; to know to just what extent a thing is a reality, it is necessary and sufficient to determine to what extent it exists in the minds of speakers. Diachronic linguistics, on the contrary, must distinguish two perspectives. One of these, the *prospective*, follows the course of time; the other, the *retrospective*, goes back in time; the result is a duplication in methodology with which we shall deal in Part Five.

(b) A second difference results from delimiting the fields embraced by each of the two disciplines. Synchronic study has as its object, not everything that is simultaneous, but only the totality of facts corresponding to each language; separation will go as far as dialects and subdialects when necessary. The term *synchronic* is really not precise enough; it should be replaced by another—rather long to be sure—*idiosynchronic*. Against this, diachronic linguistics not only does not need but even rejects such specialization; the terms that it studies do not necessarily belong to the same language (compare Proto-Indo-European **esti*, Greek *esti*,

German *ist*, and French *est*). The succession of diachronic events and their multiplication in space are precisely what creates the diversity of idioms. To justify the associating of two forms, it is enough to show that they are connected by a historical bond, however indirect it may be.

The foregoing oppositions are neither the most striking nor the most profound. One consequence of the radical antimony between the evolutionary and the static fact is that all notions associated with one or the other are to the same extent mutually irreducible. Any notion will point up this truth. The synchronic and diachronic "phenomenon," for example, have nothing in common (see p. 85). One is a relation between simultaneous elements, the other the substitution of one element for another in time, an event.

We shall also see (p. 107) that diachronic and synchronic identities are two very different things; historically the French negation *pas* is identical to the substantive *pas* 'step,' whereas the two forms are distinct in modern French. These observations would suffice to show the necessity of not confusing the two viewpoints, but nowhere is this necessity more apparent than in the distinction we are about to make.

6. *Synchronic and Diachronic Law*

It is a popular practice to speak of laws in linguistics. But are the facts of language actually governed by laws? If so, what are they like? Since language is a social institution, one might assume *a priori* that it is governed by prescriptions analogous to those that control communities. Now every social law has two basic characteristics: it is *imperative* and it is *general;* it comes in by force and it covers all cases—within certain limits of time and place, of course.

Do the laws of language fit this definition? The first step in answering the question—in line with what has just been said—is to separate once more the synchronic and diachronic areas. The two problems must not be confused; speaking of linguistic law in general is like trying to pin down a ghost.

Here are some examples, taken from Greek, in which the two classes are intentionally jumbled:

1. Proto-Indo-European voiced aspirates became voiceless: **dhūmos* → *thūmos* 'breath of life,' **bherō* → *phérō* 'I bear,' etc.

2. The accent never falls farther back than the antepenult.

3. All words end in a vowel or in *s*, *n*, or *r*, to the exclusion of all other consonants.

4. Prevocalic initial *s* became *h* (sign of aspiration): **septm* (Latin *septem*) → *heptá*.

5. Final *m* changed to *n*: **jugom* → *zugón* (cf. Latin *jugum*).[5]

6. Final occlusives fell: **gunaik* → *gúnai*, **epherst* → *éphere*, **epheront* → *épheron*.

Law 1 is diachronic: *dh* became *th*, etc. Law 2 expresses a relation between the word-unit and accent, a sort of contract between two coexisting terms; it is a synchronic law. The same is true of Law 3 since it concerns the word-unit and its ending. Laws 4, 5, and 6 are diachronic: *s* became *h*; *–n* replaced *–m*; *–t*, *–k*, etc. disappeared without leaving a trace.

We should also notice that Law 3 is the result of 5 and 6; two diachronic facts created a synchronic fact.

After we separate the two classes of laws, we see that Laws 2 and 3 are basically different from Laws 1, 4, 5, and 6.

The synchronic law is general but not imperative. Doubtless it is imposed on individuals by the weight of collective usage (see p. 73), but here I do not have in mind an obligation on the part of speakers. I mean that *in language* no force guarantees the maintenance of a regularity when established on some point. Being a simple expression of an existing arrangement, the synchronic law reports a state of affairs; it is like a law that states that trees in a certain orchard are arranged in the shape of a quincunx. And the arrangement that the law defines is precarious precisely because it is not imperative. Nothing is more regular than the synchronic law that governs Latin accentuation (a law comparable in every way to Law 2 above); but the accentual rule did not resist the

[5] According to Meillet (*Mem. de la Soc. de Ling.*, IX, pp. 365 ff.) and Gauthiot (*La fin du mot indo-européen*, pp. 158 ff.), final *–m* did not exist in Proto-Indo-European, which used only *–n*; if this theory is accepted, Law 5 can be stated in this way: Greek preserved every final *–n*; its demonstrative value is not diminished since the phonetic phenomenon that results in the preservation of a former state is the same in nature as the one that manifests a change (see p. 145). [Ed.]

forces of alteration and gave way to a new law, the one of French (see above p. 86). In short, if one speaks of law in synchrony, it is in the sense of an arrangement, a principle of regularity.

Diachrony, on the contrary, supposes a dynamic force through which an effect is produced, a thing executed. But this imperativeness is not sufficient to warrant applying the concept of law to evolutionary facts; we can speak of law only when a set of facts obeys the same rule, and in spite of certain appearances to the contrary, diachronic events are always accidental and particular.

The accidental and particular character of semantic facts is immediately apparent. That French *poutre* 'mare' has acquired the meaning 'piece of wood, rafter' is due to particular causes and does not depend on other changes that might have occurred at the same time. It is only one accident among all those registered in the history of the language.

As for syntactical and morphological transformations, the issue is not so clear from the outset. At a certain time almost all old subject-case forms disappeared in French. Here a set of facts apparently obeys the same law. But such is not the case, for all the facts are but multiple manifestations of one and the same isolated fact. The particular notion of subject was affected, and its disappearance naturally caused a whole series of forms to vanish. For one who sees only the external features of language, the unique phenomenon is drowned in the multitude of its manifestations. Basically, however, there is but one phenomenon, and this historical event is just as isolated in its own order as the semantic change undergone by *poutre*. It takes on the appearance of a "law" only because it is realized within a system. The rigid arrangement of the system creates the illusion that the diachronic fact obeys the same rules as the synchronic fact.

Finally, as regards phonetic changes, exactly the same is true. Yet the popular practice is to speak of phonetic laws. Indeed, it is said that at a given time and in a given area all words having the same phonic features are affected by the same change; for example, Law 1 on page 92 (**dhūmos* → Greek *thūmos*) affects all Greek words containing a voiced aspirate (cf. **nebhos* → *néphos*, **medhu* → *méthu*, **anghō* → *ánkhō*, etc.); Law 4 (**septm* → *heptá*) applies to **serpō* → *hérpō*, **sūs* → *hûs*, and to all words that begin with *s*. This regularity, which has at times been disputed, is apparently firmly established; obvious exceptions do not lessen the inevitability of such changes, for they can be explained either by more special phonetic laws (see the example of *trikhes: thriksi*, p. 97) or by the interference of facts of another class (analogy, etc.). Nothing seems to fit better the definition given above for the word law. And yet, regardless of the number of instances where a phonetic law holds, all facts embraced by it are but manifestations of a single particular fact.

The real issue is to find out whether phonetic changes affect words or only sounds, and there is no doubt about the answer: in *nephos, methu, ankhō*, etc. a certain phoneme—a voiced Proto-Indo-European aspirate—became voiceless, Proto-Greek initial *s* became *h*, etc.; each fact is isolated, independent of the other events of the same class, independent also of the words in which the change took place.[6] The phonic substance of all the words was of course modified, but this should not deceive us as to the real nature of the phenomenon.

What supports the statement that words themselves are not directly involved in phonetic transformations? The very simple observation that these transformations are basically alien to words and cannot touch their essence. The word-unit is not constituted solely by the totality of its phonemes but by characteristics other than its material quality. Suppose that one string of a piano is out of tune: a discordant note will be heard each time the one who is playing a melody strikes the corresponding key. But where is the discord? In the melody? Certainly not; the melody has not been affected; only the piano has been impaired. Exactly the same is true in phonetics. Our system of phonemes is the instrument we play in order to articulate the words of language; if one of its elements is modified, diverse consequences may ensue, but the modification itself is not concerned with the words which are, in a manner of speaking, the melodies of our repertory.

[6] Of course the examples cited above are purely schematic: linguistics is right in trying currently to relate to the same initial principle the largest possible series of phonetic changes; for instance, Meillet explains all the transformations of Greek occlusives by progressive weakening of their articulation (see *Mém. de la Soc. de Ling.*, IX, pp. 163 ff.). Naturally the conclusions on the nature of phonetic changes are in the last analysis applicable to these general facts, wherever they exist. [Ed.]

Diachronic facts are then particular; a shift in a system is brought about by events which not only are outside the system (see p. 84), but are isolated and form no system among themselves.

To summarize: synchronic facts, no matter what they are, evidence a certain regularity but are in no way imperative; diachronic facts, on the contrary, force themselves upon language but are in no way general.

In a word—and this is the point I have been trying to make—neither of the two classes of facts is governed by laws in the sense defined above, and if one still wishes to speak of linguistic laws, the word will embrace completely different meanings, depending on whether it designates facts of one class or the other.

7. *Is There a Panchronic Viewpoint?*

Up to this point the term law has been used in the legal sense. But cannot the term also be used in language as in the physical and natural sciences, i.e. in the sense of relations that are everywhere and forever verifiable? In a word, can not language be studied from a panchronic viewpoint?

Doubtless. Since phonetic changes have always occurred and are still occurring, this general phenomenon is a permanent characteristic of speech; it is therefore one of the laws of speech. In linguistics as in chess (see pp. 88 ff.) there are rules that outlive all events. But they are general principles existing independently of concrete facts. When we speak of particular, tangible facts, there is no panchronic viewpoint. Each phonetic change, regardless of its actual spread, is limited to a definite time and territory; no change occurs at all times and in all places; change exists only diachronically. These general principles are precisely what serve as a criterion for determining what belongs to language and what does not. A concrete fact that lends itself to panchronic explanation cannot belong to language. Take the French word *chose* 'thing': from the diachronic viewpoint it stands in opposition to the Latin word from which it derives, *causa;* from the synchronic viewpoint it stands in opposition to every word that might be associated with it in Modern French. Only the sounds of the word considered independently (*šǫz*) are susceptible of panchronic observation, but they have no linguistic value. Even from the panchronic viewpoint *šọz*, considered in a chain like *ün šọz admirablə* 'an admirable thing,' is not a unit but a shapeless mass; indeed, why *šọz* rather than *ọza* or *nšọ?* It is not a value, for it has no meaning. From the panchronic viewpoint the particular facts of language are never reached.

8. *Consequences of the Confusing of Synchrony and Diachrony*

Two instances will be cited:

(a) Synchronic truth seems to be the denial of diachronic truth, and one who has a superficial view of things imagines that a choice must be made; this is really unnecessary; one truth does not exclude the other. That French *dépit* 'spite' originally meant contempt does not prevent the word from having a completely different meaning now; etymology and synchronic value are distinct. Similarly, traditional grammar teaches that the present participle is variable and shows agreement in the same manner as an adjective in certain cases in Modern French (cf. une eau *courante* '*running* water') but is invariable in others (cf. une personne *courant* dans la rue 'a person *running* in the street'). But historical grammar shows that it is not a question of one and the same form: the first is the continuation of the variable Latin participle (*currentum*) while the second comes from the invariable ablative form of the gerund (*currendō*).[7] Does synchronic truth contradict diachronic truth, and must one condemn traditional grammar in the name of historical grammar? No, for that would be seeing only half of the facts; one must not think that the historical fact alone matters and is sufficient to constitute language. Doubtless from the viewpoint of its origin the participle *courant* has two elements, but in the collective mind of the community of speakers, these are drawn together and fused into one. The synchronic truth is just as absolute and indisputable as the diachronic truth.

(b) Synchronic truth is so similar to diachronic truth that people confuse the two or think it superfluous to separate them. For example, they try to explain the meaning of French *père* 'father'

[7] This generally accepted theory has been recently but, we believe, unsuccessfully attacked by M. E. Larch (*Das invariable Participium praesentis*, Erlangen, 1913); there was then no reason for eliminating an example that would retain its didactic value. [Ed.]

by saying that Latin *pāter* meant the same thing. Another example: Latin short *a* became *i* in noninitial open syllables; beside *faciō* we have *conficiō*, beside *amīcus, inimīcus*, etc. The law is often stated in this way: "The *a* of *faciō* becomes *i* in *conficiō* because it is no longer in the first syllable." That is not true: never did the *a* "become" *i* in *conficiō*. To re-establish the truth one must single out two periods and four terms. Speakers first said *facio—confacio;* then, *confaciō* having been changed to *conficiō* while *faciō* remained unchanged, they said *faciō—conficiō:*

faciō ⟷	*confaciō*	Period A
faciō ⟷	*conficiō*	Period B

If a "change" occurred, it is between *confaciō* and *conficiō;* but the rule, badly formulated, does not even mention *confaciō!* Then beside the diachronic change there is a second fact, absolutely distinct from the first and having to do with the purely synchronic opposition between *faciō* and *conficiō*. One is tempted to say that it is not a fact but a result. Nevertheless, it *is* a fact in its own class; indeed, all synchronic phenomena are like this. The true value of the opposition *faciō: conficiō* is not recognized for the very reason that the opposition is not very significant. But oppositions like *Gast: Gäste* and *gebe: gibt*, though also fortuitous results of phonetic evolution, are nonetheless basic grammatical phenomena of the synchronic class. The fact that both classes are in other respects closely linked, each conditioning the other, points to the conclusion that keeping them apart is not worthwhile; in fact, linguistics has confused them for decades without realizing that such a method is worthless.

The mistake shows up conspicuously in certain instances. To explain Greek *phuktós*, for example, it might seem sufficient to say that in Greek *g* or *kh* became *k* before voiceless consonants, and to cite by way of explanation such synchronic correspondences as *phugeîn: phuktós, lékhos: léktron*, etc. But in a case like *tríkhes: thriksí* there is a complication, the "passing" of *t* to *th*. The forms can be explained only historically, by relative chronology. The Proto-Greek theme **thrikh*, followed by the ending *-si*, became *thriksí*, a very old development identical to the one that produced *léktron* from the root *lekh–*. Later every aspirate followed by another aspirate in the same word was changed into an occlusive, and **thríkhes* became *tríkhes;* naturally *thriksi* escaped this law.

9. *Conclusions*

Linguistics here comes to its second bifurcaton. We had first to choose between language and speaking (see pp. 17 ff.); here we are again at the intersection of two roads, one leading to diachrony and the other to synchrony.

Once in possession of this double principle of classification, we can add that everything diachronic in language is diachronic only by virtue of speaking. It is in speaking that the germ of all change is found. Each change is launched by a certain number of individuals before it is accepted for general use. Modern German uses *ich war, wir waren,* whereas until the sixteenth century the conjugation was *ich was, wir waren* (cf. English *I was, we were*). How did the substitution of *war* for *was* come about? Some speakers, influenced by *waren,* created *war* through analogy; this was a fact of speaking; the new form, repeated many times and accepted by the community, became a fact of language. But not all innovations of speaking have the same success, and so long as they remain individual, they may be ignored, for we are studying language; they do not enter into our field of observation until the community of speakers has adopted them.

An evolutionary fact is always preceded by a fact, or rather by a multitude of similar facts, in the sphere of speaking. This in no way invalidates but rather strengthens the distinction made above since in the history of any innovation there are always two distinct moments: (1) when it sprang up in individual usage; and (2) when it became a fact of language, outwardly identical but adopted by the community.

The following table indicates the rational form that linguistic study should take:

		Synchrony
(Human) Speech	Language	
		Diachrony
	Speaking	

One must recognize that the ideal, theoretical form of a science is not always the one imposed upon it by the exigencies of practice; in linguistics these exigencies are more imperious than anywhere else; they account to some extent for the confusion that now predominates in linguistic research. Even if the distinctions set up here were accepted once and for all, a precise orientation probably could not be imposed on investigations in the name of the stated ideal.

In the synchronic study of Old French, for instance, the linguist works with facts and principles that have nothing in common with those that he would find out by tracing the history of the same language from the thirteenth to the twentieth century; on the contrary, he works with facts and principles similar to those that would be revealed in the description of an existing Bantu language, Attic Greek of 400 B.C. or present-day French, for that matter. These diverse descriptions would be based on similar relations; if each idiom is a closed system, all idioms embody certain fixed principles that the linguist meets again and again in passing from one to another, for he is staying in the same class. Historical study is no different. Whether the linguist examines a definite period in the history of French (for example, from the thirteenth to the twentieth century) Javanese, or any other language whatsoever, everywhere he works with similar facts which he needs only compare in order to establish the general truths of the diachronic class. The ideal would be for each scholar to devote himself to one field of investigation or the other and deal with the largest possible number of facts in this class; but it is very difficult to command scientifically such different languages. Against this, each language in practice forms a unit of study, and we are induced by force of circumstances to consider it alternately from the historical and static viewpoints. Above all else, we must never forget that this unit is superficial in theory, whereas the diversity of idioms hides a profound unity. Whichever way we look in studying a language, we must put each fact in its own class and not confuse the two methods.

The two parts of linguistics respectively, as defined, will be the object of our study.

Synchronic linguistics will be concerned with the logical and psychological relations that bind together coexisting terms and form a system in the collective mind of speakers.

Diachronic linguistics, on the contrary, will study relations that bind together successive terms not perceived by the collective mind but substituted for each other without forming a system.

PART TWO

Synchronic Linguistics

Chapter I

GENERALITIES

The aim of general synchronic linguistics is to set up the fundamental principles of any idiosynchronic system, the constituents of any language-state. Many of the items already explained in Part One belong rather to synchrony; for instance, the general properties of the sign are an integral part of synchrony although they were used to prove the necessity of separating the two linguistics.

To synchrony belongs everything called "general grammar," for it is only through language-states that the different relations which are the province of grammar are established. In the following chapters we shall consider only the basic principles necessary for approaching the more special problems of static linguistics or explaining in detail a language-state.

The study of static linguistics is generally much more difficult than the study of historical linguistics. Evolutionary facts are more concrete and striking; their observable relations tie together successive terms that are easily grasped; it is easy, often even amusing, to follow a series of changes. But the linguistics that penetrates values and coexisting relations presents much greater difficulties.

In practice a language-state is not a point but rather a certain span of time during which the sum of the modifications that have supervened is minimal. The span may cover ten years, a generation, a century, or even more. It is possible for a language to change hardly at all over a long span and then to undergo radical transformations within a few years. Of two languages that exist side by side during a given period, one may evolve drastically and the other practically not at all; study would have to be diachronic in the former instance, synchronic in the latter. An absolute state is defined by the absence of changes, and since language changes somewhat in spite of everything, studying a language-state means in practice disregarding changes of little importance, just as mathematicians disregard infinitesimal quantities in certain calculations, such as logarithms.

Political history makes a distinction between *era*, a point in time, and *period*, which embraces a certain duration. Still, the historian speaks of the Antoninian Era, the Era of the Crusades, etc. when he considers a set of characteristics which remained constant during those times. One might also say that static linguistics deals with eras. But *state* is preferable. The beginning and the end of an era are generally characterized by some rather brusque revolution that tends to modify the existing state of affairs. The word state avoids giving the impression that anything similar occurs in language. Besides, precisely because it is borrowed from history, the term era makes one think less of language itself than of the circumstances that surround it and condition it; in short, it suggests rather the the idea of what we called external linguistics (see p. 20).

Besides, delimitation in time is not the only difficulty that we encounter in defining a language-state: space presents the same problem. In short, a concept of a language-state can be only approximate. In static linguistics, as in most sciences, no course of reasoning is possible without the usual simplification of data.

Chapter II

THE CONCRETE ENTITIES OF LANGUAGE

1. *Definition: Entity and Unit*

The signs that make up language are not abstractions but real objects (see p. 15); signs and their relations are what linguistics studies; they are the *concrete entities* of our science.

Let us first recall two principles that dominate the whole issue:

1) The linguistic entity exists only through the associating of the signifier with the signified (see p. 66 ff.). Whenever only one ele-

ment is retained, the entity vanishes; instead of a concrete object we are faced with a mere abstraction. We constantly risk grasping only a part of the entity and thinking that we are embracing it in its totality; this would happen, for example, if we divided the spoken chain into syllables, for the syllable has no value except in phonology. A succession of sounds is linguistic only if it supports an idea. Considered independently, it is material for a physiological study, and nothing more than that.

The same is true of the signified as soon as it is separated from its signifier. Considered independently, concepts like "house," "white," "see," etc. belong to psychology. They become linguistic entities only when associated with sound-images; in language, a concept is a quality of its phonic substance just as a particular slice of sound is a quality of the concept.

The two-sided linguistic unit has often been compared with the human person, made up of the body and the soul. The comparison is hardly satisfactory. A better choice would be a chemical compound like water, a combination of hydrogen and oxygen; taken separately, neither element has any of the properties of water.

2) The linguistic entity is not accurately defined until it is *delimited*, i.e. separated from everything that surrounds it on the phonic chain. These delimited entities or units stand in opposition to each other in the mechanism of language.

One is at first tempted to liken linguistic signs to visual signs, which can exist in space without becoming confused, and to assume that separation of the significant elements can be accomplished in the same way, without recourse to any mental process. The word "form," which is often used to indicate them (cf. the expression "verbal form," "noun form") gives support to the mistake. But we know that the main characteristic of the sound-chain is that it is linear (see p. 70). Considered by itself, it is only a line, a continuous ribbon along which the ear perceives no self-sufficient and clear-cut division; to divide the chain, we must call in meanings. When we hear an unfamiliar language, we are at a loss to say how the succession of sounds should be analyzed, for analysis is impossible if only the phonic side of the linguistic phenomenon is considered. But when we know the meaning and function that must be attributed to each part of the chain, we see the parts detach themselves from each other and the shapeless ribbon break into segments. Yet there is nothing material in the analysis.

To summarize: language does not offer itself as a set of predelimited signs that need only be studied according to their meaning and arrangement; it is a confused mass, and only attentiveness and familiarization will reveal its particular elements. The unit has no special phonic character, and the only definition that we can give it is this: it is *a slice of sound which to the exclusion of everything that precedes and follows it in the spoken chain is the signifier of a certain concept.*

2. *Method of Delimitation*

One who knows a language singles out its units by a very simple method—in theory, at any rate. His method consists of using speaking as the source material of language and picturing it as two parallel chains, one of concepts (*A*) and the other of sound-images (*B*).

In an accurate delimitation, the division along the chain of sound-images (*a*, *b*, *c*) will correspond to the division along the chain of concepts (*a′*, *b′*, *c′*):

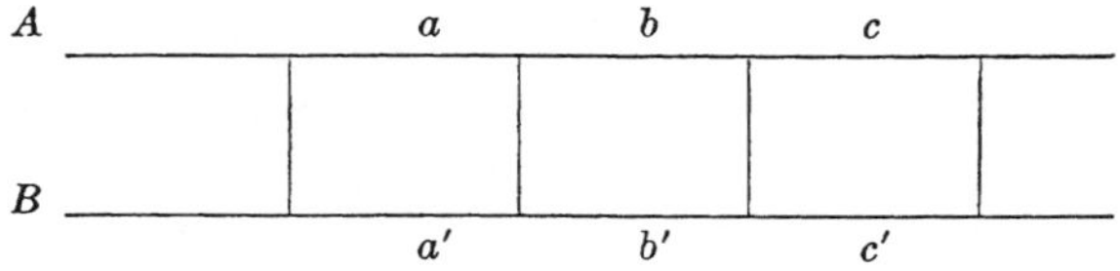

Take French *sižlaprã*. Can we cut the chain after *l* and make *sižl* a unit? No, we need only consider the concepts to see that the division is wrong. Neither is the syllabic division *siž-la-prã* to be taken for granted as having linguistic value. The only possible divisions are these: (1) *si-ž-la-prã* (*si je la prends* 'if I take it') and (2) *si-ž-l-aprã* (*si je l'apprends* 'if I learn it'), and they are determined by the meaning that is attached to the words.[1]

To verify the result of the procedure and be assured that we are really dealing with a unit, we must be able in comparing a series of

[1] Cf. the sounds [jurmɑm] in English: "your mine" or "you're mine." [Tr.]

sentences in which the same unit occurs to separate the unit from the rest of the context and find in each instance that meaning justifies the delimitation. Take the two French phrases *lafǫrsdüvã* (la *force* du vent 'the *force* of the wind'), and *abudfǫrs* (a bout de *force* 'exhausted'; *literally:* 'at the end of one's *force*'). In each phrase the same concept coincides with the same phonic slice, *fǫrs;* thus it is certainly a linguistic unit. But in *ilməfǫrsaparle* (il me *force* a parler 'he *forces* me to talk') *fǫrs* has an entirely different meaning: it is therefore another unit.

3. *Practical Difficulties of Delimitation*

The method outlined above is very simple in theory, but is it easy to apply? We are tempted to think so if we start from the notion that the units to be isolated are words. For what is a sentence except a combination of words? And what can be grasped more readily than words? Going back to the example given above, we may say that the analysis of the spoken chain *sižlaprã* resulted in the delimiting of four units, and that the units are words: *si-je-l-apprends*. But we are immediately put on the defensive on noting that there has been much disagreement about the nature of the word, and a little reflection shows that the usual meaning of the term is incompatible with the notion of concrete unit.

To be convinced, we need only think of French *cheval* 'horse' and its plural from *chevaux*. People readily say that they are two forms of the same word; but considered as wholes, they are certainly two distinct things with respect to both meaning and sound. In *mwa* (*mois,* as in le *mois* de Septembre 'the *month* of September') and *mwaz* (*mois*, in un *mois* après 'a *month* later') there are also two forms of the same word, and there is no question of a concrete unit. The meaning is the same, but the slices of sound are different. As soon as we try to liken concrete units to words, we face a dilemma: we must either ignore the relation—which is nonetheless evident—that binds *cheval* and *chevaux,* the two sounds of *mwa* and *mwaz*, etc. and say that they are different words, or instead of concrete units be satisfied with the abstraction that links the different forms of the same word. The concrete unit must be sought, not in the word, but elsewhere. Besides, many words are complex units, and we can easily single out their subunits (suffixes, prefixes, radicals). Derivatives like *pain-ful* and *delight-ful* can be divided into distinct parts, each having an obvious meaning and function. Conversely, some units are larger than words: compounds (French *porte-plume* 'penholder'), locutions (*s'il vous plaît* 'please'), inflected forms (*il a été* 'he has been'), etc. But these units resist delimitation as strongly as do words proper, making it extremely difficult to disentangle the interplay of units that are found in a sound-chain and to specify the concrete elements on which a language functions.

Doubtless speakers are unaware of the practical difficulties of delimiting units. Anything that is of even the slightest significance seems like a concrete element to them and they never fail to single it out in discourse. But it is one thing to feel the quick, delicate interplay of units and quite another to account for them through methodical analysis.

A rather widely held theory makes sentences the concrete units of language: we speak only in sentences and subsequently single out the words. But to what extent does the sentence belong to language (see p. 124)? If it belongs to speaking, the sentence cannot pass for the linguistic unit. But let us suppose that this difficulty is set aside. If we picture to ourselves in their totality the sentences that could be uttered, their most striking characteristic is that in no way do they resemble each other. We are at first tempted to liken the immense diversity of sentences to the equal diversity of the individuals that make up a zoological species. But this is an illusion: the characteristics that animals of the same species have in common are much more significant than the differences that separate them. In sentences, on the contrary, diversity is dominant, and when we look for the link that bridges their diversity, again we find, without having looked for it, the word with its grammatical characteristics and thus fall back into the same difficulties as before.

4. *Conclusion*

In most sciences the question of units never even arises: the units are delimited from the outset. In zoology, the animal immediately presents itself. Astronomy works with units that are separated in space, the stars. The chemist can study the nature and composition of potassium bichromate without doubting for an instant that this is a well-defined object.

When a science has no concrete units that are immediately recognizable, it is because they are not necessary. In history, for example, is the unit the individual, the era, or the nation? We do not know. But what does it matter? We can study history without knowing the answer.

But just as the game of chess is entirely in the combination of the different chesspieces, language is characterized as a system based entirely on the opposition of its concrete units. We can neither dispense with becoming acquainted with them nor take a single step without coming back to them; and still, delimiting them is such a delicate problem that we may wonder at first whether they really exist.

Language then has the strange, striking characteristic of not having entities that are perceptible at the outset and yet of not permitting us to doubt that they exist and that their functioning constitutes it. Doubtless we have here a trait that distinguishes language from all other semiological institutions.

Chapter III

IDENTITIES, REALITIES, VALUES

The statement just made brings us squarely up against a problem that is all the more important because any basic notion in static linguistics depends directly on our conception of the unit and even blends with it. This is what I should like successively to demonstrate with respect to the notions of synchronic identity, reality, and value.

A. What is a synchronic *identity?* Here it is not a question of the identity that links the French negation *pas* 'not' to Latin *passum,* a diachronic identity that will be dealt with elsewhere (see p. 181), but rather of the equally interesting identity by virtue of which we state that two sentences like je ne sais *pas* 'I *don't* know' and ne dîtes *pas* cela '*don't* say that' contain the same element. An idle question, one might say; there is identity because the same slice of sound carries the same meaning in the two sentences. But that explanation is unsatisfactory, for if the correspondence of slices of sound and concepts is proof of identity (see above, p. 105, la *force* du vent: a bout de *force*), the reverse is not true. There can be identity without this correspondence. When *Gentlemen!* is repeated several times during a lecture, the listener has the feeling that the same expression is being used each time, and yet variations in utterance and intonation make for appreciable phonic differences in diverse contexts—differences just as appreciable as those that elsewhere separate different words (cf. French *pomme* 'apple' and *paume* 'palm,' *goutte* 'drop' and *je goute* 'I taste,' *fuir* 'flee,' and *fouir* 'stuff,' etc.);[2] besides, the feeling of identity persists even though there is no absolute identity between one *Gentlemen!* and the next from a semantic viewpoint either. In the same vein, a word can express quite different ideas without compromising its identity (cf. French *adopter* une mode '*adopt* a fashion' and *adopter* un enfant '*adopt* a child,' la *fleur* du pommier 'the *flower* of the apple tree' and la *fleur* de la noblesse 'the *flower* of nobility,' etc.).

The linguistic mechanism is geared to differences and identities, the former being only the counterpart of the latter. Everywhere then, the problem of identities appears; moreover, it blends partially with the problem of entities and units and is only a complication—illuminating at some points—of the larger problem. This characteristic stands out if we draw some comparisons with facts taken from outside speech. For instance, we speak of the identity of two "8:25 p.m. Geneva-to-Paris" trains that leave at twenty-four hour intervals. We feel that it is the same train each day, yet everything—the locomotive, coaches, personnel—is probably different. Or if a street is demolished, then rebuilt, we say that it is the same street even though in a material sense, perhaps nothing of the old one remains. Why can a street be completely rebuilt and still be the same? Because it does not constitute a purely material entity; it is based on certain conditions that are distinct from the materials

[2] Cf. English *bought: boat, naught: note, far: for: four* (for many speakers). [Tr.]

that fit the conditions, e.g. its location with respect to other streets. Similarly, what makes the express is its hour of departure, its route, and in general every circumstance that sets it apart from other trains. Whenever the same conditions are fulfilled, the same entities are obtained. Still, the entities are not abstract since we cannot conceive of a street or train outside its material realization.

Let us contrast the preceding examples with the completely different case of a suit which has been stolen from me and which I find in the window of a second-hand store. Here we have a material entity that consists solely of the inert substance—the cloth, its lining, its trimmings, etc. Another suit would not be mine regardless of its similarity to it. But linguistic identity is not that of the garment; it is that of the train and the street. Each time I say the word *Gentlemen!* I renew its substance; each utterance is a new phonic act and a new psychological act. The bond between the two uses of the same word depends neither on material identity nor on sameness in meaning but on elements which must be sought after and which will point up the true nature of linguistic units.

B. What is a synchronic *reality?* To what concrete or abstract elements of language can the name be applied?

Take as an example the distinction between the parts of speech. What supports the classing of words as substantives, adjectives, etc.? Is it done in the name of a purely logical, extra-linguistic principle that is applied to grammar from without like the degrees of longitude and latitude on the globe? Or does it correspond to something that has its place in the system of language and is conditioned by it? In a word, is it a synchronic reality? The second supposition seems probable, but the first could also be defended. In the French sentence *ces gants sont bon marché* 'these gloves are cheap,' is *bon marché* an adjective? It is apparently an adjective from a logical viewpoint but not from the viewpoint of grammar, for *bon marché* fails to behave as an adjective (it is invariable, it never precedes its noun, etc.); in addition, it is composed of two words. Now the distinction between parts of speech is exactly what should serve to classify the words of language. How can a group of words be attributed to one of the "parts"? But to say that *bon* 'good' is an adjective and *marché* 'market' a substantive explains nothing. We are then dealing with a defective or incomplete classification; the division of words into substantives, verbs, adjectives, etc. is not an undeniable linguistic reality.[3]

Linguistics accordingly works continuously with concepts forged by grammarians without knowing whether or not the concepts actually correspond to the constituents of the system of language. But how can we find out? And if they are phantoms, what realities can we place in opposition to them?

To be rid of illusions we must first be convinced that the concrete entities of language are not directly accessible. If we try to grasp them, we come into contact with the true facts. Starting from there, we can set up all the classifications that linguistics needs for arranging all the facts at its disposal. On the other hand, to base the classifications on anything except concrete entities—to say, for example, that the parts of speech are the constituents of language simply because they correspond to categories of logic—is to forget that there are no linguistic facts apart from the phonic substance cut into significant elements.

C. Finally, not every idea touched upon in this chapter differs basically from what we have elsewhere called *values*. A new comparison with the set of chessmen will bring out this point (see pp. 88 ff.). Take a knight, for instance. By itself is it an element in the game? Certainly not, for by its material make-up—outside its square and the other conditions of the game—it means nothing to the player; it becomes a real, concrete element only when endowed with value and wedded to it. Suppose that the piece happens to be destroyed or lost during a game. Can it be replaced by an equivalent piece? Certainly. Not only another knight but even a figure shorn of any resemblance to a knight can be declared identical provided the same value is attributed to it. We see then that in semiological systems like language, where elements hold each other in equilibrium in accordance with fixed rules, the notion of identity blends with that of value and *vice versa*.

In a word, that is why the notion of value envelopes the notions of unit, concrete entity, and reality. But if there is no fundamental

[3] Form, function, and meaning combine to make the classing of the parts of speech even more difficult in English than in French. Cf. *ten-foot: ten feet* in *a ten-foot pole: the pole is ten feet long*. [Tr.]

difference between these diverse notions, it follows that the problem can be stated successively in several ways. Whether we try to define the unit, reality, concrete entity, or value, we always come back to the central question that dominates all of static linguistics.

It would be interesting from a practical viewpoint to begin with units, to determine what they are and to account for their diversity by classifying them. It would be necessary to search for the reason for dividing language into words—for in spite of the difficulty of defining it, the word is a unit that strikes the mind, something central in the mechanism of language—but that is a subject which by itself would fill a volume. Next we would have to classify the subunits, then the larger units, etc. By determining in this way the elements that it manipulates, synchronic linguistics would completely fulfill its task, for it would relate all synchronic phenomena to their fundamental principle. It cannot be said that this basic problem has ever been faced squarely or that its scope and difficulty have been understood; in the matter of language, people have always been satisfied with ill-defined units.

Still, in spite of their capital importance, it is better to approach the problem of units through the study of value, for in my opinion value is of prime importance.

Chapter IV

LINGUISTIC VALUE

1. *Language as Organized Thought Coupled with Sound*

To prove that language is only a system of pure values, it is enough to consider the two elements involved in its functioning: ideas and sounds.

Psychologically our thought—apart from its expression in words—is only a shapeless and indistinct mass. Philosophers and linguists have always agreed in recognizing that without the help of signs we would be unable to make a clear-cut, consistent distinction between two ideas. Without language, thought is a vague, uncharted nebula. There are no pre-existing ideas, and nothing is distinct before the appearance of language.

Against the floating realm of thought, would sounds by themselves yield predelimited entities? No more so than ideas. Phonic substance is neither more fixed nor more rigid than thought; it is not a mold into which thought must of necessity fit but a plastic substance divided in turn into distinct parts to furnish the signifiers needed by thought. The linguistic fact can therefore be pictured in its totality—i.e. language—as a series of contiguous subdivisions marked off on both the indefinite plane of jumbled ideas (*A*) and the equally vague plane of sounds (*B*). The following diagram gives a rough idea of it:

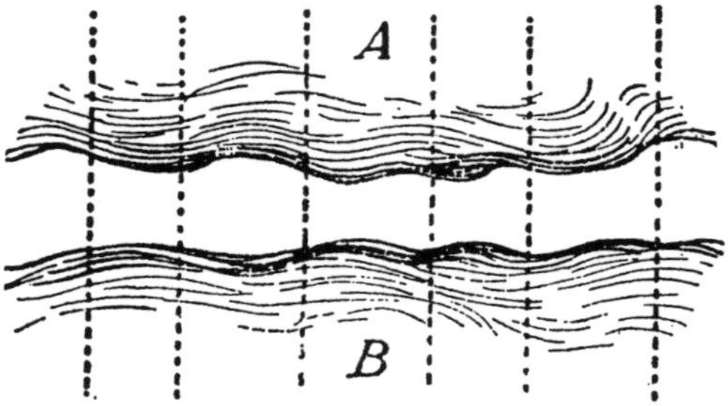

The characteristic role of language with respect to thought is not to create a material phonic means for expressing ideas but to serve as a link between thought and sound, under conditions that of necessity bring about the reciprocal delimitations of units. Thought, chaotic by nature, has to become ordered in the process of its decomposition. Neither are thoughts given material form nor are sounds transformed into mental entities; the somewhat mysterious fact is rather that "thought-sound" implies division, and that language works out its units while taking shape between two shapeless masses. Visualize the air in contact with a sheet of water; if the atmospheric pressure changes, the surface of the water will be broken up into a series of divisions, waves; the waves resemble the union or coupling of thought with phonic substance.

Language might be called the domain of articulations, using the word as it was defined earlier (see p. 10). Each linguistic term is a member, an *articulus* in which an idea is fixed in a sound and a sound becomes the sign of an idea.

Language can also be compared with a sheet of paper: thought is the front and the sound the back; one cannot cut the front without cutting the back at the same time; likewise in language, one can neither divide sound from thought nor thought from sound; the division could be accomplished only abstractedly, and the result would be either pure psychology or pure phonology.

Linguistics then works in the borderland where the elements of sound and thought combine; *their combination produces a form, not a substance.*

These views give a better understanding of what was said before (see pp. 67 ff.) about the arbitrariness of signs. Not only are the two domains that are linked by the linguistic fact shapeless and confused, but the choice of a given slice of sound to name a given idea is completely arbitrary. If this were not true, the notion of value would be compromised, for it would include an externally imposed element. But actually values remain entirely relative, and that is why the bond between the sound and the idea is radically arbitrary.

The arbitrary nature of the sign explains in turn why the social fact alone can create a linguistic system. The community is necessary if values that owe their existence solely to usage and general acceptance are to be set up; by himself the individual is incapable of fixing a single value.

In addition, the idea of value, as defined, shows that to consider a term as simply the union of a certain sound with a certain concept is grossly misleading. To define it in this way would isolate the term from its system; it would mean assuming that one can start from the terms and construct the system by adding them together when, on the contrary, it is from the interdependent whole that one must start and through analysis obtain its elements.

To develop this thesis, we shall study value successively from the viewpoint of the signified or concept (Section 2), the signifier (Section 3), and the complete sign (Section 4).

Being unable to seize the concrete entities or units of language directly, we shall work with words. While the word does not conform exactly to the definition of the linguistic unit (see p. 105), it at least bears a rough resemblance to the unit and has the advantage of being concrete; consequently, we shall use words as specimens equivalent to real terms in a synchronic system, and the principles that we evolve with respect to words will be valid for entities in general.

2. *Linguistic Value from a Conceptual Viewpoint*

When we speak of the value of a word, we generally think first of its property of standing for an idea, and this is in fact one side of linguistic value. But if this is true, how does *value* differ from *signification?* Might the two words be synonyms? I think not, although it is easy to confuse them, since the confusion results not so much from their similarity as from the subtlety of the distinction that they mark.

From a conceptual viewpoint, value is doubtless one element in signification, and it is difficult to see how signification can be dependent upon value and still be distinct from it. But we must clear up the issue or risk reducing language to a simple naming-process (see p. 65).

Let us first take signification as it is generally understood and as it was pictured on page 67. As the arrows in the drawing show, it is only the counterpart of the sound-image. Everything that occurs concerns only the sound-image and the concept when we look upon the word as independent and self-contained.

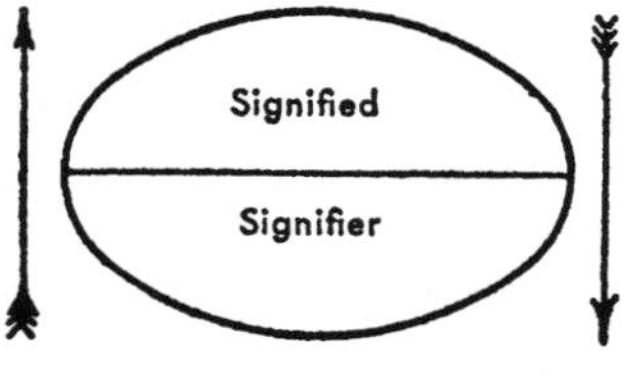

But here is the paradox: on the one hand the concept seems to be the counterpart of the sound-image, and on the other hand the sign itself is in turn the counterpart of the other signs of language.

Language is a system of interdependent terms in which the value of each term results solely from the simultaneous presence of the others, as in the diagram:

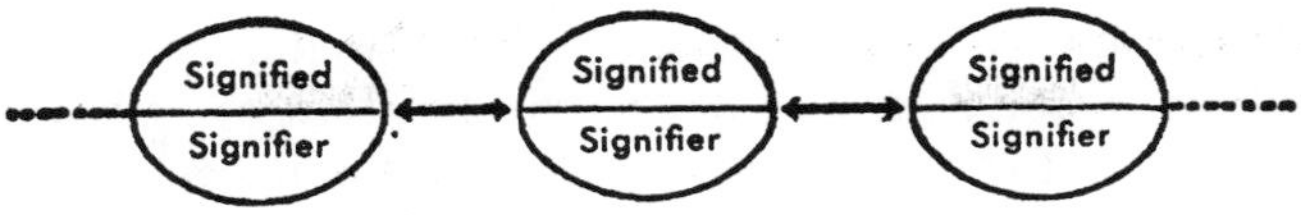

How, then, can value be confused with signification, i.e. the counterpart of the sound-image? It seems impossible to liken the relations represented here by horizontal arrows to those represented above (p. 114) by vertical arrows. Putting it another way—and again taking up the example of the sheet of paper that is cut in two (see p. 113)—it is clear that the observable relation between the different pieces A, B, C, D, etc. is distinct from the relation between the front and back of the same piece as in A/A′, B/B′, etc.

To resolve the issue, let us observe from the outset that even outside language all values are apparently governed by the same paradoxical principle. They are always composed:

(1) of a *dissimilar* thing that can be *exchanged* for the thing of which the value is to be determined; and

(2) of *similar* things that can be *compared* with the thing of which the value is to be determined.

Both factors are necessary for the existence of a value. To determine what a five-franc piece is worth one must therefore know: (1) that it can be exchanged for a fixed quantity of a different thing, e.g. bread; and (2) that it can be compared with a similar value of the same system, e.g. a one-franc piece, or with coins of another system (a dollar, etc.). In the same way a word can be exchanged for something dissimilar, an idea; besides, it can be compared with something of the same nature, another word. Its value is therefore not fixed so long as one simply states that it can be "exchanged" for a given concept, i.e. that it has this or that signification: one must also compare it with similar values, with other words that stand in opposition to it. Its content is really fixed only by the concurrence of everything that exists outside it. Being part of a system, it is endowed not only with a signification but also and especially with a value, and this is something quite different.

A few examples will show clearly that this is true. Modern French *mouton* can have the same signification as English *sheep* but not the same value, and this for several reasons, particularly because in speaking of a piece of meat ready to be served on the table, English uses *mutton* and not *sheep*. The difference in value between *sheep* and *mouton* is due to the fact that *sheep* has beside it a second term while the French word does not.

Within the same language, all words used to express related ideas limit each other reciprocally; synonyms like French *redouter* 'dread,' *craindre* 'fear,' and *avoir peur* 'be afraid' have value only through their opposition: if *redouter* did not exist, all its content would go to its competitors. Conversely, some words are enriched through contact with others: e.g. the new element introduced in *décrépit* (un vieillard *décrépit*, see p. 83) results from the co-existence of *décrépi* (un mur *décrépi*). The value of just any term is accordingly determined by its environment; it is impossible to fix even the value of the word signifying "sun" without first considering its surroundings: in some languages it is not possible to say "sit in the *sun*."

Everything said about words applies to any term of language, e.g. to grammatical entities. The value of a French plural does not coincide with that of a Sanskrit plural even though their signification is usually identical; Sanskrit has three numbers instead of two (*my eyes, my ears, my arms, my legs,* etc. are dual);[4] it would be wrong to attribute the same value to the plural in Sanskrit and in French; its value clearly depends on what is outside and around it.

If words stood for pre-existing concepts, they would all have exact equivalents in meaning from one language to the next; but this is not true. French uses *louer* (*une maison*) 'let (a house)' indifferently to mean both "pay for" and "receive payment for," whereas German uses two words, *mieten* and *vermieten;* there is obviously no exact correspondence of values. The German verbs *schätzen* and *urteilen* share a number of significations, but that correspondence does not hold at several points.

Inflection offers some particularly striking examples. Distinctions of time, which are so familiar to us, are unknown in certain languages. Hebrew does not recognize even the fundamental

[4] The use of the comparative form for two and the superlative for more than two in English (e.g. *may the* better *boxer win: the* best *boxer in the world*) is probably a remnant of the old distinction between the dual and the plural number. [Tr.]

distinctions between the past, present, and future. Proto-Germanic has no special form for the future; to say that the future is expressed by the present is wrong, for the value of the present is not the same in Germanic as in languages that have a future along with the present. The Slavic languages regularly single out two aspects of the verb: the perfective represents action as a point, complete in its totality; the imperfective represents it as taking place, and on the line of time. The categories are difficult for a Frenchman to understand, for they are unknown in French; if they were predetermined, this would not be true. Instead of pre-existing ideas then, we find in all the foregoing examples *values* emanating from the system. When they are said to correspond to concepts, it is understood that the concepts are purely differential and defined not by their positive content but negatively by their relations with the other terms of the system. Their most precise characteristic is in being what the others are not.

Now the real interpretation of the diagram of the signal becomes apparent. Thus

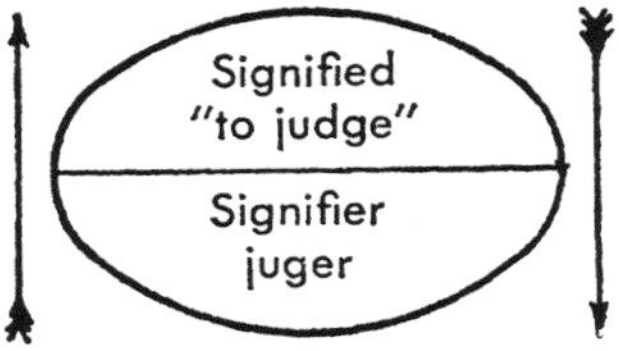

means that in French the concept "to judge" is linked to the sound-image *juger;* in short, it symbolizes signification. But it is quite clear that initially the concept is nothing, that is only a value determined by its relations with other similar values, and that without them the signification would not exist. If I state simply that a word signifies something when I have in mind the associating of a sound-image with a concept, I am making a statement that may suggest what actually happens, but by no means am I expressing the linguistic fact in its essence and fullness.

3. *Linguistic Value from a Material Viewpoint*

The conceptual side of value is made up solely of relations and differences with respect to the other terms of language, and the same can be said of its material side. The important thing in the word is not the sound alone but the phonic differences that make it possible to distinguish this word from all others, for differences carry signification.

This may seem surprising, but how indeed could the reverse be possible? Since one vocal image is no better suited than the next for what it is commissioned to express, it is evident, even *a priori*, that a segment of language can never in the final analysis be based on anything except its noncoincidence with the rest. *Arbitrary* and *differential* are two correlative qualities.

The alteration of linguistic signs clearly illustrates this. It is precisely because the terms *a* and *b* as such are radically incapable of reaching the level of consciousness—one is always conscious of only the *a/b* difference—that each term is free to change according to laws that are unrelated to its signifying function. No positive sign characterizes the genitive plural in Czech *žen* (see p. 86); still the two forms *žena: žen* function as well as the earlier forms *žena: ženb; žen* has value only because it is different.

Here is another example that shows even more clearly the systematic role of phonic differences: in Greek, *éphēn* is an imperfect and *éstēn* an aorist although both words are formed in the same way; the first belongs to the system of the present indicative of *phēmī* 'I say,' whereas there is no present **stēmi*; now it is precisely the relation *phēmī: éphēn* that corresponds to the relation between the present and the imperfect (cf. *déiknūmi: edéiknūn*, etc.). Signs function, then, not through their intrinsic value but through their relative position.

In addition, it is impossible for sound alone, a material element, to belong to language. It is only a secondary thing, substance to be put to use. All our conventional values have the characteristic of not being confused with the tangible element which supports them. For instance, it is not the metal in a piece of money that fixes its value. A coin nominally worth five francs may contain less than half its worth of silver. Its value will vary according to the amount stamped upon it and according to its use inside or outside a political boundary. This is even more true of the linguistic signifier, which is not phonic but incorporeal—constituted not by its material substance but by the differences that separate its sound-image from all others.

The foregoing principle is so basic that it applies to all the material elements of language, including phonemes. Every language forms its words on the basis of a system of sonorous elements, each element being a clearly delimited unit and one of a fixed number of units. Phonemes are characterized not, as one might think, by their own positive quality but simply by the fact that they are distinct. Phonemes are above all else opposing, relative, and negative entities.

Proof of this is the latitude that speakers have between points of convergence in the pronunciation of distinct sounds. In French, for instance, general use of a dorsal *r* does not prevent many speakers from using a tongue-tip trill; language is not in the least disturbed by it; language requires only that the sound be different and not, as one might imagine, that it have an invariable quality. I can even pronounce the French *r* like German *ch* in *Bach, doch,* etc., but in German I could not use *r* instead of *ch,* for German gives recognition to both elements and must keep them apart. Similarly, in Russian there is no latitude for *t* in the direction of *t'* (palatalized *t*), for the result would be the confusing of two sounds differentiated by the language (cf. *govorit'* 'speak' and *goverit* 'he speaks'), but more freedom may be taken with respect to *th* (aspirated *t*) since this sound does not figure in the Russian system of phonemes.

Since an identical state of affairs is observable in writing, another system of signs, we shall use writing to draw some comparisons that will clarify the whole issue. In fact:

1) The signs used in writing are arbitrary; there is no connection, for example, between the letter *t* and the sound that it designates.

2) The value of letters is purely negative and differential. The same person can write *t*, for instance, in different ways:

The only requirement is that the sign for *t* not be confused in his script with the signs used for *l*, *d*, etc.

3) Values in writing function only through reciprocal opposition within a fixed system that consists of a set number of letters. This third characteristic, though not identical to the second, is closely related to it, for both depend on the first. Since the graphic sign is arbitrary, its form matters little or rather matters only within the limitations imposed by the system.

4) The means by which the sign is produced is completely unimportant, for it does not affect the system (this also follows from characteristic 1). Whether I make the letters in white or black, raised or engraved, with pen or chisel—all this is of no importance with respect to their signification.

4. *The Sign Considered in Its Totality*

Everything that has been said up to this point boils down to this: in language there are only differences. Even more important: a difference generally implies positive terms between which the difference is set up; but in language there are only differences *without positive terms*. Whether we take the signified or the signifier, language has neither ideas nor sounds that existed before the linguistic system, but only conceptual and phonic differences that have issued from the system. The idea or phonic substance that a sign contains is of less importance than the other signs that surround it. Proof of this is that the value of a term may be modified without either its meaning or its sound being affected, solely because a neighboring term has been modified (see p. 115).

But the statement that everything in language is negative is true only if the signified and the signifier are considered separately; when we consider the sign in its totality, we have something that is positive in its own class. A linguistic system is a series of differences of sound combined with a series of differences of ideas; but the pairing of a certain number of acoustical signs with as many cuts made from the mass of thought engenders a system of values; and this system serves as the effective link between the phonic and psychological elements within each sign. Although both the signified and the signifier are purely differential and negative when considered separately, their combination is a positive fact; it is even the sole type of facts that language has, for maintaining the parallelism between the two classes of differences is the distinctive function of the linguistic institution.

Certain diachronic facts are typical in this respect. Take the countless instances where alteration of the signifier occasions a conceptual change and where it is obvious that the sum of the ideas distinguished corresponds in principle to the sum of the distinctive signs. When two words are confused through phonetic alteration (e.g. French *décrépit* from *dĕcrepitus* and *décrépi* from *crispus*), the ideas that they express will also tend to become confused if only they have something in common. Or a word may have different forms (cf. *chaise* 'chair' and *chaire* 'desk'). Any nascent difference will tend invariably to become significant but without always succeeding or being successful on the first trial. Conversely, any conceptual difference perceived by the mind seeks to find expression through a distinct signifier, and two ideas that are no longer distinct in the mind tend to merge into the same signifier.

When we compare signs—positive terms—with each other, we can no longer speak of difference; the expression would not be fitting, for it applies only to the comparing of two sound-images, e.g. *father* and *mother*, or two ideas, e.g. the idea "father" and the idea "mother"; two signs, each having a signified and signifier, are not different but only distinct. Between them there is only *opposition*. The entire mechanism of language, with which we shall be concerned later, is based on oppositions of this kind and on the phonic and conceptual differences that they imply.

What is true of value is true also of the unit (see pp. 110 ff.). A unit is a segment of the spoken chain that corresponds to a certain concept; both are by nature purely differential.

Applied to units, the principle of differentiation can be stated in this way: *the characteristics of the unit blend with the unit itself*. In language, as in any semiological system, whatever distinguishes one sign from the others constitutes it. Difference makes character just as it makes value and the unit.

Another rather paradoxical consequence of the same principle is this: in the last analysis what is commonly referred to as a "grammatical fact" fits the definition of the unit, for it always expresses an opposition of terms; it differs only in that the opposition is particularly significant (e.g. the formation of German plurals of the type *Nacht: Nächte*). Each term present in the grammatical fact (the singular without umlaut or final *e* in opposition to the plural with umlaut and *-e*) consists of the interplay of a number of oppositions within the system. When isolated, neither *Nacht* nor *Nächte* is anything: thus everything is opposition. Putting it another way, the *Nacht: Nächte* relation can be expressed by an algebraic formula a/b in which *a* and *b* are not simple terms but result from a set of relations. Language, in a manner of speaking, is a type of algebra consisting solely of complex terms. Some of its oppositions are more significant than others; but units and grammatical facts are only different names for designating diverse aspects of the same general fact: the functioning of linguistic oppositions. This statement is so true that we might very well approach the problem of units by starting from grammatical facts. Taking an opposition like *Nacht: Nächte*, we might ask what are the units involved in it. Are they only the two words, the whole series of similar words, *a* and *ä*, or all singulars and plurals, etc.?

Units and grammatical facts would not be confused if linguistic signs were made up of something besides differences. But language being what it is, we shall find nothing simple in it regardless of our approach; everywhere and always there is the same complex equilibrium of terms that mutually condition each other. Putting it another way, *language is a form and not a substance* (see p. 113). This truth could not be overstressed, for all the mistakes in our terminology, all our incorrect ways of naming things that pertain to language, stem from the involuntary supposition that the linguistic phenomenon must have substance.

Chapter V

SYNTAGMATIC AND ASSOCIATIVE RELATIONS

1. *Definitions*

In a language-state everything is based on relations. How do they function?

Relations and differences between linguistic terms fall into two distinct groups, each of which generates a certain class of values. The opposition between the two classes gives a better understanding of the nature of each class. They correspond to two forms of our mental activity, both indispensable to the life of language.

In discourse, on the one hand, words acquire relations based on the linear nature of language because they are chained together. This rules out the possibility of pronouncing two elements simultaneously (see p. 70). The elements are arranged in sequence on the chain of speaking. Combinations supported by linearity are *syntagms*.[5] The syntagm is always composed of two or more consecutive units (e.g. French *re-lire* 're-read,' *contre tous* 'against everyone,' *la vie humaine* 'human life,' *Dieu est bon* 'God is good,' *s'il fait beau temps, nous sortirons* 'if the weather is nice, we'll go out,' etc.). In the syntagm a term acquires its value only because it stands in opposition to everything that precedes or follows it, or to both.

Outside discourse, on the other hand, words acquire relations of a different kind. Those that have something in common are associated in the memory, resulting in groups marked by diverse relations. For instance, the French word *enseignement* 'teaching' will unconsciously call to mind a host of other words (*enseigner* 'teach,' *renseigner* 'acquaint,' etc.; or *armement* 'armament,' *changement* 'amendment,' etc.; or *éducation* 'education,' *apprentissage* 'apprenticeship,' etc.). All those words are related in some way.

We see that the co-ordinations formed outside discourse differ strikingly from those formed inside discourse. Those formed outside discourse are not supported by linearity. Their seat is in the brain; they are a part of the inner storehouse that makes up the language of each speaker. They are *associative relations*.

The syntagmatic relation is *in praesentia*. It is based on two or more terms that occur in an effective series. Against this, the associative relation unites terms *in absentia* in a potential mnemonic series.

From the associative and syntagmatic viewpoint a linguistic

[5] It is scarcely necessary to point out that the study of *syntagms* is not to be confused with syntax. Syntax is only one part of the study of syntagms (see pp. 134 ff.). [Ed.]

unit is like a fixed part of a building, e.g. a column. On the one hand, the column has a certain relation to the architrave that it supports; the arrangement of the two units in space suggests the syntagmatic relation. On the other hand, if the column is Doric, it suggests a mental comparison of this style with others (Ionic, Corinthian, etc.) although none of these elements is present in space: the relation is associative.

Each of the two classes of co-ordination calls for some specific remarks.

2. *Syntagmatic Relations*

The examples on page 123 have already indicated that the notion of syntagm applies not only to words but to groups of words, to complex units of all lengths and types (compounds, derivatives, phrases, whole sentences).

It is not enough to consider the relation that ties together the different parts of syntagms (e.g. French *contre* 'against' and *tous* 'everyone' in *contre tous, contre* and *maître* 'master' in *contremaître* 'foreman');[6] one must also bear in mind the relation that links the whole to its parts (e.g. *contre tous* in opposition on the one hand to *contre* and on the other *tous*, or *contremaître* in opposition to *contre* and *maître*).

An objection might be raised at this point. The sentence is the ideal type of syntagm. But it belongs to speaking, not to language (see p. 14). Does it not follow that the syntagm belongs to speaking? I do not think so. Speaking is characterized by freedom of combinations; one must therefore ask whether or not all syntagms are equally free.

It is obvious from the first that many expressions belong to language. These are the pat phrases in which any change is prohibited by usage, even if we can single out their meaningful elements (cf. *à quoi bon?* 'what's the use?' *allons donc!* 'nonsense!'). The same is true, though to a lesser degree, of expressions like *prendre la mouche* 'take offense easily,'[7] *forcer la main à quelqu'un* 'force someone's hand,' *rompre une lance* 'break a lance,'[8] or even *avoir mal* (*à la*

[6] Cf. English *head* and *waiter* in *headwaiter*. [Tr.]
[7] Literally 'take the fly.' Cf. English *take the bull by the horns*. [Tr.]
[8] Cf. English *bury the hatchet*. [Tr.]

tête, etc.) 'have (a headache, etc.),' *à force de* (*soins*, etc.) 'by dint of (care, etc.),' *que vous en semble?* 'how do you feel about it?' *pas n'est besoin de . . .* 'there's no need for . . .,' etc., which are characterized by peculiarities of signification or syntax. These idiomatic twists cannot be improvised; they are furnished by tradition. There are also words which, while lending themselves perfectly to analysis, are characterized by some morphological anomaly that is kept solely by dint of usage (cf. *difficulté* 'difficulty' beside *facilité* 'facility,' etc., and *mourrai* '[I] shall die' beside *dormirai* '[I] shall sleep').[9]

There are further proofs. To language rather than to speaking belong the syntagmatic types that are built upon regular forms. Indeed, since there is nothing abstract in language, the types exist only if language has registered a sufficient number of specimens. When a word like *indécorable* arises in speaking (see pp. 167 ff.), its appearance supposes a fixed type, and this type is in turn possible only through remembrance of a sufficient number of similar words belonging to language (*impardonable* 'unpardonable,' *intolérable* 'intolerable,' *infatigable* 'indefatigable,' etc.). Exactly the same is true of sentences and groups of words built upon regular patterns. Combinations like *la terre tourne* 'the world turns,' *que vous dit-il?* 'what does he say to you?' etc. correspond to general types that are in turn supported in the language by concrete remembrances.

But we must realize that in the syntagm there is no clear-cut boundary between the language fact, which is a sign of collective usage, and the fact that belongs to speaking and depends on individual freedom. In a great number of instances it is hard to class a combination of units because both forces have combined in producing it, and they have combined in indeterminable proportions.

3. *Associative Relations*

Mental association creates other groups besides those based on the comparing of terms that have something in common; through its grasp of the nature of the relations that bind the terms together, the mind creates as many associative series as there are diverse relations. For instance, in *enseignement* 'teaching,' *enseigner* 'teach,'

[9] The anomaly of the double *r* in the future forms of certain verbs in French may be compared to irregular plurals like *oxen* in English. [Tr.]

enseignons '(we) teach,' etc., one element, the radical, is common to every term; the same word may occur in a different series formed around another common element, the suffix (cf. *enseignement, armement, changement,* etc.); or the association may spring from the analogy of the concepts signified (*enseignement, instruction, apprentissage, éducation,* etc.); or again, simply from the similarity of the sound-images (e.g. *enseignement* and *justement* 'precisely').[10] Thus there is at times a double similarity of meaning and form, at times similarity only of form or of meaning. A word can always evoke everything that can be associated with it in one way or another.

Whereas a syntagm immediately suggests an order of succession and a fixed number of elements, terms in an associative family occur neither in fixed numbers nor in a definite order. If we associate *painful, delightful, frightful,* etc. we are unable to predict the number of words that the memory will suggest or the order in which they will appear. A particular word is like the center of a constellation; it is the point of convergence of an indefinite number of co-ordinated terms (see the illustration on page 127).

But of the two characteristics of the associative series—indeterminate order and indefinite number—only the first can always be verified; the second may fail to meet the test. This happens in the case of inflectional paradigms, which are typical of associative groupings. Latin *dominus, dominī, dominō,* etc. is obviously an associative group formed around a common element, the noun theme *domin-*, but the series[11]

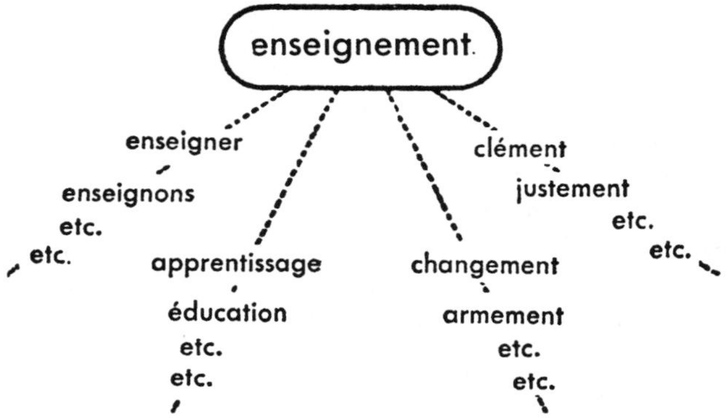

[10] The last case is rare and can be classed as abnormal, for the mind naturally

is not indefinite as in the case of *enseignement, changement,* etc.; the number of cases is definite. Against this, the words have no fixed order of succession, and it is by a purely arbitrary act that the grammarian groups them in one way rather than in another; in the mind of speakers the nominative case is by no means the first one in the declension, and the order in which terms are called depends on circumstances.

Chapter VI

THE MECHANISM OF LANGUAGE

1. *Syntagmatic Solidarities*

The set of phonic and conceptual differences that constitutes language results from two types of comparisons; the relations are sometimes associative, sometimes syntagmatic. The groupings in both classes are for the most part fixed by language; this set of common relations constitutes language and governs its functioning.

What is most striking in the organization of language are *syntagmatic solidarities;* almost all units of language depend on what surrounds them in the spoken chain or on their successive parts.

This is shown by word formation. A unit like *painful* decomposes

---

discards associations that becloud the intelligibility of discourse. But its existence is proved by a lower category of puns based on the ridiculous confusions that can result from pure and simple homonomy like the French statement: "Les musiciens produisent les *sons* ['sounds, bran'] et les grainetiers les vendent" 'musicians produce *sons* and seedsmen sell them.' [Cf. Shakespeare's "Not on thy *sole*, but on thy *soul.*" (Tr.)] This is distinct from the case where an association, while fortuitous, is supported by a comparison of ideas (cf. French *ergot* 'spur': *ergoter* 'wrangle'; German *blau* 'blue': *durchblauen* 'thrash soundly'); the point is that one member of the pair has a new interpretation. Folk etymologies like these (see pp. 173 ff.) are of interest in the study of semantic evolution, but from the synchronic viewpoint they are in the same category as *enseigner: enseignement.* [Ed.]

[11] Cf. English *education* and the corresponding associative series: *educate, educates,* etc.; *internship, training,* etc.; *vocation, devotion,* etc.; and *lotion, fashion,* etc. [Tr.]

into two subunits (*pain-ful*), but these subunits are not two independent parts that are simply lumped together (*pain* + *ful*). The unit is a product, a combination of two interdependent elements that acquire value only through their reciprocal action in a higher unit (*pain* × *ful*). The suffix is nonexistent when considered independently; what gives it a place in the language is a series of common terms like *delight-ful, fright-ful,* etc. Nor is the radical independent. It exists only through combining with a suffix. In *gos-ling,* the element *gos–* is nothing without its suffix. The whole has value only through its parts, and the parts have value by virtue of their place in the whole. That is why the syntagmatic relation of the part to the whole is just as important as the relation of the parts to each other.

This general principle holds true for every type of syntagm enumerated above (pp. 124 ff.), for larger units are always composed of more restricted units linked by their reciprocal solidarity.

To be sure, language has independent units that have syntagmatic relations with neither their parts nor other units. Sentence equivalents like *yes, no, thanks,* etc. are good examples. But this exceptional fact does not compromise the general principle. As a rule we do not communicate through isolated signs but rather through groups of signs, through organized masses that are themselves signs. In language everything boils down to differences but also to groupings. The mechanism of language, which consists of the interplay of successive terms, resembles the operation of a machine in which the parts have a reciprocating function even though they are arranged in a single dimension.

2. *Simultaneous Functioning of the Two Types of Groupings*

Between the syntagmatic groupings, as defined, there is a bond of interdependence; they mutually condition each other. In fact, spatial co-ordinations help to create associative co-ordinations, which are in turn necessary for analysis of the parts of the syntagm.

Take the French compound *dé-faire* 'un-do.' [12] We can picture it as a horizontal ribbon that corresponds to the spoken chain:

[12] Cf. English *misplace.* To the French series correspond English *mistake, misspell, misrepresent,* etc. and *place, replace, displace,* etc. [Tr.]

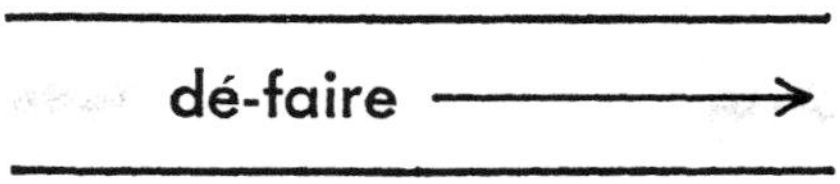

But simultaneously and on another axis there exists in the subconscious one or more associative series comprising units that have an element in common with the syntagm:

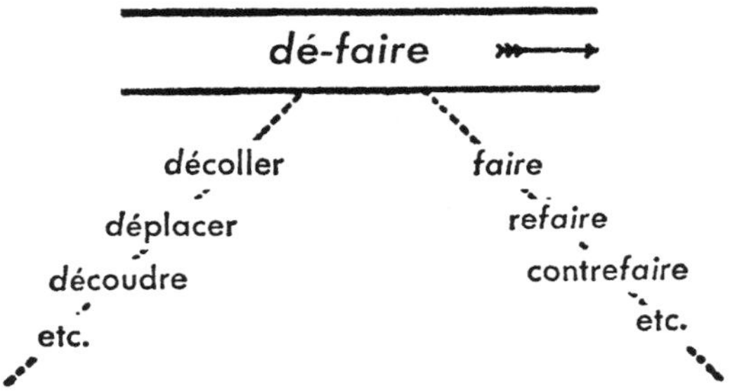

In the same way, if Latin *quadruplex* is a syntagm, this is because it too is supported by a double associative series:

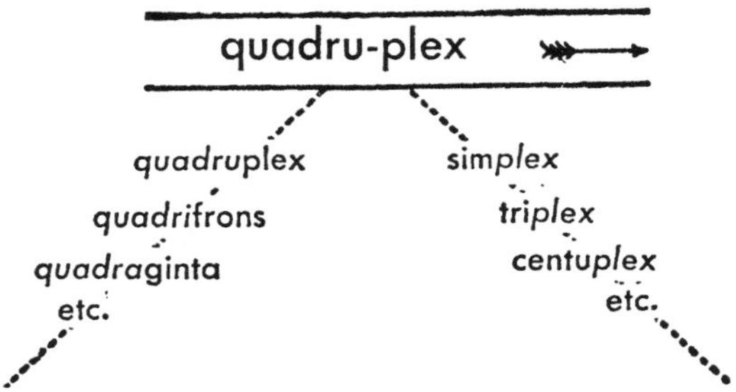

To the extent that the other forms float around *défaire* or *quadruplex*, these words can be decomposed into subunits. This is just another way of saying that they are syntagms. *Défaire* could not be analyzed, for instance, if the other forms containing *dé–* or *faire* disappeared from the language. It would be but a simple unit, and its two parts could not be placed in opposition.

Now the functioning of the dual system in discourse is clear.

Our memory holds in reserve all the more or less complex types of syntagms, regardless of their class or length, and we bring in the associative groups to fix our choice when the time for using them arrives. When a Frenchman says *marchons!* '(let's) walk!' he thinks unconsciously of diverse groups of associations that converge on the syntagm *marchons!* The syntagm figures in the series *marche!* '(thou) walk!' *marchez!* '(you) walk!' and the opposition between *marchons!* and the other forms determines his choice; in addition, *marchons!* calls up the series *montons!* '(let's) go up!' *mangeons* '(let's) eat!' etc. and is selected from the series by the same process. In each series the speaker knows what he must vary in order to produce the differentiation that fits the desired unit. If he changes the idea to be expressed, he will need other oppositions to bring out another value; for instance, he may say *marchez!* or perhaps *montons!*

It is not enough to say, looking at the matter positively, that the speaker chooses *marchons!* because it signifies what he wishes to express. In reality the idea evokes not a form but a whole latent system that makes possible the oppositions necessary for the formation of the sign. By itself the sign would have no signification. If there were no forms like *marche! marchez!* against *marchons!*, certain oppositions would disappear, and the value of *marchons!* would be changed *ipso facto*.

This principle applies to even the most complex types of syntagms and sentences. To frame the question que *vous* dit-il? 'what does he say to *you?*' the speaker varies one element of a latent syntactical pattern, e.g. que *te* dit-il? 'what does he say to *thee?*' que *nous* dit-il? 'what does he say to *us?*' etc., until his choice is fixed on the pronoun *vous*. In this process, which consists of eliminating mentally everything that does not help to bring out the desired differentiation at the desired point, associative groupings and syntagmatic patterns both play a role.

Conversely, the process of fixation and choice governs the smallest units and even phonological elements wherever they are endowed with a value. I am thinking not only of cases like French *pətit* 'small' (feminine form, written *petite*) in opposition to *pəti* (masculine form, written *petit*) or Latin *dominī* against *dominō*, where the difference happens to be based on a simple phoneme, but also of the more subtle and characteristic fact that a phoneme by itself plays a role in the system of a language-state. For example, if *m*, *p*, *t*, etc. can never occur at the end of a word in Greek, this means that their presence or absence in a definite position counts in the structure of the word and in the structure of the sentence. In every such case the isolated sound, like every other unit, is chosen after a dual mental opposition. In the imaginary grouping *anma*, for instance, the sound *m* stands in syntagmatic opposition to its environing sounds and in associative opposition to all other sounds that may come to mind:

a n m a
v
d

3. *Absolute and Relative Arbitrariness*

The mechanism of language can be presented from another especially important angle.

The fundamental principle of the arbitrariness of the sign does not prevent our singling out in each language what is radically arbitrary, i.e. unmotivated, and what is only relatively arbitrary. Some signs are absolutely arbitrary; in others we note, not its complete absence, but the presence of degrees of arbitrariness: *the sign may be relatively motivated.*

For instance, both *vingt* 'twenty' and *dix-neuf* 'nineteen' are unmotivated in French, but not in the same degree, for *dix-neuf* suggests its own terms and other terms associated with it (e.g. *dix* 'ten,' *neuf* 'nine,' *vingt-neuf* 'twenty-nine,' *dix-huit* 'eighteen,' *soixante-dix* 'seventy,' etc.). Taken separately, *dix* and *neuf* are in the same class as *vingt*, but *dix-neuf* is an example of relative motivation. The same is true of *poirier* 'pear-tree,' which recalls the simple word *poire* 'pear' and, through its suffix, *cerisier* 'cherry-tree,' *pommier* 'apple-tree,' etc.[13] For *frêne* 'ash,' *chêne* 'oak,' etc. there is nothing comparable. Again, compare *berger* 'shepherd,' which is completely unmotivated, and *vacher* 'cowherd,' which is relatively motivated.[14] In the same way, the pairs *geôle* 'jail' and

[13] Cf. English *flaxen*, which suggests *flax*, *silken*, *woolen*, etc. [Tr.]
[14] Cf. English *clerk*, unmotivated, against *farmer*, relatively motivated. [Tr.]

cachot 'dungeon,' *hache* 'ax' and *couperet* 'chopper,' *concierge* 'porter' and *portier* 'doorman,' *jadis* 'of old' and *autrefois* 'formerly,' *souvent* 'often' and *frequemment* 'frequently,' *aveugle* 'blind' and *boiteux* 'limping,' *sourd* 'deaf' and *bossu* 'hunchbacked,' *second* 'second' and *deuxième* 'second (of a series),' German *Laub* and French *feuillage* 'foliage,' and French *métier* 'handicraft' and German *Handwerk*.[15] The English plural *ships* suggests through its formation the whole series *flags, birds, books*, etc., while *men* and *sheep* suggest nothing. In Greek *dṓsō* 'I shall give' the notion of futurity is expressed by a sign that calls up the association *lū́so, stesō, túpsō*, etc.; *eîmi* 'I shall go,' on the other hand, is completely isolated.

This is not the place to search for the forces that condition motivation in each instance; but motivation varies, being always proportional to the ease of syntagmatic analysis and the obviousness of the meaning of the subunits present. Indeed, while some formative elements like *-ier* in *poir-ier* against *ceris-ier, pomm-ier*, etc. are obvious, others are vague or meaningless. For instance, does the suffix *-ot* really correspond to a meaningful element in French *cachot* 'dungeon'? On comparing words like *coutelas* 'cutlas,' *fatras* 'pile,' *platras* 'rubbish,' *canevas* 'canvas,' etc., one has no more than the vague feeling that *-as* is a formative element characteristic of substantives. At any rate, even in the most favorable cases motivation is never absolute. Not only are the elements of a motivated sign themselves unmotivated (cf. *dix* and *neuf* in *dix-neuf*), but the value of the whole term is never equal to the sum of the value of the parts. *Teach* + *er* is not equal to *teach* × *er* (see p. 128).

Motivation is explained by the principles stated in Section 2. The notion of relative motivation implies: (1) analysis of a given term, hence a syntagmatic relation; and (2) the summoning of one or more other terms, hence an associative relation. It is the mechanism through which any term whatever lends itself to the expression of an idea, and is no more than that. Up to this point units have appeared as values, i.e. as elements of a system, and we

[15] For examples not similar in English and French, compare completely unmotivated *jail, slave, then* and relatively motivated *reformatory, servant, heretofore*. [Tr.]

have given special consideration to their opposition; now we recognize the solidarities that bind them; they are associative and syntagmatic, and they are what limits arbitrariness. *Dix-neuf* is supported associatively by *dix-huit, soixante-dix*, etc. and syntagmatically by its elements *dix* and *neuf* (see p. 128). This dual relation gives it a part of its value.

Everything that relates to language as a system must, I am convinced, be approached from this viewpoint, which has scarcely received the attention of linguists: the limiting of arbitrariness. This is the best possible basis for approaching the study of language as a system. In fact, the whole system of language is based on the irrational principle of the arbitrariness of the sign, which would lead to the worst sort of complication if applied without restriction. But the mind contrives to introduce a principle of order and regularity into certain parts of the mass of signs, and this is the role of relative motivation. If the mechanism of language were entirely rational, it could be studied independently. Since the mechanism of language is but a partial correction of a system that is by nature chaotic, however, we adopt the viewpoint imposed by the very nature of language and study it as it limits arbitrariness.

There is no language in which nothing is motivated, and our definition makes it impossible to conceive of a language in which everything is motivated. Between the two extremes—a minimum of organization and a minimum of arbitrariness—we find all possible varieties. Diverse languages always include elements of both types—radically arbitrary and relatively motivated—but in proportions that vary greatly, and this is an important characteristic that may help in classifying them.

In a certain sense—one which must not be pushed too far but which brings out a particular form that the opposition may take—we might say that languages in which there is least motivation are more *lexicological*, and those in which it is greatest are more *grammatical*. Not because "lexical" and "arbitrary" on the one hand and "grammar" and "relative motivation" on the other, are always synonymous, but because they have a common principle. The two extremes are like two poles between which the whole system moves, two opposing currents which share the movement of language: the tendency to use the lexicological instrument (the unmotivated sign) and the preference given to the grammatical instrument (structural rules).

We would see, for example, that motivation plays a much larger role in German than in English. But the ultra-lexicological type is Chinese while Proto-Indo-European and Sanskrit are specimens of the ultra-grammatical type. Within a given language, all evolutionary movement may be characterized by continual passage from motivation to arbitrariness and from arbitrariness to motivation; this see-saw motion often results in a perceptible change in the proportions of the two classes of signs. Thus with respect to Latin, French is characterized, among other things, by a huge increase in arbitrariness. Latin *inimīcus* recalls *in–* and *amicus* and is motivated by them; against this, *ennemi* 'enemy' is motivated by nothing—it has reverted to absolute arbitrariness, which is really the prime characteristic of the linguistic sign. We would notice this shift in hundreds of instances: cf. *constāre* (*stāre*): *coûter* 'cost,' *fabrica* (*faber*): *forge* 'forge,' *magister* (*magis*): *maître* 'master,' *berbicarius* (*berbix*): *berger* 'shepherd,' etc. French owes its characteristic appearance to this fact.

Chapter VII

GRAMMAR AND ITS SUBDIVISIONS

1. *Definitions: Traditional Divisions*

Static linguistics or the description of a language-state is *grammar* in the very precise, and moreover usual, sense that the word has in the expressions "grammar of the Stock Exchange," etc., where it is a question of a complex and systematic object governing the interplay of coexisting values.

Grammar studies language as a system of means of expression. Grammatical means synchronic and significant, and since no system straddles several periods, there is no such thing as "historical grammar"; the discipline so labeled is really only diachronic linguistics.

My definition disagrees with the narrower one usually given. *Morphology* and *syntax* together are what is generally called grammar while lexicology, or the science of words, is excluded.

But first, do these divisions fit the facts? Do they agree with the principles that have just been posited?

Morphology deals with different classes of words (verbs, nouns, adjectives, pronouns, etc.) and with different inflectional forms (conjugation, declension, etc.). To separate this study from syntax, it is alleged that syntax has as its object the functions attached to linguistic units while morphology considers only their form. For instance, morphology says simply that the genitive of Greek *phúlax* 'guardian' is *phúlakos*, and syntax explains the use of the two forms.

But the distinction is illusory. The series of forms of the substantive *phúlax* becomes an inflectional paradigm only through comparison of the functions attached to the different forms; reciprocally, the functions are morphological only if each function corresponds to a definite phonic sign. A declension is neither a list of forms nor a series of logical abstractions but a combination of the two (see pp. 102 ff.). Forms and functions are interdependent and it is difficult, if not impossible, to separate them. Linguistically, morphology has no real, autonomous object. It cannot form a discipline distinct from syntax.

Second, is it logical for us to exclude lexicology from grammar? As they are registered in the dictionary, words do not seem at first glance to lend themselves to grammatical study, which is generally restricted to the relations between units. But we notice at once that innumerable relations may be expressed as efficiently by words as by grammar. For instance, Latin *fīō* and *faciō* stand in opposition to each other in the same way as *dīcor* and *dicō*, two grammatical forms of the same word. The distinction between the perfective and imperfective is expressed grammatically in Russian *sprosít′: sprášivat′* 'ask' and lexicologically in *skazát′: govorít′* 'say.' Prepositions are usually assigned to grammar, but the prepositional locution *en considération de* 'in consideration of' is basically lexicological since the word *considération* retains its own meaning in the French phrase. If we compare Greek *peíthō: peíthomai* with French *je persuade* 'I persuade': *j'obéis* 'I obey,' we see that the opposition is expressed grammatically in the first instance and lexicologically in the second. A large number of relations that are expressed in certain languages by cases or prepositions are rendered in others by compounds, more like words proper (French *royaume des cieux* 'kingdom of heaven' and German *Himmelreich*), or by derivatives (French *moulin à vent* 'windmill' and Polish *wiatr-ak*) or finally, by simple words (French *bois de chauffage* 'firewood' and Russian *drová*, French *bois de construction* 'timber' and Russian *lês*). The interchange of simple words and phrases within the same language also occurs very frequently (cf. French *considérer* 'consider' and *prendre en considération* 'take into consideration,' *se venger de* 'avenge' and *tirer vengeance de* 'take revenge on').

Functionally, therefore, the lexical and the syntactical may blend. There is basically no distinction between any word that is not a simple, irreducible unit and a phrase, which is a syntactical fact. The arrangement of the subunits of the word obeys the same fundamental principles as the arrangement of groups of words in phrases.

In short, although the traditional divisions of grammar may be useful in practice, they do not correspond to natural distinctions. To build a grammar, we must look for a different and a higher principle.

2. *Rational Divisions*

Morphology, syntax, and lexicology interpenetrate because every synchronic fact is identical. No line of demarcation can be drawn in advance. Only the distinction established above between syntagmatic and associative relations can provide a classification that is not imposed from the outside. No other base will serve for the grammatical system.

We should first gather together all that makes up a language-state and fit this into a theory of syntagms and a theory of associations. Immediately certain parts of traditional grammar would seem to fall effortlessly into one category or the other. Inflection is evidently a typical kind of association of forms in the mind of speakers; and syntax (i.e. the theory of word groupings, according to the most common definition) goes back to the theory of syntagms, for the groupings always suppose at least two units distributed in space. Not every syntagmatic fact is classed as syntactical, but every syntactical fact belongs to the syntagmatic class.

To prove the necessity of the dual approach, almost any point of grammar will do. The notion of word, for instance, poses two distinct problems, depending on whether the word is studied from the associative or the syntagmatic viewpoint. In French, the adjective *grand* 'big' offers a duality of form from the syntagmatic viewpoint (*grã garçon* written *grand garçon* 'big boy' and *grãt ãfã*, written *grand enfant* 'big baby') and another duality from the associative viewpoint (masculine *grã*, written *grand*, and feminine *grãd*, written *grande*).

Each fact should in this way be fitted into its syntagmatic or associative class, and the whole subject matter of grammar should be arranged along its two natural co-ordinates; no other division will show what must be changed in the usual framework of synchronic linguistics. I cannot undertake that task here, for my aim is limited to stating only the most general principles.

Chapter VIII

ROLE OF ABSTRACT ENTITIES IN GRAMMAR

One important subject, not yet touched upon, points up this very necessity of examining every grammatical question from the two viewpoints specified in Chapter VII: abstract entities in grammar. Let us consider them first associatively.

To associate two forms is not only to feel that they have something in common but also to single out the nature of the relations that govern associations. For instance, speakers are aware that the relation between *enseigner* and *enseignement* or *juger* and *jugement* is not the same as the relation between *enseignement* and *jugement* 'judgment' (see p. 125). This is how the system of associations is tied to the system of grammar. We can say that the sum of the conscious and methodical classifications made by the grammarian who studies a language-state without bringing in history must coincide with the associations, conscious or not, that are set up in speaking. These associations fix word-families, inflectional paradigms, and formative elements (radicals, suffixes, inflectional endings, etc.) in our minds (see pp. 185 ff.).

But does association single out only material elements? No, of course not. We have already seen that it brings together words that are related only through meaning (cf. *enseignement, apprentissage, éducation*, etc.). The same must apply in grammar. Take the three Latin genitive forms *domin-ī, rēg-is, ros-ārum*. The sounds of the three endings offer no basis for association, yet the endings are connected by the feeling that they have a common value which prescribes an identical function. This suffices to create the association in the absence of any material support, and the notion of the genitive in this way takes its place in the language. Through a similar procedure, the inflectional endings *–us, –ī, –ō*, etc. (in *dominus, dominī, dominō*, etc.) are linked together in the mind and are the basis for the more general notions of case and case endings. Associations of the same class, but larger still, combine all substantives, adjectives, etc. and fix the notion of parts of speech.

All these things exist in language, but as *abstract entities;* their study is difficult because we never know exactly whether or not the awareness of speakers goes as far as the analyses of the grammarian. But the important thing is that *abstract entities are always based, in the last analysis, on concrete entities.* No grammatical abstraction is possible without a series of material elements as a basis, and in the end we must always come back to these elements.

Now we turn to the syntagmatic viewpoint. The value of a cluster is often linked to the order of its elements. In analyzing a syntagm, the speaker does not restrict himself to singling out its parts; he observes a certain order of succession among them. The meaning of English *pain-ful* or Latin *signi-fer* depends on the respective positions of their subunits: we cannot say *ful-pain* or *fer-signum.* A value may have no relations with a concrete element (like *–ful* or *–fer*) and result solely from the arrangement of the terms; for instance, the different significations of the two clusters in French *je dois* 'I must' and *dois-je?* 'must I?' are due only to word order. One language sometimes expresses through word order an idea that another would convey through one or more concrete terms. In the syntagmatic pattern *gooseberry wine, gold watch,* etc., English expresses through the mere order of the terms relations that are denoted in Modern French by prepositions (cf. *vin de groseilles, montre en or,* etc.). Modern French in turn expresses the notion of direct complement solely through putting the substantive after the transitive verb (cf. *je cueille une fleur* 'I pick a flower'), while Latin and some other languages use the accusative, which is characterized by special case endings, etc.

Word order is unquestionably an abstract entity, but it owes its existence solely to the concrete units that contain it and that flow in a single dimension. To think that there is an incorporeal syntax outside material units distributed in space would be a mistake. In English, *the man I have seen* apparently uses a zero-sign to stand for a syntactical fact which French expresses by *que* 'that' (l'homme *que* j'ai vu). But the comparing of the English with the French syntactical fact is precisely what produces the illusion that nothingness can express something. The material units alone actually create the value by being arranged in a certain way. We cannot study a syntactical value outside a number of concrete terms, and the very fact that we understand a linguistic complex (e.g. the English words cited above) shows that word-order alone expresses the thought.

A material unit exists only through its meaning and function. This principle is especially important in understanding smaller units, for one is tempted to think that they exist by virtue of their sheer material quality—that *love,* for example, owes its existence solely to its sounds. Conversely—as we have just seen—a meaning and function exist only through the support of some material form. This principle was formulated with respect to larger syntagms or syntactical patterns, but only because one is inclined to see these as immaterial abstractions hovering over the terms of the sentence. By complementing each other, the two principles bear out my statements relative to the delimiting of units (see p. 103).

PART THREE

Diachronic Linguistics

Chapter I

GENERALITIES

What diachronic linguistics studies is not relations between coexisting terms of a language-state but relations between successive terms that are substituted for each other in time.

There is really no such thing as absolute immobility (see pp. 75 ff.). Every part of language is subjected to change. To each period there corresponds some appreciable evolution. Evolution may vary in rapidity and intensity, but this does not invalidate the principle. The stream of language flows without interruption; whether its course is calm or torrential is of secondary importance.

That we often fail to see this uninterrupted evolution is due to the attention paid to the literary language which, as will appear later (pp. 195 ff.) is superimposed on the vulgar language (i.e. the natural language) and is subjected to other forces. The literary language, once it has been formed, generally remains fairly stable and tends to keep its identity; its dependence on writing gives it special guarantees of preservation; therefore it cannot show us how much natural languages change when freed from any literary regimentation.

Phonetics—and all of phonetics—is the prime object of diachronic linguistics. In fact, the evolution of sounds is incompatible with the notion of states; to compare phonemes or groups of phonemes with what they were previously means to set up a diachrony. One period may be closely related to the next, but when the two merge, phonetics ceases to play a part. Nothing is left but the description of the sounds of a language-state, and that is the task of phonology.

The diachronic character of phonetics fits in very well with the principle that anything which is phonetic is neither significant nor grammatical in the broad sense of the word phonetic (see p. 18). In studying the history of the sounds of a word, we may ignore meaning and, by considering only the material envelope of a word, cut out phonic slices without asking whether they have a signification. For instance, we may try to trace the meaningless group *-ewo-* in Attic Greek. If the evolution of language meant nothing more than the evolution of its sounds, the opposition between the objects that belong to each of the two parts of linguistics would immediately be crystal clear. It would be obvious that diachronic is equivalent to nongrammatical and synchronic to grammatical.

But sounds are not the only things that change with time. Words change their signification. Grammatical classes evolve. Some of them disappear along with the forms that were used to express them (e.g. the dual number in Latin). And if all associative and syntagmatic facts in a synchronic state have their history, how is the absolute distinction between diachrony and synchrony to be maintained? This becomes very difficult when we leave the domain of phonetics.

It is worth noting, however, that many changes often considered grammatical are really only phonetic. Such "grammatical" creations as German *Hand: Hände*, which replaced *hant: hanti* (see p. 83), yield completely to a phonetic explanation. Another phonetic fact is at the base of compounds of the type *Springbrunnen*, *Reitschule*, etc. In Old High German the first element was not verbal but substantival. *Beta-hūs* meant 'house of prayer'; but after a phonetic change brought about the fall of the final vowel (*beta* → *bet-*, etc.), a semantic contact was established with the verb (*beten*, etc.), and *Bethaus* then signified 'house for praying.'

Something similar occurred in compounds formed with the word *līch* 'outward appearance' in Old High German (cf. *mannolīch* 'having the appearance of a man,' *redolīch* 'having the appearance of reason,' etc.). Today, in a number of adjectives (cf. *verzeihlich*, *glaublich*, etc.), *-lich* is comparable to the suffix in *pardon-able*, *believ-able*, etc., and at the same time the interpretation of the first element, through loss of the final vowel (e.g. *redo* → *red-*), is likened to a verbal root (*red-* from *reden*).

In *glaublich*, *glaub-* is accordingly linked to *glauben* rather than to *Glaube*, and in spite of the difference in the radical, *sichtlich* is associated with *sehen* and not *Sicht*.

In all the preceding instances and in many other similar ones, the distinction between the two classes remains clear-cut. The linguist must keep this distinction in mind or risk thinking that he is studying historical grammar when he is actually moving successively from diachrony, where he studies phonetic changes, to synchrony, where he examines the consequences that issue from these changes.

But this restriction does not remove all difficulties. The evolution of any grammatical fact, regardless of its syntagmatic or grammatical character, is not like the evolution of a sound. It is not simple but decomposes into a great number of particular facts of which only a part are phonetic. In the genesis of a syntagmatic pattern like the French future *prendre ai* '(I) have to take,' which became *prendrai* '(I) shall take,' there are at least two distinct facts, one psychological (the synthesis of the two elements of the concept) and the other phonetic and dependent on the first (the reduction of the two accents of the combination to one: *préndre ai* → *prendraí*).

The inflection of the strong Germanic verb (like Modern German *geben, gab, gegeben,* etc., cf. Greek *leípo, élipon, léloipa,* etc.) is based chiefly on the ablaut of radical vowels. These alternations (see p. 157), which began as a relatively simple system, doubtless result from a mere phonetic fact. But for the oppositions to acquire such functional importance, the original inflectional system had to be simplified through a series of diverse processes: the disappearance of multiple varieties of the present and of the shades of meaning attached to them; the disappearance of the imperfect, the future, and the aorist; the elimination of reduplication of the perfect, etc. These nonphonetic changes reduced verbal inflection to a restricted group of forms in which radical alternations became very important in signaling meaning. Thus the opposition *e: a* is more significant in *geben: gab* than is the opposition *e: o* in Greek *leípo: léloipa,* for the German perfect lacks reduplication and the Greek has it.

Phonetic change, though it does generally affect evolution in some way, cannot explain it entirely. Once the phonetic force is eliminated, we find a residue that seems to justify the idea of a "history of grammar," and therein lies the real difficulty. This indispensable distinction between diachrony and synchrony would call for detailed explanations that are outside the scope of this course.[1]

In the following chapters we shall study, successively, phonetic changes, alternation, and analogical facts, and conclude with some remarks about folk etymology and agglutination.

Chapter II

PHONETIC CHANGES

1. *Their Absolute Regularity*

We saw earlier (p. 93) that a phonetic change affects not words but sounds. What is transformed is a phoneme. This event, though isolated like all other diachronic events, results in the identical alteration of all words containing the same phoneme. It is in this sense that phonetic changes are absolutely regular.

In German, every ī became *ei*, then *ai: wīn, trīben, līhen, zīt* became *Wein, treiben, leihen, Zeit;* every ū became *au: hūs, zūn, rūch* became *Haus, Zaun, Rauch;* in the same way ü changed to *eu: hüser* became *Häuser*, etc. On the contrary, the diphthong *ie* became ī, which is still written *ie:* cf. *biegen, lieb, Tier*. In addition, every *uo* became *ū: muot* became *Mut*, etc. Every *z* became *s* (writ-

[1] To this didactic external reason might be added another: in his lectures F. de Saussure never approached linguistics of speaking (see pp. 17 ff.). We recall that a new speech form always owes its origin to a series of individual facts (see p. 98). We might say that the author refused to classify these as grammatical in the sense that an isolated act is necessarily foreign to language and to its system, which depends only on the set of collective patterns. As long as these facts remain in the province of speaking, they are only very special, occasional uses of the established system. It is only when an innovation becomes engraved in the memory through frequent repetition and enters the system that it effects a shift in the equilibrium of values and that language changes, spontaneously and *ipso facto*. We might apply to grammatical evolution what was said on pages 18 and 84 about phonetic evolution: its end result is outside the system, for the system is never observed in its evolution; it differs from one moment to the next. This attempted explanation is just a simple suggestion on our part. [Ed.]

ten *ss*, see p. 36): *wazer* → *Wasser*, *fliezen* → *fliessen*, etc. Every intervocalic *h* disappeared: *līhen*, *sehen* → *leien*, *seen* (written *leihen*, *sehen*). Every *w* was changed to labiodental *v* (written *w*): *wazer* → *waser* (*Wasser*).

In French, every palatalized *l* became *y*: *piller* 'pillar' and *bouillir* 'boil' are pronounced *piyẹ*, *buyir*, etc.

In Latin, what was once intervocalic *s* appears as *r* in another period: **genesis*, **asēna* → *generis*, *arēna*, etc.

Any phonetic change at all, when seen in its true light, would confirm the perfect regularity of these transformations.

2. *Conditioned Phonetic Changes*

The preceding examples have already shown that phonetic phenomena, far from always being absolute, are more often linked to fixed conditions. Putting it another way, what is transformed is not the phonological species but the phoneme as it occurs under certain conditions—its environment, accentuation, etc. For instance, *s* became *r* in Latin only between vowels and in certain other positions; elsewhere it remains (cf. *est*, *senex*, *equos*).

Absolute changes are extremely rare. That changes often appear to be absolute is due to the obscure or extremely general nature of the conditions. In German, for example, *ī* became *ei*, *ai*, but only in a tonic syllable. Proto-Indo-European k_1 became *h* in Germanic (cf. Proto-Indo-European *k_1*olsom*, Latin *collum*, German *Hals*), but the change did not occur after *s* (cf. Greek *skótos* and Gothic *skadus* 'shadow').

Besides, the classing of changes as absolute or conditioned is based on a superficial view of things. It is more logical, in line with the growing trend, to speak of *spontaneous* and *combinatory* phonetic phenomena. Changes are spontaneous when their cause is internal and combinatory when they result from the presence of one or more other phonemes. The passing of Proto-Indo-European *o* to Germanic *a* (cf. Gothic *skadus*, German *Hals*, etc.) is thus a spontaneous fact. Germanic consonantal mutations or *Lautverschiebungen* typify spontaneous change: Proto-Indo-European k_1 became *h* in Proto-Germanic (cf. Latin *collum* and Gothic *hals*) and Proto-Germanic *t*, which is preserved in English, became *z* (pronounced *ts*) in High German (cf. Gothic *taihun*, English *ten*,

German *zehn*). Against this, the passing of Latin *ct, pt* to Italian *tt* (cf. *factum* → *fatto, captīvum* → *cattivo*) is a combinatory fact, for the first element was assimilated to the second. The German umlaut is also due to an external cause, the presence of *i* in the following syllable: while *gast* did not change, *gasti* became *gesti, Gäste*.

The result is not an issue in either case, and whether or not there is a change is of no importance. For instance, on comparing Gothic *fisks* with Latin *piscis* and Gothic *skadus* with Greek *skótos*, we observe in the first pair the persistence of *i* and in the second the passing of *o* to *a*. The first phoneme remained while the second one changed, but what matters is that each acted independently.

A combinatory phonetic fact is always conditioned, but a spontaneous fact is not necessarily absolute, for it may be conditioned negatively by the absence of certain forces of change. In this way Proto-Indo-European k_2 spontaneously became *qu* in Latin (cf. *quattuor, inquilīna*, etc.) but not, for instance, when followed by *o* or *u* (cf. *cottīdie, colō secundus*, etc.). In the same way the persistence of Proto-Indo-European *i* in Gothic *fisks*, etc. is linked to a condition—the *i* could not be followed by *r* or *h*, for then it became *e*, written *ai* (cf. *wair* → Latin *vir* and *maihstus* → German *Mist*).

3. *Points on Method*

In devising formulas to express phonetic changes we must consider the preceding distinctions or risk presenting the facts incorrectly.

Here are some examples of inaccuracies.

According to the old formulation of Verner's law, "in Germanic every noninitial þ changed to ð if the accent came after it": cf. on the one hand **faþer* → **faðer* (German *Vater*), **liþumé* → **liðumé* (German *litten*), and on the other **þris* (German *drei*), **broþer* (German *Bruder*), **liþo* (German *leide*), where þ remains. This formula gives the active role to accent and introduces a restrictive clause for initial þ. What actually happened is quite different. In Germanic, as in Latin, þ tended to sonorize spontaneously within a word; only the placing of the accent on the preceding vowel could prevent it. Everything is therefore reversed. The fact is spontaneous, not combinatory, and the accent is an obstacle rather than the precipitating cause. We should say: "Every internal þ became ð unless the change was opposed by the placing of the accent on the preceding vowel."

In order to separate what is spontaneous from what is combinatory, we must analyze the stages of the transformation and not mistake the mediate result for the immediate one. It is wrong to explain rhotacization, for instance (cf. Latin **genesis* → *generis*), by saying that *s* became *r* between two vowels, for *s*, having no laryngeal sound, could never become *r* directly. There are really two acts. First, *s* became *z* through a combinatory change. Second, this sound was replaced by closely related *r* since *z* had not been retained in the sound system of Latin. The second change was spontaneous. It is therefore a serious mistake to consider the two dissimilar facts as a single phenomenon. The fault is on the one hand in mistaking the mediate result for the immediate one (*s* → *r* instead of *z* → *r*) and on the other, in regarding the total phenomenon as combinatory when this is true of only its first part. This is the same as saying that *e* became *a* before a nasal in French. The fact is that there were in succession a combinatory change—nasalization of *e* by *n* (cf. Latin *ventum* → French *vẽnt*, Latin *fēmina* → French *femə, fẽmə*)—and a spontaneous change of *ẽ* to *ã* (cf. *vãnt, fãmə*, now *vã, fãm*). To raise the objection that the change could occur only before a nasal consonant would be pointless. The question is not why *e* was nasalized but only whether the transformation of *ẽ* into *ã* is spontaneous or combinatory.

The most serious mistake in method that I can recall at this point—although it is not related to the principles stated above—is that of formulating a phonetic law in the present tense, as if the facts embraced by it existed once and for all instead of being born and dying within a span of time. The result is chaos, for in this way any chronological succession of events is lost sight of. I have already emphasized this point (p. 97) in analyzing the successive phenomena that explain the duality of *tríkhos: thriksí*. Whoever says "*s* became *r* in Latin" gives the impression that rhotacization is inherent in the nature of language and finds it difficult to account for exceptions like *causa, rīsus*, etc. Only the formula "intervocalic *s* became *r* in Latin" justifies our believing that *causa, rīsus*, etc.

had no *s* at the moment when *s* became *r* and were sheltered from change. The fact is that speakers still said *caussa, rīssus,* etc. For a similar reason we must say "*ā* became *ē* in the Ionian dialect (cf. *mấter mếter*, etc.), for otherwise we would not know what to make of forms like *pâsa, phāsi,* etc. (which were still *pansa, phansi,* etc. during the period of the change).

4. *Causes of Phonetic Changes*

The search for the causes of phonetic changes is one of the most difficult problems of linguistics. Many explanations have been proposed, but none of them thoroughly illuminates the problem.

1) One supposition is that racial predispositions trace beforehand the direction of phonetic changes. This raises a question of comparative anthropology: Does the phonational apparatus vary from one race to the next? No, scarcely more than from one individual to the next. A newborn Negro transplanted to France speaks French as well as a native Frenchman. Furthermore, expressions like "the Italian vocal apparatus" or "the mouth of Germanic speakers does not allow that" imply that a mere historical fact is a permanent characteristic. This is similar to the mistake of stating a phonetic law in the present tense. To pretend that the Ionian vocal apparatus finds long *ā* difficult and changes it to *ē* is just as erroneous as to say that *ā* "becomes" *ē* in Ionian.

The Ionian vocal apparatus had no aversion to *ā*, for this sound was used in certain instances. This is obviously an example, not of racial incapacity, but of a change in articulatory habits. In the same way Latin, which had not retained intervocalic *s* (**genesis* → *generis*), reintroduced it a short time later (cf. **rīssus* → *rīsus*). These changes do not indicate a permanent disposition of the Latin voice.

There is doubtless a general direction that phonetic phenomena follow during a particular period and within a specific nation. The monophthongizations of diphthongs in Modern French are manifestations of one and the same tendency, but we would find similar general currents in political history and never question their being merely historical without any direct influence of race.

2) Phonetic changes have often been considered adaptions to conditions of soil and climate. Consonants abound in some

northern languages while more vowels occur in certain southern languages, giving them their harmonious sound. Climate and living conditions may well influence language, but the problem becomes complicated as soon as we enter into detail: beside the Scandinavian idioms with their many consonants are those of the Lapps and Finns, which are even more vocalic than Italian. We also notice that the accumulation of consonants in present-day German is in many instances a quite recent fact, due to the fall of posttonic vowels; that certain dialects of southern France are less opposed to consonantal clusters than the French of the north; that Serbian has as many consonantal clusters as Great Russian, etc.

3) The cause of phonetic changes has also been ascribed to the law of least effort by which two articulations are replaced by one or a difficult articulation by an easier one. This idea, regardless of what is said about it, is worth examining. It may clarify the cause of phonetic changes or at least indicate the direction that the search for it must take.

The law of least effort seems to explain a certain number of cases: the passing of an occlusive to a spirant (Latin *habēre* → French *avoir* 'have'); the fall of great clusters of final syllables in many languages; phenomena relating to assimilation (e.g. *ly* → *ll* as in **alyos* → Greek *állos*, *tn* → *nn* as in **atnos* → Latin *annus*); the monophthongization of diphthongs, which is only another type of assimilation (e.g. *ai* → *e* as in French *maizõn* → *mezõ*, written *maison* 'house'), etc.

But we might mention just as many instances where exactly the opposite occurs. Against monophthongization, for example, we can set the change of German *ī*, *ū*, *ü*, to *ei*, *au*, *eu*. If the shortening of Slavic *ā*, *ē* to *ă*, *ĕ* is due to least effort, then the reverse phenomenon offered by German (*fater* → *Vāter*, *geben* → *gēben*) must be due to greatest effort. If voicing is easier than nonvoicing (cf. *opera* → Provençal *obra*), the reverse must necessitate greater effort, and yet Spanish passed from *z* to χ (cf. *hiχo*, written *hijo*) and Germanic changed *b*, *d*, *g* to *p*, *t*, *k*. If loss of aspiration (cf. Proto-Indo-European **bherō* → Germanic *beran*) is considered a lessening of effort, what is to be said of German, which inserts aspiration where it did not exist (*Tanne*, *Pute*, etc., pronounced *Thanne*, *Phute*)?

The foregoing remarks do not pretend to refute the proposed

solution. In fact, we can scarcely determine what is easiest or most difficult for each language to pronounce. Shortening means less effort in the sense of duration, but it is equally true that long sounds allow careless pronunciations while short sounds require more care. Given different predispositions, we can therefore present two opposing facts from the same viewpoint. Thus where *k* became *tš* (cf. Latin *cēdere* → Italian *cedere*), there is apparently an increase in effort if we consider only the end terms of the change, but the impression would probably differ if we reconstructed the chain: *k* became palatalized *k'* through assimilation to the following vowel; then *k'* passed to *ky;* the pronunciation did not become more difficult; two tangled elements in *k'* were clearly differentiated; then from *ky* speakers passed successively to *ty*, *tχ*, *tš*, everywhere with less effort.

The law of least effort would require extensive study. It would be necessary to consider simultaneously the physiological viewpoint (the question of articulation) and the psychological viewpoint (the question of attention).

4) An explanation that has been favored for several years attributes changes in pronunciation to our phonetic education during childhood. After much groping and many trials and corrections, the child succeeds in pronouncing what he hears around him; here would be the starting point of all changes; certain uncorrected inaccuracies would win out in the individual and become fixed in the generation that is growing up. Children often pronounce *t* for *k*, and our languages offer no corresponding phonetic change in their history. But this is not true of other deformations. In Paris, for instance, many children pronounce *fl'eur* (*fleur* 'flower') and *bl'anc* (*blanc* 'white') with palatalized *l;* now it was through a similar process that *florem* became *fl'ore*, then *fiore*, in Italian.

The preceding observations deserve careful attention but leave the problem undented. Indeed, what prompts a generation to retain certain mistakes to the exclusion of others that are just as natural is not clear. From all appearances the choice of faulty pronunciations is completely arbitrary, and there is no obvious reason for it. Besides, why did the phenomenon break through at one time rather than another?

The same question applies to all the preceding causes of phonetic changes if they are accepted as real. Climatic influence, racial predisposition, and the tendency toward least effort are all permanent or lasting. Why do they act sporadically, sometimes on one point of the phonological system and sometimes on another? A historical event must have a determining cause, yet we are not told what chances in each instance to unleash a change whose general cause has existed for a long time. This is the most difficult point to explain.

5) Phonetic changes are sometimes linked to the general state of the nation at a particular moment. Languages go through some periods that are more turbulent than others. There have been attempts to relate phonetic changes to turbulent periods in a nation's history and in this way to discover a link between political instability and linguistic instability; this done, some think that they can apply conclusions concerning language in general to phonetic changes. They observe, for example, that the sharpest upheavals of Latin in its development into the Romance languages coincided with the highly disturbed period of invasions. Two distinctions will serve as guideposts:

a) Political stability does not influence language in the same way as political instability; here there is no reciprocity. When political equilibrium slows down the evolution of language, a positive though external cause is involved. But instability, which has the opposite effect, acts only negatively. Immobility—the relative fixation of an idiom—may have an external cause (the influence of a court, school, an academy, writing, etc.) which in turn is positively favored by social and political equilibrium. But if some external upheaval that has affected the equilibrium of the nation precipitates linguistic evolution, this is because language simply reverts back to its free state and follows its regular course. The immobility of Latin of the classical period is due to external facts; the changes that it later underwent, however, were self-generated in the absence of certain external conditions.

b) Here we are dealing only with phonetic phenomena and not with every type of modification of language. Grammatical changes are obviously similar. Because they are always closely linked to thought, grammatical facts are more easily affected by the impact of external upheavals, which have a more immediate repercussion on the mind. But there is no solid basis for the belief that sudden evolutions of the sounds of an idiom correspond to turbulent periods in the history of a nation.

Still, it is impossible to cite a single period—even among those where language is in a deceptive state of immobility—that has witnessed no phonetic changes.

6) The "linguistic substratum" has also been posited as the cause of phonetic changes. The absorption of an indigenous population by newcomers brings about certain changes. The difference between Provençal and French (*langue d'oc* and *langue d'oïl*) would accordingly correspond to a different proportion of the autochthonous Celtic element in the two parts of Gaul. This theory has also been used to trace the dialectal differences of Italian and the influence of Ligurian, Etruscan, etc., depending on the region. But first, this hypothesis supposes circumstances that are rarely found. Second, one must be more specific: Did earlier populations introduce some of their own articulatory habits into the new language on adopting it? This is admissible and quite natural. But if the imponderable forces of race, etc. are called in anew, the pitfalls described earlier reappear.

7) A final explanation—which scarcely merits the name—compares phonetic changes to changes in fashion. But no one has explained these changes. We know only that they depend on laws of imitation, which are the concern of the psychologist. This explanation, though it does not solve our problem, has the advantage of fitting it into another larger problem and positing a psychological basis for phonetic changes. But where is the starting point of imitation? That is the mystery, in phonetic changes as well as in changes of fashion.

5. *The Effect of Phonetic Changes Is Unlimited*

If we try to determine how far phonetic changes will go, we see immediately that they are unlimited and incalculable, i.e. we cannot foresee where they will stop. It is childish to think that the word can be changed only up to a certain point, as if there were something about it that could preserve it. Phonetic modifications derive their character from the arbitrariness of the linguistic sign,[2] which is distinct from the signified.

We can easily observe that the sounds of a word have been affected at a certain moment and see the extent of the damage, but we cannot say beforehand how far the word has become or will become unrecognizable.

Like every word having the same ending, Proto-Indo-European **aiwom* (cf. Latin *aevom*) changed to **aiwan*, **aiwa*, **aiw* in Proto-Germanic; next, **aiw* became *ew* in Old High German, as did every word that contained the cluster *aiw;* then the change of final *w* to *o* resulted in *ēo*, which in turn passed to *eo*, *io* in accordance with other equally general rules; finally *io* became *ie*, *je*, giving Modern German *jē* (cf. das schönste, was ich *je* gesehen habe 'the prettiest that I have *ever* seen').

The modern word does not contain a single one of its original elements when considered from the viewpoint of the starting point and the end result. Each step, when viewed separately, is absolutely certain and regular and limited in its effect; viewed as a whole, however, the word gives the impression of an unlimited number of modifications. We might make the same observation about Latin *calidum* by first leaving out the transitional forms and comparing this form with Modern French *šọ* (written *chaud* 'warm'), then retracing the steps: *calidum*, *calidu*, *caldu*, *cald*, *calt*, *tsalt*, *tsaut*, *šaut*, *šọt*, *šọ*. Compare also Vulgar Latin **waidanju* → *gẽ* (written *gain* 'gain'), *minus* → *mwẽ* (written *moins* 'less'), *hoc illī* → *wi* (written *oui* 'yes').

A phonetic change is also unlimited and incalculable in that it affects all types of signs, making no distinction between radicals, suffixes, etc. This must be true *a priori*, for if grammar interfered, the phonetic phenomenon would mingle with the synchronic fact, a thing that is radically impossible. It is in this sense that we can speak of the blind nature of the evolutions of sounds.

For instance, *s* fell in Greek after *n* not only in **khānses* 'geese,' **menses* 'months' (giving *khênes*, *mênes*), where it had no grammatical value, but also in verbal forms like **etensa*, **ephansa*, etc. (giving *éteina*, *éphēna*, etc.), where it marked the aorist. In Middle High German the posttonic vowels *i*, *e*, *a*, *o* regularly became *e*

[2] Meaning *signifier*. See p. 75, note. [Tr.]

(*gibil* → *Giebel*, *meistar* → *Meister*) even though the difference in timbre marked a number of inflectional endings; that is how the accusative singular *boton* and the genitive and dative singular *boten* merged into *boten*.

Phonetic changes will thus cause a profound disturbance in the grammatical organism if they are not stopped by some barrier. This will be the subject matter of the next chapter.

Chapter III

GRAMMATICAL CONSEQUENCES OF PHONETIC EVOLUTION

1. *The Breaking of the Grammatical Bond*

One of the first consequences of the phonetic phenomenon is the breaking of the grammatical bond that unites two or more terms. The result is that one word is no longer felt to be derived from another:

> *mansiō*—**mansiōnāticus*
> *maison* 'house' || *ménage* 'housekeeping'

The collective mind of the community of speakers formerly saw **mansiō-nāticus* as a derivative of *mansiō;* then phonetic vicissitudes separated them. Similarly:

> (*vervēx*—*vervēcārius*)
> Vulgar Latin *berbīx*—*berbīcārius*
> *brebis* 'ewe' || *berger* 'shepherd'

The separation naturally has its countereffect on value. In certain local dialects *berger* means specifically 'a herder of oxen.' Other examples:

> *Grātiānopolis*—*grātiānopolitānus* ||||| *decem*—*undecim*
> *Grenoble* || *Grésivaudan* |||||||||||||| *dix* 'ten' || *onze* 'eleven'

Gothic *bītan* 'bite'—*bitum* 'we have bitten'—*bitr* 'bitter, biting' is a similar example. Following the change of *t* to *ts* (*z*) on the one hand and the conservation of the cluster *tr* on the other, West Germanic had *bīzan, bizum* || *bitr.*

In addition, phonetic evolution may break the normal relation between two inflected forms of the same word. In Old French, for instance, *comes—comitem* became *cuens* || *comte, barō—barōnem* → *ber* || *baron, presbiter—presbiterum* → *prestre* || *provoire.*

Or an ending may split in two. All accusative singulars were characterized by the same final *-m* in Proto-Indo-European (**ek₁ wom, *owim, *podm, *māterm,* etc.).[3] In Latin there was no radical change in this respect, but in Greek the very different treatment of the sonant and con-sonant nasal created two distinct series of forms: *híppon, ó(w)in* against *póda, matera.* The accusative plural evinces a similar fact (cf. *híppous* and *pódas*).

2. *Effacement of the Structure of Words*

Another grammatical effect of phonetic changes is that the distinct parts that helped to fix the value of a word become unanalyzable. The word becomes an indivisible whole. Examples: French *ennemi* 'enemy' (cf. Latin *in-imīcus—amīcus*); Latin *perdere* (cf. older *per-dare—dare*), *amiciō* (for **ambjaciō—jaciō*); German *Drittel* (for *drit-teil—Teil*).

Effacement of the structure of words is obviously related at several points to the breaking of grammatical bonds (see Section 1 above). For instance, stating that *ennemi* cannot be analyzed is another way of saying that its parts can no longer be compared as in *in-imīcus* from simple *amīcus*. The formula:

amīcus—inimīcus
ami || *ennemi*

is very similar to:

mansiō—mansiōnāticus
maison || *ménage.*

Cf. also: *decem—undecim* against *dix* || *onze.*

[3] Or *-n*? See p. 92, note. [Ed.]

The simple Classical Latin forms *hunc, hanc, hāc,* etc. go back to *hon-ce, han-ce, ha-ce,* etc. (attested by epigraphic forms) and are the result of the agglutination of a pronoun with a particle *–ce.* Once *hon-ce,* etc. could be compared with *ec-ce,* etc., but comparison was no longer possible after *–e* had fallen. That is just another way of saying that the elements of *hunc, hanc, hāc,* etc. are no longer distinct.

Phonetic evolution first obscures analysis, then makes it completely impossible. The inflection of nouns in Proto-Indo-European is a case in point.

The Proto-Indo-European declension was as follows: nominative singular **pod-s,* accusative **pod-m,* dative **pod-ai,* locative **pod-i,* nominative plural **pod-es,* accusative **pod-ns,* etc. At first the inflection of *ek_1wos* was identical: *ek_1wo-s,* *ek_1wo-m,* *ek_1wo-ai,* *ek_1wo-i,* *ek_1wo-es,* *ek_1wo-ns,* etc.; during that period *ek_1wo–* was singled out as easily as **pod–*. But vocalic contractions later modified that state, giving dative *$ek_1w\bar{o}i$,* locative *ek_1woi,* nominative plural *$ek_1w\bar{o}s$.* From that moment the distinctness of the radical *ek_1wo–* was compromised and its analysis became elusive. Still later, new changes like the differentiation between accusatives (see p. 154) wiped out the last trace of the original state. The contemporaries of Xenophon probably had the impression that the radical was *hipp–* and that the inflectional endings were vocalic (*hipp-os,* etc.), with the result that the endings of words like *ek_1wo-s* and **pod-s* were distinct. In inflection as elsewhere, anything which interferes with analysis helps to loosen grammatical bonds.

3. *There Are No Phonetic Doublets*

In the two cases that we have examined (Sections 1 and 2), evolution radically separated two terms that originally were united grammatically. This phenomenon might give rise to a serious mistake in interpretation.

On observing the relative identity of Vulgar Latin *barō: barōnem* and the dissimilarity of Old French *ber: baron,* is one not justified in saying that one and the same original unit (*bar–*) developed in divergent directions and produced two forms? No, for the same unit cannot be subjected at the same time and in the same place to two different transformations; that would be contrary to the very definition of phonetic changes. By itself, phonetic evolution cannot create two forms to replace one.

Here, introduced by way of examples, are the objections that might be raised against my thesis:

Collocāre gave both *coucher* 'sleep' and *colloquer* 'place,' someone might say. No, it gave only *coucher; colloquer* is only a learned borrowing from Latin (cf. *rançon* 'ransom' and *rédemption* 'redemption').

Another objection might be that *cathedra* gave two authentic French words, *chaire* 'pulpit' and *chaise* 'chair.' The fact that *chaise* is a dialectal form is forgotten. The Parisian dialect changed intervocalic *r* to *z*. For instance, speakers said *pèse, mèse* for *père* 'father,' *mère* 'mother'; literary French has kept only two specimens of the localism: *chaise* and *bésicles*, the doublet of *béricles* 'spectacles,' derived from *béryl* 'beryl.' The same is true of Picard *rescapé* 'one who has escaped (death or injury),' which has just gained currency in French and now stands in contrast to *réchappé* 'one who has (voluntarily) escaped (from confinement).' French *cavalier* 'rider' and *chevalier* 'knight' and *cavalcade* 'ride' and *chevauchée* 'distance traversed' are found side by side simply because *cavalier* and *cavalcade* were borrowed from Italian. The development of *calidum*, which became *chaud* 'warm' in French and *caldo* in Italian, is essentially the same. All the foregoing examples are instances of borrowings.

The answer to the objection that the Latin pronoun *mē* resulted in two forms in French, *me* and *moi* (cf. il *me* voit 'he sees *me*' and c'est *moi* qu'il voit 'it's *me* that he sees') is this: unstressed Latin *mē* became *me* while stressed *mē* became *moi;* now the presence or absence of stress depends, not on the phonetic laws that made *mē* become *me* and *moi*, but on the function of the word in the sentence; it is a grammatical duality. In the same way, German **ur–* remained *ur–* when stressed and became *er–* when protonic (cf. *úrlaub* and *erlaúben*); but the functioning of the accent is itself linked to the structural patterns that contained *ur–* and thus to a grammatical and synchronic condition. Finally, to come back to the first example, differences of form and accent in the pair *bárō: barṓnem* evidently antedate phonetic changes.

In fact, phonetic doublets do not exist. The evolution of sounds only emphasizes previous differences. Wherever these differences are not due to external causes (as in borrowings), they imply grammatical and synchronic dualities that are absolutely unrelated to phonetic changes.

4. *Alternation*

Two words like *maison: ménage* seldom tempt us to try to discover what is responsible for the difference, either because the differential elements (*–ezõ* and *–en–* do not lend themselves well to comparison, or because no other pair offers a parallel opposition. But often it happens that the two related words differ in only one or two elements which are easily singled out, and that the same difference is regularly repeated in a series of like pairs; this is *alternation*, the largest and most common of the grammatical facts in which phonetic changes play a part.

In French, every Latin *ō* in an open syllable became *eu* when stressed and *ou* when protonic; this produced pairs like *pouvons* '(we) can': *peuvent* '(they) can,' *oeuvre* 'work': *ouvrier* 'worker,' *nouveau: neuf* 'new,' etc., where it is easy to single out a differential and regularly variable element. In Latin, rhotacization causes *gerō* to alternate with *gestus, oneris* with *onus, maeor* with *maestus*, etc. Since *s* was treated differently according to the position of the accent in Germanic, Middle High German has *ferliesen: ferloren, kiessen: gekoren, friesen: gefroren*, etc. The fall of Proto-Indo-European *e* is reflected in Modern German in the oppositions *beissen: biss, leiden: litt, reiten: ritt*, etc.

In all the preceding examples the radical element is the part that is affected. But of course all parts of a word may have similar oppositions. Nothing is more common, for instance, than a prefix that takes different forms according to the make-up of the first part of the radical (cf. Greek *apo-didōmi: ap-érchomai*, French *inconnu* 'unknown': *inutile* 'useless'). The Proto-Indo-European alternation *e: o*, which certainly must, in the last analysis, have a phonetic basis, is found in a great number of suffixal elements (Greek *híppos: híppe, phér-o-men: phér-e-te, gén-os: gén-e-os* for **gén-es-os*, etc.). Old French gives special treatment to Latin accented *a* after palatals; this results in an *e: ie* alternation in a number of inflectional endings (cf. *chant-er: jug-ier, chant-é; jug-ié, chant-ez: jug-iez*, etc.).

Alternation is then defined as *a correspondence existing between two definite sounds or groups of sounds and shifting regularly between two series of coexisting forms.*

Phonetic changes alone do not explain doublets, and are obviously neither the sole cause nor the main cause of alternation. Whoever says that Latin *nov–* became *neuv–* and *nouv–* (French *neuve* and *nouveau*) through a phonetic change is fabricating an imaginary unity and failing to see a pre-existing synchronic duality. The different position of *nov–* in *nov-us* and *nov-ellus* is both antecedent to the phonetic change and distinctly grammatical (cf. *barō: barōnem*). The synchronic duality is what originates and makes possible any alternation. The phonetic phenomenon broke no unity; it merely made an opposition between coexisting terms more obvious by discarding certain sounds. It is a mistake—and one shared by many linguists—to assume that alternation is phonetic simply because sounds make up its substance and play a part in its genesis through their alterations. The fact is that alternation, whether considered from its starting point or end result, is always both grammatical and synchronic.

5. *Laws of Alternation*

Can alternation be reduced to laws? If so, what is the nature of these laws?

Take the alternation *e: i*, which occurs so frequently in Modern German. If we lump all examples together and consider them indiscriminately (*geben: gibt, Feld: Gefilde, Wetter: wittern, helfen: Hilfe, sehen: Sicht*, etc.), we can formulate no general principle. But if we extract from this mass the pair *geben: gibt* and set it in opposition to *schelten: schilt, helfen: hilft, nehmen: nimmt*, etc., we see that the alternation coincides with distinctions of tense, person, etc. In *lang: Länge, stark: Stärke, hart: Härte*, etc., a similar opposition is linked to the formation of substantives from adjectives; in *Hand: Hände, Gast: Gäste*, etc., to the formation of the plural, and so on for all the many cases that Germanic students class under ablaut (consider also *finden: fand*, or *finden: Fund, binden: band*, or *binden: Bund, schiessen: schoss: Schuss, fliessen: floss:*

Fluss, etc.). Ablaut, or radical vocalic variation coinciding with a grammatical opposition, is a prime example of alternation but is distinguished from the general phenomenon by no particular characteristic.

Ordinarily, then, alternation is distributed regularly among several terms and coincides with an important opposition of function, class, or determination. It is possible to speak of grammatical laws of alternation, but these laws are only a fortuitous result of the underlying phonetic facts. When phonetic facts create a regular opposition between two series of terms that have an opposition of value, the mind seizes upon the material difference, gives it significance, and makes it the carrier of the conceptual difference (see pp. 84 ff.). The laws of alternation, like all synchronic laws, are simple structural principles; they are not imperative. It is completely wrong to say, as people so readily do, that the *a* of *Nacht* changes to *ä* in the plural *Nächte*, for this gives the illusion that a transformation governed by an imperative principle comes between one term and the next. What we are actually dealing with is a simple opposition of forms resulting from phonetic evolution. To be sure analogy (to be considered later in Chapter VI) may create new pairs that show the same phonic difference (cf. *Kranz: Kränze*, modeled on *Gast: Gäste*, etc.). The law thus seems to apply like a rule that governs usage to the extent of modifying it. But we recall that in language these permutations are at the mercy of conflicting analogical influences, and this suffices to show that such rules are always precarious and fit perfectly the definition of synchronic law.

Sometimes the phonetic cause of the alternation is still evident. In Old High German, for instance, the pairs cited on page 158 had the forms *geban: gibit*, *feld: gefildi*, etc. During that period the radical itself appeared with *i* instead of *e* wherever *i* followed but with *e* in every other instance. The alternation of Latin *faciō: conficiō*, *amīcus: inimīcus*, *facilis: difficilis*, etc., is likewise linked to a phonic condition which speakers would have expressed in this way: the *a* of such words as *faciō* and *amīcus* alternates with *i* in medial syllables of words in the same family.

But the foregoing phonic oppositions suggest exactly the same observations as all grammatical laws: they are synchronic. To forget this is to risk making the mistake in interpretation pointed out above (see pp. 96 ff.). Faced with a pair like *faciō: conficiō*, we must indeed guard against confusing the relation between these coexisting terms and the relation that ties together the successive terms of the diachronic fact (*confaciō* → *conficiō*). We may be tempted to confuse them since the cause of phonetic differentiation is still apparent in the pair, but the phonetic fact belongs to the past, and for speakers there is only a single synchronic opposition.

All of this confirms what was said about the strictly grammatical nature of alternation. The word permutation, which is apt in some ways, has been used for alternation but should be avoided for the very reason that it has often been applied to phonetic changes and suggests a false notion of movement where there is only a state.

6. *Alternation and Grammatical Bond*

We have seen how phonetic evolution may cause a break in the grammatical bonds that unite words by changing the form of the words. But this is true only of isolated pairs like *maison: ménage, Teil: Drittel*, etc., not of alternation.

It is obvious from the first that any slightly regular phonic opposition of two elements tends to establish a bond between them. *Wetter* is instinctively related to *wittern* because speakers are accustomed to seeing *e* alternate with *i*. As soon as speakers feel that there is a general law governing a phonic opposition, the usual correspondence has all the more reason for forcing itself on their attention and helping to tighten rather than loosen the grammatical bond. This is how the German ablaut reinforces recognitions of the radical unit across vocalic variations (see p. 158).

The same is true of nonsignificant alternations that are linked to a mere phonic condition. In French, the prefix *re-* (*rependre* 'retake,' *regagner* 'regain,' *retoucher* 'retouch,' etc.) is reduced to *r-* before a vowel (*rouvrir* 'reopen,' *racheter* 'buy back,' etc.). Similarly, under the same conditions the prefix *in-*, still very much alive although of learned origin, has two distinct forms: *ẽ-* (in *inconnu* 'unknown,' *indigne* 'unworthy,' *invertébré* 'invertebrate,' etc.) and *in-* (in *inavouable* 'inadmissible,' *inutile* 'useless,' *inesthétique* 'unaesthetic,' etc.). In no way does this difference break unity of conception, for meaning and function are apprehended as identical, and language has determined where it will use one form or the other.

Chapter IV

ANALOGY

1. *Definition and Examples*

That phonetic evolution is a disturbing force is now obvious. Wherever it does not create alternations, it helps to loosen the grammatical bonds between words; the total number of forms is uselessly increased; the linguistic mechanism is obscured and complicated to the extent that the irregularities born of phonetic changes win out over the forms grouped under general patterns; in other words, to the extent that absolute arbitrariness wins out over relative arbitrariness (see p. 133).

Fortunately, analogy counterbalances the effect of phonetic transformations. To analogy are due all normal, nonphonetic modifications of the external side of words.

Analogy supposes a model and its regular imitation. *An analogical form is a form made on the model of one or more other forms in accordance with a definite rule.*

The nominative form of Latin *honor*, for instance, is analogical. Speakers first said *honōs: honōsem*, then through rhotacization of the *s*, *honōs: honōrem*. After that, the radical had a double form. This duality was eliminated by the new form *honor*, created on the pattern of *ōrātor: ōrātōrem*, etc., through a process which subsequently will be set up as a proportion:

ōrātōrem: ōrātor = hōnōrem: x
x = honor

Thus analogy, to offset the diversifying action of a phonetic change (*honōs: honōrem*), again unified the forms and restored regularity (*honor: honōrem*).

For a long time French speakers said *il preuve, nous prouvons, ils* *preuvent*. Today they say *il prouve* 'he proves,' *ils prouvent* 'they prove,' using forms that have no phonetic explanation. *Il aime* 'he loves' is derived from Latin *amat* while *nous aimons* 'we love' is the analogical form for *amons;* speakers should also say *amable* instead of *aimable* 'amiable.' In Greek, intervocalic *s* disappeared: *-eso-* became *-eo-* (cf. *géneos* for **génesos*). Still, intervocalic *s* is found in the future and aorist of all verbs with vowels: *lūso, élūsa,* etc. Analogy with forms like *túpsō* and *étupsa,* where *s* did not fall, preserved the memory of the future and of the aorist in *s*. In German, *Gast: Gäste, Balg: Bälge,* etc. are phonetic, but *Kranz: Kränze* (previously *kranz: kranza*), *Hals: Hälse* (previously *halsa*), etc. are due to imitation.

Analogy favors regularity and tends to unify structural and inflectional procedures. But it is capricious; beside *Kranz: Kränze,* etc., stand *Tag: Tage, Salz: Salze,* etc., which for one reason or another have resisted analogy. Thus we cannot say beforehand how far imitation of a model will go or which types will bring it about. The most numerous forms do not necessarily unleash analogy. The Greek perfect has the active forms *pépheuga, pépheugas, pephéugamen,* but all the middle forms are inflected without *a: pephugmai, pephúgmetha,* etc., and the language of Homer shows that the *a* was formerly missing in the plural and in the dual of the active (cf. *ídmen, éikion,* etc.). Analogy started solely from the first person singular of the active and won over almost the whole paradigm of the perfect indicative. This development is also noteworthy because here analogy attached *-a-*, originally an inflectional element, to the radical, forming *pepheúga-men*. The reverse—attaching the radical element to the suffix—is much more common (see p. 170).

Two or three words often suffice to create a general form such as an inflectional ending. In Old High German, weak verbs like *habēn, lobōn,* etc. had an *-m* in the first person singular of the present: *habēm, lobōm,* etc. The *-m* derives from a few verbs similar to *-mi* verbs in Greek (*bim, *stām, gōm, tuom*), which by themselves forced the ending on the whole weak conjugation. Notice that here analogy did not eliminate a phonetic difference but generalized a formative method.

2. *Analogical Phenomena Are Not Changes*

The first linguists did not understand the nature of the phenomenon of analogy, which they called "false analogy." They thought that in inventing *honor*, Latin "had made a mistake" concerning the prototype *honōs*. For them, everything that deviated from the original state was an irregularity, a distortion of an ideal form. The fact is that, through an illusion characteristic of their time, they saw in the original state of the language something superior and perfect, with the result that they did not even ask themselves whether this state had been preceded by another. Every liberty taken with respect to this state was then an anomaly. The neogrammarian school was the first to assign analogy to its proper place by showing that it is, along with phonetic changes, the prime force in the evolution of languages, the procedure through which languages pass from one state of organization to another.

But exactly what are analogical phenomena? People generally think of them as changes. But are they?

Every analogical fact is a play with a cast of three: (1) the traditional, legitimate heir (e.g. *honōs*); (2) the rival (*honor*); and (3) a collective character made up of the forms that created the rival (*honōrem, ōrātor, ōrātōrem*, etc.). One might readily suppose that *honor* is a modification, a "metaplasm," of *honōs* and say that it drew most of its substance from *honōs*. But the only form that had no part in the production of *honor* is this very *honōs!*

The phenomenon of analogy may be pictured by the diagram:

TRADITIONAL FORMS		NEW FORM
Honōs	*honōrem,*	
(which plays	*ōrātor, ōrātōrem,* etc.	*honor*
no part)	(productive group)	

Here we obviously have a "paraplasm," the installation of a rival beside a traditional form—in short, a creation. Whereas phonetic change introduces nothing new without annulling what has preceded it (*honōrem* replaces *honōsem*), the analogical form does not necessarily entail the disappearance of its double. *Honor* and *honōs* coexisted for a time and were used interchangeably. Still, since language is reluctant to keep two signifiers for a single idea, the original form, which is less regular, generally falls into disuse and disappears. The result is what gives the impression of a transformation. Once analogy has completed its work, the opposition between the old state (*honōs: honōrem*) and the new (*honor: honōrem*) is apparently the same as the opposition that results from the evolution of sounds. At the moment when *honor* was born, however, nothing was changed since *honor* replaced nothing; nor is the disappearance of *honōs* a change, for this phenomenon is independent of the first. Wherever we can follow the course of linguistic events, we see that analogical innovation and the elimination of the older form are two distinct things, and that nowhere do we come upon a transformation.

So little does analogy have the characteristic of replacing one form by another that it often produces forms which replace nothing at all. German can make a diminutive in *-chen* from any substantive with a concrete meaning; if the form *Elefantchen* were introduced into the language, it would supplant nothing that already exists. Similarly in French, on the model of *pension* 'pension': *pensionnaire* 'pensionary,' *réaction*, 'reaction': *réactionnaire* 'reactionary,' etc., someone might create *interventionnaire, répressionnaire*, etc., meaning 'one who favors intervention,' 'one who favors repression,' etc. The process is evidently the same as the one that engendered *honor;* both recall the same formula:

réaction: réactionnaire = répression: x
x = répressionnaire

In neither case is there the slightest pretext for speaking of change; *répressionnaire* replaces nothing. Another example: some French speakers use the analogical form *finaux* instead of *finals*, which is generally assumed to be the correct form; someone might coin the adjective *firmamental* and give it the plural form *firmamentaux*. Should we say that there is change in *finaux* and creation in *firmamentaux?* In both cases there is creation. On the pattern of *mur* 'wall': *enmurer* 'wall in,' speakers formed *tour* 'turn': *entourer* 'surround,' and *jour* 'light': *ajourer* 'open' (in *un travail ajouré* 'work that admits light, i.e. lacework,' etc.). These rather recent derivatives seem to be creations. But if I notice that *entorner* and *ajorner*, built on *torn* and *jorn*, were used during an earlier period, must I change my mind and say that *entourer* and *ajourer* are modifications of the older words? The illusion of analogical change comes from setting up a relation between the new form and the one replaced by it. But this is a mistake since formations classed as changes (like *honor*) are basically the same as those I call creations (like *répressionnaire*).

3. *Analogy as a Creative Force in Language*

When, after seeing what analogy is not, we begin to study it for what it is, we find that it seems very simply to blend with the principle of linguistic creativity in general. What is that principle?

Analogy is psychological, but this does not suffice to separate it from phonetic phenomena, for they may also be considered psychological (see p. 151). We must go further and say that analogy is grammatical. It supposes awareness and understanding of a relation between forms. Meaning plays no part in phonetic changes, but it must intervene in analogy.

As far as we can tell, neither comparison with other forms nor meaning had anything to do with the passing from intervocalic *s* to *r* in Latin. The skeleton of the form *honōsem* passed to *honōrem*. Other forms must be introduced to account for the appearance of *honor* beside *honōs*. This is shown by the proportion:

$$\textit{ōrātōrem}: \textit{ōrātor} = \textit{honōrem}: x$$
$$x = \textit{honor}$$

The new combination would have no basis if the mind did not associate its forms through their meanings.

Analogy is grammatical throughout, but let us hasten to add that its end result—creation—belongs at first only to speaking. It is the chance product of an isolated speaker. Here, at the very fringe of language, is where the phenomenon must first be sought. Still, two things must be kept apart: (1) awareness of the relation that ties together the productive forms; and (2) the result suggested by the comparison, the form improvised by the speaker to express his thought. Only the result belongs to speaking.

Analogy, then, is one more lesson in separating language from speaking (see pp. 17 ff.). It shows us that the second depends on the first, and it points to the essence of the linguistic mechanism as described on page 130. Any creation must be preceded by an unconscious comparison of the materials deposited in the storehouse of language, where productive forms are arranged according to their syntagmatic and associative relations.

A major part of the analogical phenomenon is therefore completed before the new form appears. Speech is continuously engaged in decomposing its units, and this activity contains not only every possibility of effective talk, but every possibility of analogical formation. It is wrong to suppose that the productive process is at work only when the new formation actually occurs. The elements were already there. A newly formed word like *in-décor-able* already has a potential existence in language; all its elements are found in syntagms like *décor-er* 'decorate,' *décor-ation* 'decoration,' *pardonn-able* 'pardonable,' *mani-able* 'manageable': *in-connu* 'unknown,' *in-sensé* 'insane,' etc., and the final step of realizing it in speaking is a small matter in comparison with the build-up of forces that makes it possible.

In short analogy, considered by itself, is only one side of the phenomenon of interpretation, one manifestation of the general activity that singles out units for subsequent use. That is why I say that analogy is entirely grammatical and synchronic.

The grammatical and synchronic character of analogy suggests two observations that confirm my views on absolute and relative arbitrariness (see pp. 131 ff.).

1) Words can be rated for capacity to engender other words to the extent to which they themselves are decomposable. Simple words are by definition unproductive (cf. French *magasin* 'warehouse,' *arbre* 'tree,' *racine* 'root,' etc.). *Magasinier* 'warehouse-keeper' was not engendered by *magasin*. It was formed on the pattern of *prisonier* 'prisoner': *prison* 'prison,' etc. In the same way *emmagisiner* 'to warehouse' owes its existence to the analogy of *enmailloter* 'swathe,' *encadrer* 'frame,' *encapuchonner* 'put on a cowl,' etc., which contain *maillot* 'swaddling-clothes,' *cadre* 'frame,' *capuchon* 'cowl,' etc.

Each language then has both productive and sterile words, in varying proportions. This takes us back to the distinction between "lexicological" and "grammatical" languages (see p. 133). In Chinese, most words are not decomposable; in an artificial language, however, almost all words are. An Esperantist has unlimited freedom to build new words on a given root.

2) We have seen (p. 161) that any analogical creation may be pictured as similar to a proportion. This formula is frequently used

to explain the phenomenon of analogical creation itself, but we have sought its explanation in the analysis and reconstruction of elements furnished by language.

There is a conflict between the two notions. If proportion is a satisfactory explanation, why posit an analysis of elements? To form *indécorable,* there is no point in extracting its elements (*in-décor-able*). All we need do is to take the whole and put it in the equation:

pardonner: impardonnable, etc. = *décorer: x*
x = *indécorable*

Here, no complicated operation such as the grammarian's conscious analysis is presumed on the part of the speaker. In *Krantz: Kränze,* modeled on *Gast: Gäste* and the like, decomposition seems less probable than proportion since the radical of the model may be either *Gast–* or *Gäst–*. A phonic characteristic of *Gäste* might simply have been carried over to *Kranze.*

Of the two theories, which fits the facts? (Bear in mind that *Kranz* does not necessarily exclude analysis. We have observed alternations in roots and prefixes, and the feeling for alternation may well exist alongside positive analysis; see p. 158.)

The two contrasting notions are reflected in two different grammatical doctrines. European grammars work with proportion; they explain the formation of the German preterite, for example, by starting from whole words. On the model of *setzen: setzte* the pupil is told to form the preterite of *lachen,* etc. Against this, Hindu grammar would study roots (*setz–*, *lach–*, etc.) in one chapter and preterite endings (*–te*, etc.) in another. The elements that result from analysis would be given, and from these elements whole words would have to be reconstructed. In every Sanskrit dictionary, verbs are arranged in the order assigned to them by their roots.

Theoreticians of grammar will incline toward whichever method is predominant in their linguistic group.

Old Latin apparently favors the analytical procedure. Here is obvious proof: quantity is not the same in *făctus* and *āctus* despite *făciō* and *agō;* we must assume that *actus* goes back to **ăgtos* and attribute lengthening of the vowel to the voiced consonant that followed; this hypothesis is fully confirmed by the Romance languages. The opposition *spĕciō: spĕctus* against *tĕgō: tēctus* is reflected in French *dépit* 'despite' (= *despĕctus*) and *toit* 'roof' (= *tēctum*); cf. *conficiō: confectus* (French *confit* 'candied') against *regō: rēctus* (*dīrēctus* → French *droit* 'straight'). But **agtos, *tegtos, *regtos* were not inherited from Proto-Indo-European, which certainly had **aktos, *tektos*, etc.; prehistoric Latin introduced them, and this despite the difficulty of pronouncing a voiced consonant before a voiceless one. This was made possible only by acute awareness of the radical units *ag–*, *teg–*, *reg–*. The feeling for word-parts (radicals, suffixes, etc.) and their arrangement was therefore strong in Old Latin. In all probability the feeling is not so acute in modern languages but is stronger in German than in French (see p. 186 f.).

Chapter V

ANALOGY AND EVOLUTION

1. *How an Analogical Innovation Enters Language*

Nothing enters language without having been tested in speaking, and every evolutionary phenomenon has its roots in the individual. This principle, which was stated previously (see p. 98), applies particularly to analogical innovations. Before *honor* could become a rival strong enough to replace *honōs*, one speaker had to coin the new word, then others had to imitate and repeat it until it forced itself into standard usage.

But not every analogical innovation is so fortunate. Abortive combinations that language will probably never adopt are always at hand. Children, because they are not well acquainted with standard usage and are not yet bound by it, clutter their speech with them: in French they say *viendre* for *venir* 'come,' *mouru* for *mort* 'dead,' etc. But adults use them too. For instance, many people say *traisait* (which, incidentally, is found in the writings of Rousseau) instead of *trayait* '(he) milked.' All such innovations are perfectly regular; they are explained in the same way as those that language has accepted; *viendre*, for example, stems from the proportion:

$$\textit{éteindrai: éteindre} = \textit{viendrai: } x$$
$$x = \textit{viendre}$$

and *traisait* was formed on the model of *plaire* 'please': *plaisait* '(he) pleased,' etc.

Language retains only a minimal part of the creations of speaking, but those that endure are numerous enough to change completely the appearance of its vocabulary and grammar from one period to the next.

From what was said in the preceding chapter, it is evident that analogy by itself could not be a force in evolution, and that the constant substitution of new forms for old ones is one of the most striking features in the transformation of languages. Each time a new formation becomes definitely installed and eliminates its rival, something is actually created and something else abandoned, with the result that analogy occupies a preponderant place in the theory of evolution.

This is the point that I should like to emphasize.

2. *Analogical Innovations as Symptoms of Changes in Interpretation*

Language never stops interpreting and decomposing its units. But why does interpretation vary constantly from one generation to the next? The cause of change must be sought in the great mass of forces that constantly threaten the analysis adopted in a particular language-state. I shall recall a few of them.

The first and most important force is phonetic evolution (see Chapter II). By making some analyses ambiguous and others impossible, phonetic changes affect both the conditions and the results of decomposition, thereby shifting the boundaries and changing the nature of units (see p. 141 concerning compounds like *beta-hūs* and *redo-līch*, and p. 155 concerning noun inflection in Proto-Indo-European).

In addition to the phonetic fact there is agglutination (to be discussed later), which welds a combination of elements into one unit, and every imaginable circumstance which, though external, may modify the analysis of words. For it is obvious that analysis, because it results from a set of comparisons, depends constantly on the associative environment of the term. The Proto-Indo-European superlative **swād-is-to-s* contained two independent suffixes, *–is–*, which carried the idea of comparative degree (cf. Latin *mag-is*) and *–to–*, which designated the definite place of an object in a series (cf. Greek *tri-to-s* 'third'). The two prefixes were agglutinated (cf. Greek *hēd-isto-s*, or rather *hēd-ist-os*). But agglutination was in turn greatly aided by a fact unrelated to the concept of the superlative degree: comparatives in *is–* had dropped out of usage, having been supplanted by formations in *–jōs;* since *–is–* was no longer recognized as an independent element, it was no longer singled out in *–isto–*.

We note in passing the general tendency to shorten the radical in favor of the formative element, especially when the former ends in a vowel. Thus the Latin suffix *–tāt–* (*vēri-tāt-em* for *vēro-tāt-em*, cf. Greek *deinó-tet-a*) took over the *i* of the theme, giving the analysis *vēr-itāt-em;* in the same way *Rōmā-nus*, *Albā-nus* (cf. *aēnus* for **aesno-s*) became *Rōm-ānus*, etc.

Changes in interpretation, no matter how they start, always become apparent through the existence of analogical forms. Indeed, if living units perceived by speakers at a particular moment can by themselves give birth to analogical formations, every definite redistribution of units also implies a possible expansion of their use. Analogy is therefore proof positive that a formative element exists at a given moment as a significant unit. *Merīdiōnālis* (Lactantius) for *merīdiālis* shows that the division was *septentri-ōnālis*, *regi-ōnālis*, and to prove that the suffix *–tāt* had been enlarged by an *i* element borrowed from the radical, we need only cite *celer-itātem;* *pāg-ānus*, built on *pāg-us*, suffices to show how Latin speakers analyzed *Rōm-ānus;* and the analysis of *redlich* (see p. 141) is confirmed by the existence of *sterblich*, formed with a verbal root.

A particularly unusual example will show how analogy works out new units from period to period. In Modern French, *somnolent* 'sleepy' is analyzed *somnol-ent*, as if it were a present participle. Proof of this is the existence of the verb *somnoler* 'be sleepy.' But in Latin the division was *somno-lentus*, like *succu-lentus*, etc., and before that it was *somn-olentus* 'smelling of sleep,' from *olēre*, as in *vīn-olentus* 'smelling of wine.'

The most obvious and important effect of analogy is thus the substituting of more regular forms composed of living elements for older irregular and obsolescent forms.

Doubtless things do not always run so smoothly. The functioning of language is disturbed by many hesitations, approximations, and semianalyses. At no time does an idiom have a perfectly stable system of units. From what was said about the inflection of **ekwos* against **pods*, it is obvious that imperfect analyses sometimes lead to muddled analogical creations. The Proto-Indo-European forms **geus-etai*, **gus-tos*, **gus-tis* allow us to single out the root **geus–*, *gus–*. But intervocalic *s* fell in Greek, and the analysis of *geúomai*, *geustós* was accordingly beclouded. Fluctuation resulted, and the root singled out was sometimes *geus–*, sometimes *geu–*. Analogy in turn bears witness to this fluctuation, for even roots in *eu–* take final *–s* (e.g. *pneu–*, *pneûma*, and the verbal adjective *pneus-tós*).

But analogy influences language even when there is groping and hesitation. For analogy, though not an evolutionary fact in itself, usually reflects the changes that have affected the functioning of language and sanctions them through new combinations. It collaborates efficiently with all the forces that constantly modify the architecture of an idiom and is in this way a powerful force in evolution.

3. *Analogy as a Renovating and Conservative Force*

One is sometimes tempted to ask whether analogy actually has the importance attributed to it here and whether its action is as far-reaching as that of phonetic changes. As a matter of fact, the history of each language discloses a motley accumulation of analogical facts. Collectively, these continuous reshufflings play an even more important part in the evolution of language than do sound changes.

But one thing in particular interests the linguist. In the enormous mass of analogical phenomena built up through centuries of evolution, almost all elements are preserved; they are only distributed differently. Analogical innovations are more apparent than real. Language is a garment covered with patches cut from its own cloth. Four-fifths of French is Proto-Indo-European if we think of the substance that constitutes sentences, but the words that have been transmitted in their totality without analogical change from the mother language to Modern French would occupy less than the space of one page (e.g. *est* 'is' = **esti,* numbers, words like *ours* 'bear,' *nez* 'nose,' *père* 'father,' *chien* 'dog,' etc.). The vast majority of words are, in one way or another, new combinations of phonic elements torn from older forms. In this sense analogy, for the very reason that it always uses old material for its innovations, is remarkably conservative.

But analogy has an equally important role as a conservative force pure and simple. It intervenes not only when old materials are redistributed in new units but also when forms remain unchanged. To realize this, we need only recall that analogical creation and the mechanism of speech have a common basis (see p. 165).

Latin *agunt* was transmitted almost intact from the prehistoric period (when people said **agonti*) until the beginning of the Romance period. During that span of time successive generations used the form over and over without there being a rival form to replace it. Here analogy played a part in the retention of the form. The stability of *agunt* is just as much the work of analogy as is any innovation. *Agunt* is integrated in a system; it is supported by forms like *dīcunt* and *legunt* as well as by *agimus*, *agitis*, and the like. Outside this frame, *agunt* might easily have been replaced by a form made up of new elements. What was transmitted was not *agunt* but *ag-unt*. The form did not change because *ag–* and *–unt* regularly appeared in other series, and the support of these forms preserved *agunt* from start to finish. Compare also *sex-tus*, which is supported by two compact series: *sex*, *sex-āginta,* etc. on the one hand and *quar-tus*, *quin-tus*, etc. on the other.

Forms are then preserved because they are constantly renewed by analogy. A word is apprehended simultaneously as a unit and as a syntagm, and is preserved to the extent that its elements do not change. Conversely, the existence of the form is threatened only to the extent that its elements disappear from usage. Consider what is happening to French *dites* '(you) say' and *faites* '(you) do,' which are direct descendants of Latin *dic-itis* and *fac-itis*. Because they have no support from present-day verbal inflection, language is trying to replace them. *Disez*, *faisez* (on the pattern of *plaisez* 'please,' *lisez* 'read,' etc.) are heard today, and the new endings are already common in most compounds (*contredisez* 'contradict,' etc.).

The only forms left untouched by analogy are of course isolated words like proper nouns, especially place names (cf. *Paris*, *Geneva*, *Agen*, etc.), which allow no analysis and consequently no interpretation of their elements. No rival creation springs up beside them.

It follows that a form may be preserved for either of two diametrically opposed reasons: complete isolation or complete integration in a system that has kept the basic parts of the word intact and that always comes to its rescue. It is within the intermediate group of forms not supported firmly enough by their environment that innovating analogy may unfold its effects.

But whether we deal with the preservation of a form composed of several elements or a redistribution of linguistic material in new constructions, analogy is there. It always plays an important role.

Chapter VI

FOLK ETYMOLOGY

We sometimes mangle words that have unfamiliar forms and meanings, and usage sometimes sanctions these deformations. In this way Old French *coute-pointe* (from *coute*, variant of *couette* 'cover' and *pointe*, past participle of *poindre* 'quilt') was changed to *courtepointe* 'counterpane,' as if formed from the adjective *court* 'short' and the noun *pointe* 'point.'[4] Such innovations, no matter how odd they may seem, are not due entirely to chance; they are crude attempts to explain refractory words by relating them to something known.

At first blush this phenomenon, called folk etymology, can

[4] Cf. Old English *scam-faest* 'confirmed in shame.' In early Modern English this became *shame-fast*, then *shame-faced*. [Tr.]

hardly be distinguished from analogy. When a speaker forgets that French *surdité* 'deafness' exists and coins analogical *sourdité*,[5] the result is the same as if he had misunderstood *surdité* and deformed it through remembrance of the adjective *sourd* 'deaf'; the only apparent difference is that analogical constructions are rational while folk etymology works somewhat haphazardly and results only in absurdities.

But this difference, which concerns only the results, is not basic. Their basic dissimilarity goes much deeper. In order to see what it is, let us begin by citing a few examples of the main types of folk etymology.

First come words that receive new interpretations with no corresponding change of form. In German, *durchbläuen* 'thrash soundly' goes back etymologically to *bliuwan* 'flog' but is associated with *blau* 'blue' because of the "blues" produced by flogging. In the Middle Ages German borrowed *adventure* 'adventure' from French and formed regularly *ābentüre, Abenteuer;* without deformation the word was associated with *Abend* ("a story related in the evening"); the result was that during the eighteenth century the word was written *Abendteuer*. Old French *soufraite* 'privation' (= *suffracta* from *subfrangere*) produced the adjective *souffreteux* 'sickly,' now associated with *souffrir* 'suffer,' with which it has nothing in common.[6] French *lais* is the noun form of *laisser* 'leave' but is associated nowadays with *léguer* 'bequeath' and written *legs;* some people even pronounce it *le-g-s*.[7] This might suggest that a change of form resulted from the new interpretation, but the change actually relates to the influence of the written form through which people tried to show their idea of the origin of the word without changing its pronunciation. Similarly, French *homard* 'lobster,' borrowed from Old Norse *hummar* (cf. Danish *hummer*), added a final *d* through analogy with French words in *-ard;* only here the mistake in interpretation that is marked by orthography affects the ending, which was confused with a common suffix (cf. *bavard* 'chatterbox,' etc.).

But people more often deform words in order to adapt them to

[5] Cf. English *pronounciation* against *pronunciation*. [Tr.]

[6] Cf. English *liquorice* (from Latin *liquiritia*), which has only a graphic relation to liquor. [Tr.]

[7] Cf. English *gooseberry* (from French *groseille*). [Tr.]

the elements which they think they recognize in them. German *Sauerkraut* became *choucroute* (*chou* 'cabbage' and *croute* 'crust') in French. In German, *dromedārius* became *trampeltier* 'animal that paws' in a new compound which includes existing words, *trampeln* and *Tier*. Old High German changed Latin *margarita* to *mari-greos* 'sea-pebble' by combining two known words.

A last example, especially instructive: Latin *carbunculus* 'small piece of coal' became *Karfunkel* (through association with *funkeln* 'glow') in German and *escarboucle* 'carbuncle' (associated with *boucle* 'buckle, ring') in French. *Calfeter*, *calfetrer* became *calfeutrer* 'chink' in French under the influence of *feutre* 'felt.'[8] What strikes one at the outset is that each of the examples contains, beside an intelligible element that occurs in other contexts, one part that stands for nothing that has previously existed (*Kar–*, *escar–*, *cal–*). But it would be a mistake to think that the elements are partly creations, that something new appeared as a result of the phenomenon. The reverse is true: interpretation could not touch the parts (*Kar–*, *escar–*, *cal–*). We might say that they are parts of folk etymologies that stopped at the half-way point. *Karfunkel* is in the same class as *Abenteuer* (if *–teuer* is considered an unexplained residue); it is also comparable to *homard*, where *hom–* makes no sense by itself.

Thus the degree of deformation does not create radical differences between words corrupted by folk etymology; all these words are pure and simple interpretations of misunderstood forms in terms of known forms.

Now we see how etymology resembles analogy, yet differs from it.

The two phenomena have only one common characteristic: people use significant elements provided by language in both, but the two are diametrically opposed in everything else. Analogy always implies the forgetting of the older forms; no analysis of the older form *il trayait* is at the base of the analogical form *il traisait* (see p. 168). The older form must even be forgotten before the rival can appear. Analogy takes nothing from the substance of the signs that it replaces. Against this, folk etymology is simply an interpretation of the older form; remembrance of the older form. though muddled,

[8] Cf. English *crayfish*, derived from Old French *crevice*. [Tr.]

is the starting point of the deformation that it underwent. The basis for analysis is remembrance in one instance and forgetfulness in the other, and this difference is of prime importance.

Folk etymology works only under particular conditions, then, and affects only rare, technical, or foreign words that speakers assimilate imperfectly. But analogy, a universal fact, belongs to the normal functioning of language. These two phenomena, so similar in some ways, are basically different. They must be carefully separated.

Chapter VII

AGGLUTINATION

1. *Definition*

The importance of analogy was indicated in the last two chapters. Along with analogy there is another force at work in the production of new units: agglutination.

Aside from these two, no other formative device amounts to much. Onomatopoeia (see p. 69), words formed consciously and without recourse to analogy by an individual (e.g. *gas*), and even folk etymology are of little or no importance.

Agglutination is the welding together of two or more originally distinct terms that frequently occur as a syntagm within the sentence into one unit which is absolute or hard to analyze. Such is the agglutinative process. It is a *process*, not a *procedure*, for the latter word implies will or intention, and the absence of will is what characterizes agglutination.

Here are some examples. French speakers first said *ce ci*, using two words, then *ceci* 'this': a new word was the result even though its substance and constituents did not change. Compare also: French *tous jours* 'every day,' *toujours* 'always,' *au jour d'hui* 'on today's day,' *aujourd'hui* 'today,' *dès jà* 'since now,' *déjà* 'already,' *vert jus* 'green juice,' *verjus* 'verjuice, sour grapes.' Agglutination may also weld together the subunits of a word, as we saw (p. 170)

in the case of the Proto-Indo-European superlative **swād-is-to-s* and the Greek superlative *hḗd-isto-s.*

On closer examination we discern three phases in the phenomenon of agglutination:

1) The combining of several terms in a syntagm. The new syntagm is like all other syntagms.

2) Agglutination proper, or the synthesizing of the elements of the syntagm into a new unit. Synthesis takes place independently through a mechanical tendency; when a compound concept is expressed by a succession of very common significant units, the mind gives up analysis—it takes a short-cut—and applies the concept to the whole cluster of signs, which then become a simple unit.

3) Every other change necessary to make the old cluster of signs more like a simple word: unification of accent (*vért-jús* → *verjús*), special phonetic changes, etc.

It is often claimed that phonetic and accentual changes (3) precede conceptual changes (2), and that semantic synthesis is explained through agglutination and material synthesis. But this probably puts the cart before the horse. It is quite likely that *vert jus*, *tous jours*, etc. became simple words because they were grasped as a single idea.

2. *Agglutination and Analogy*

The contrast between analogy and agglutination is striking:

1) In agglutination two or more units are blended into one through synthesis (e.g. French *encore* 'still' from *hanc horam*), or two subunits become one (cf. *héd-isto-s* from **swad-is-to-s*). Against this, analogy starts from lesser units and builds them into greater units. To create *pāg-ānus*, analogy united the radical *pāg-* and the suffix *-ānus*.

2) Agglutination works only in the zone of syntagms. It affects only a particular cluster. It embraces nothing else. In contrast, analogy calls forth associative series as well as syntagms.

3) Above all, agglutination is neither wilful nor active. I have already said that it is a simple mechanical process in which merger takes place spontaneously. Analogy, on the contrary, is a procedure that requires analyses and combinations, intelligent action, and intention.

Construction and *structure* are often used in discussing word formation, but their meaning differs, depending on whether they are applied to agglutination or to analogy. When applied to agglutination, they suggest that the elements in contact in a syntagm slowly set, i.e. are synthesized to such an extent that their original components are wiped out completely. But when applied to analogy, construction means the arrangement obtained in one swoop, in an act of speaking, by the reuniting of a certain number of elements borrowed from different associative series.

The importance of separating the two formative methods is obvious. In Latin, for instance, *possum* is only the welding together of two words, *potis* and *sum* 'I am the master': it is an agglutinate word. In contrast, *signifer*, *agricola*, etc., are products of analogy, constructions based on models furnished by the language. Only analogical creations may be named *compounds* or *derivatives*.[9]

Often it is difficult to say whether an analyzable form arose through agglutination or as an analogical construction. Linguists have discussed endlessly the question of the Proto-Indo-European forms **es-mi*, **es-ti*, **ed-mi*, etc. Were the elements *es–*, *ed–*, etc. real words during a very old period, and were they later agglutinated with other words (*mi*, *ti*, etc.)? Or are **es-mi*, **es-ti*, etc. the result of combinations of elements drawn from other similar complex units? In the latter case, agglutination would antedate the formation of inflectional endings in Proto-Indo-European. In the

[9] This amounts to saying that the two phenomena act jointly in the history of language. But agglutination always occurs first and is what furnishes models for analogy. For instance, the type of compound that gave *hippo-dromo-s*, etc. in Greek started through partial agglutination at a period when inflectional endings were unknown in Proto-Indo-European (*ekwo dromo* was then equivalent to a compound like *country house*) but through analogy became a productive means of forming new compounds before complete welding of its elements occurred. The same is true of the future tense in French (*je ferai* 'I shall do,' etc.), which arose in Vulgar Latin through agglutination of the infinitive with the present tense of the verb *habēre* (*facere habeō* 'I have to do'). Through the intervention of analogy, agglutination thus creates syntactical types and is grammatical; left alone, it pushes the synthesis of elements to the point where the elements become complete units and produces only unanalyzable or unproductive words (e.g. *hanc hōram* → French *encore* 'still'), i.e. it is lexicological. [Ed.]

absence of historical evidence, the question is probably unanswerable.

Only history can enlighten us. Whenever we can state that a simple element was once two or more elements in the sentence, we have an agglutinate word: e.g. Latin *hunc*, which goes back to *hon ce* (*ce* is attested epigraphically). But when historical information is lacking, it is hard to determine what is due to agglutination and what results from analogy.

Chapter VIII

DIACHRONIC UNITS, IDENTITIES AND REALITIES

Static linguistics works with units that owe their existence to their synchronic arrangement. Everything that has just been said proves that in a diachronic succession the elements are not delimited once and for all as this drawing might suggest:

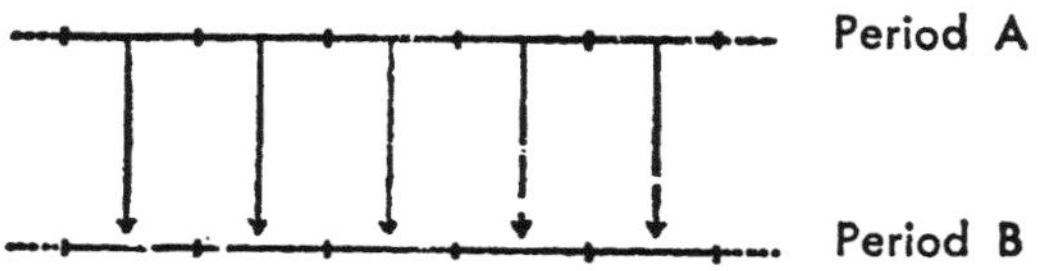

Rather, the elements are distributed differently from one moment to the next by virtue of the events enacted in the theatre of language, with the result that they would be more aptly represented by the drawing:

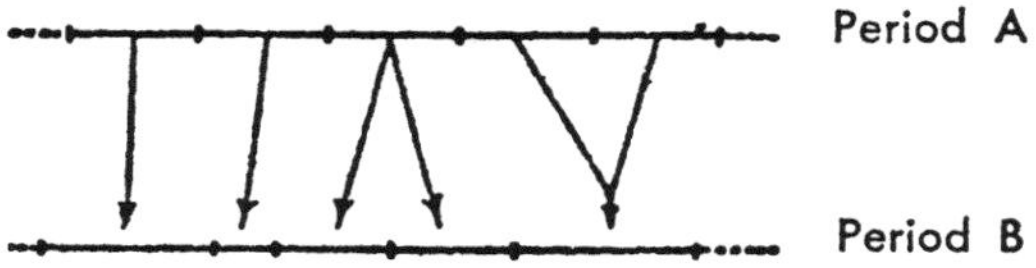

This is confirmed by all that has been said about the consequences of phonetic evolution, analogy, agglutination, etc.

Almost every example cited up to this point belongs to word-formation. Here is one from syntax. Proto-Indo-European had no prepositions; the relations that they indicate were expressed by numerous cases that had great signaling power. Nor did Proto-Indo-European use preverbs in compounding verbs; it used only particles—small words added to the sentence in order to pinpoint and modify the action of the verb. For instance, there was nothing to correspond to Latin *īre ob mortem* 'to confront death,' or to *obīre mortem;* the form would have been *īre mortem ob*. This was still the state of Proto-Greek: (1) In *óreos baínō káta, óreos baínō* by itself means "I come from the mountain," the genitive having the value of the ablative; *káta* adds the qualification "by coming down." During another period the form was (2) *katà óreos baínō*, where *katà* acts as a preposition, or even (3) *kata-baínō óreos*, through the agglutination of the verb and particle, which had become a preverb.

Here are found two or three distinct phenomena, depending on the interpretation of the units: (1) A new class of words, prepositions, was created simply by shifting existing units. A particular arrangement which was originally of no significance and probably due to chance, allowed a new grouping: *kata*, independent at first, was united with the substantive *óreos*, and the whole was joined to *baínō* to serve as its complement. (2) A new verbal class (*katabaínō*) appeared. This is another psychological grouping, also favored by a special distribution of units and consolidated by agglutination. (3) As a natural consequence, the meaning of the genitive ending (*óre-os*) was weakened. Then *katà* had to express the basic idea formerly carried by the genitive alone and the importance of the ending decreased proportionately. The starting point of the future disappearance of *–os* is in the last phenomenon.

In all three instances, there was then a new distribution of units. The old substance was given new functions. The important thing is that no phonetic change intervened to bring about any of the shifts. But we must not think that meaning alone was involved even though the substance did not change. There is no syntactical phenomenon without the uniting of a certain chain of concepts with a certain chain of phonic units (see p. 139), and this is the very relation that was modified. The sounds remained, but the significant units were no longer the same.

We saw earlier (p. 75) that what alters the sign is a shift in the relationship between the signifier and the signified. This definition applies not only to the alteration of the terms of the system but also to the evolution of the system itself. The diachronic phenomenon in its totality is only that and nothing more.

But the mere recording of a certain shift of synchronic units is by no means a complete report of what has happened in language. There is also the problem of the self-contained *diachronic unit.* With respect to every event, we must ask which element has been subjected directly to change. We have already met a similar problem in dealing with phonetic changes (see p. 94). They affect only isolated phonemes, leaving the word-unit untouched. Since diachronic events are of all kinds, many other such questions would have to be answered, and the units delimited in diachrony would not necessarily correspond to those delimited in synchrony. According to the principle laid down in Part One, our concept of the unit cannot be the same in both cases. In any event, we cannot accurately define the unit until we have studied it from both viewpoints, the static and the evolutionary. Until we solve the problem of the diachronic unit, we cannot penetrate the outer guise of evolution and reach its essence. Understanding units is just as important here as in synchrony if we are to separate illusion from reality (see p. 110).

But *diachronic identity* poses another difficult question. Indeed, before I can say that a unit has remained identical or that it has changed its form or meaning while continuing to exist as a distinct unit—for both possibilities exist—I must know the basis for stating that an element taken from one period (e.g. French *chaud* 'warm') is the same as an element taken from another period (e.g. Latin *calidum*).

The answer will doubtless be that *calidum* must have become *chaud* through regular sound changes and that therefore *chaud* = *calidum.* This is a phonetic identity. The same applies to *sevrer* 'wean' and *sēparāre. Fleurir* 'flower,' however, is not the same thing as *flōrēre* (which would have become **flouroir*), etc.

Diachronic identity seems at first glance to be satisfactorily accounted for by phonetic correspondence. But it is actually impossible for sound alone to account for identity. Doubtless it is correct to say that Latin *mare* should appear in French as *mer* 'sea' because every *a* became *e* under certain conditions, unstressed final *e* fell, etc. But to say that these correspondences (*a* → *e*, *e* → zero, etc.) account for identity is to reverse the facts, for I am using the correspondence between *mare* and *mer* to decide that *a* became *e*, that final *e* fell, etc.

One speaker may say *se facher* 'become angry' while someone who lives in another part of France says *se fôcher*, but this difference is unimportant in comparison with the grammatical facts that allow us to recognize one and the same unit of language in these two distinct forms. To say that two words as different as *calidum* and *chaud* constitute a diachronic identity means simply that speakers passed from one form to the other through a series of synchronic identities in speaking without there being a break in their common bond despite successive phonetic changes. That is why I could state that knowing how *Gentlemen!* retains its identity when repeated several times during a lecture is just as interesting as knowing why *pas* (negation) is identical to *pas* (noun) in French, or again, why *chaud* is identical to *calidum* (see p. 107 f.). The second problem is really but an extension and a complication of the first.

APPENDICES TO PARTS THREE AND FOUR

1. *Subjective and Objective Analysis*

The analysis that speakers constantly make of the units of language is *subjective analysis.* One must guard against confusing subjective analysis with *objective analysis,* which is based on history. In a form like Greek *híppos,* the grammarian singles out three elements: a root, a suffix, and an ending (*hípp-o-s*). But Greek speakers saw only two elements (*hípp-os*, see p. 155). Objective analysis reveals four subunits in *amābās* (*am-ā-bā-s*); Latin speakers recognized only three (*amā-bā-s*); perhaps they even thought of *–bās* as an inflectional whole in opposition to the radical. In French *entier* 'whole' (Latin *in-teger* 'intact'), *enfant* 'child' (Latin *in-fans* 'one who does not speak'), and *enceinte* 'pregnant' (Latin *in-cincta* 'without a girdle'), the historian may single out a common prefix *en–* that stands for Latin privative *in–;* the subjective analysis of speakers completely ignores the prefix.

The grammarian is prone to think that spontaneous analyses of language are wrong; the truth is that subjective analysis is no more false than "false" analogy (see p. 162 f.). Language never errs; it simply takes a different viewpoint. There is no common yardstick for both the analysis of speakers and the analysis of the historian although both use the same procedure—the confrontation of series that have a common element. Both analyses are justifiable, and each retains its value. In the last resort, however, only the speakers' analysis matters, for it is based directly on the facts of language.

Historical analysis is but a modified form of subjective analysis. Basically, it consists of projecting the constructions of different periods on a single plane. It resembles spontaneous analysis in that it tries to identify the subunits of words but differs in that it synthesizes all the divisions made in the course of time with a view to reaching the oldest one. The word is like a house in which the arrangement and function of different rooms has been changed several times. Objective analysis adds up and schematizes the successive arrangements, but for those who live in the house there is always but one arrangement. The analysis *hípp-o-s*, which was discussed above, is not false, for it was framed in the minds of speakers; it is merely "anachronistic"; it goes back to a period that preceded the one from which the word is taken. Older *hípp-o-s* does not contradict the *hípp-os* of Classical Greek, but the two analyses cannot be judged in the same way. This again points up the radical distinction between diachrony and synchrony.

And that allows us also to resolve a methodological issue which is still pending in linguistics. The old school divided words into roots, themes, suffixes, etc. and attached an absolute value to these distinctions. One would think, to read Bopp and his disciples, that the Greeks had carried with them from time immemorial a collection of roots and suffixes which they used in fabricating words, and that they took the trouble to manufacture their words while speaking, e.g. that *pắter* was to them the root *pă* + the suffix *-ter*, that *dōsō* stood for the sum of *dō* + *sō* + a personal ending, etc.

There had to be a reaction against the aberrations of the old school, and the appropriate slogan was this: Observe what happens in the everyday speech of present-day languages and attribute to older periods no process, no phenomenon that is not observable today. And since the living language generally does not lend itself to analyses like those made by Bopp, the neogrammarians, faithful to their principle, declared that roots, themes, suffixes, etc. are mere abstractions which should be used solely to facilitate exposition. But unless there is some justification for setting up these categories, why bother? And if they are set up, by what authority can one division like *hípp-o-s*, for instance, be declared better than another like *hípp-os*?

The new school, after pointing out the shortcomings of the old doctrine—and this was easy—was satisfied to reject the theory but remain fettered in practice to a scientific apparatus that it was powerless to discard. When we examine "abstractions" more closely, we see what part of reality they actually stand for, and a simple corrective measure suffices to give an exact and justifiable meaning to the expedients of the grammarian. That is what I have tried to do above by showing that objective analysis, which is intimately linked to subjective analysis of the living language, has a definite and rightful place in linguistic methodology.

2. *Subjective Analysis and the Defining of Subunits*

In analysis, then, we can set up a method and formulate definitions only after adopting a synchronic viewpoint. That is what I wish to show through a few observations about word-parts: prefixes, roots, radicals, suffixes, and inflectional endings.[10]

First, the *inflectional ending*, i.e. the word-final variable element that distinguishes the different forms of a noun or verb paradigm. In *zeúgnū-mi*, *zeúgnū-s*, *zeúgnū-si*, *zeúgnū-men*, etc. 'I harness,' etc., the inflectional endings *–mi*, *–s*, *–si*, etc. stand out simply because they are in opposition to each other and to the preceding part of the word (*zeugnū́–*). We recall that in Czech the absence of an inflectional ending plays the same role as a regular ending (e.g. the genitive plural *žen* in opposition to nominative singular *žena;* see p. 86 and p. 118). Similarly, Greek *zeúgnū!* '(thou) harness!' against *zeúgnu-te* '(you) harness!' or *rhêtor!* against *rhêtor-os*, etc. and French *marš!*, written *marche* '(thou) walk!' against *maršõ!* '(let's) walk!' are all inflected forms with a zero ending.

By eliminating the inflectional ending we obtain the *inflectional theme* or *radical*. This is generally the common element which emerges spontaneously when we compare a series of related words, whether inflected or not, and which conveys the idea common to every word. In the French series *roulis* 'roll,' *rouleau* 'rolling-pin,' *roulage* 'roller,' *roulement* 'rolling,' for instance, the radical *roul–* stands out. But in their analysis, speakers often single out several kinds, or rather grades, of radicals in the same family of words. *Zeugnū́–*, separated above from *zeúgnū-mi*, *zeúgnū-s*, etc., is a first-grade radical. It is not irreducible, for the division *zeug-nu* is self-evident if we compare *zeúgnu–* with other series (*zeúgnūmi*, *zeuktós*, *zeûksis*, *zeuktêr*, *zugón*, etc. on the one hand and *zeúgnūmi*,

[10] F. de Saussure did not study the question of compounds—not from the synchronic viewpoint at any rate. This part of the problem must therefore be set aside. Of course the distinction made above between compounds and agglutinate words does not apply here where analysis of a language-state is concerned. It is scarcely necessary to point out that this account of subunits does not pretend to answer the more difficult question raised above (pp. 105, 110 f.) concerning the defining of the word-unit. [Ed.]

deíknūmi, órnūmi, etc. on the other). *Zeug–* (with its alternate forms *zeug–, zeuk–, zug–;* see p. 160) is therefore a second-grade radical. But *zeug-* is irreducible. To carry its decomposition further by comparing related forms is not possible.

The *root* is the irreducible element common to all words of the same family. But any subjective and synchronic analysis separates material elements only by considering the share of meaning that matches each element, and the root is in this respect the element in which the meaning common to all related words reaches the highest degree of abstraction and generality. Naturally, indefiniteness varies from one root to the next, but it also depends somewhat on the extent to which the radical is reducible. The more the radical is shortened, the greater the likelihood that its meaning will become abstract. Thus *zeugmátion* suggests a little team, *zeûgma* any team whatsoever, and *zeug–* the indefinite notion of yoking or harnessing.

It follows that a root cannot constitute a word and have an inflectional ending joined directly to it. Indeed, a word always stands for a fairly definite idea, at least from a grammatical viewpoint, and this is contrary to the general and abstract nature of the root. But what about the numerous roots and inflectional themes that apparently mingle? Take Greek *phlôks,* genitive *phlogós* against the root *phleg–: phlog–* which is found in every word of the same family (cf. *phlég-ō,* etc.). Does this not contradict the distinction which we have just set up? No, for we must separate *phleg–: phlog–* with a general meaning from *phlog–* with its special meaning or risk considering the material form only to the exclusion of meaning. The same material element here has two different values. It therefore comprises two distinct linguistic elements (see p. 105). Above, it was shown that *zeúgnū!* is a word with an inflectional ending of zero. In the same way, *phlog–* is a theme with a zero suffix. No confusion is possible. The radical is distinct from the root even when phonetically identical to it.

The root is then a reality in the mind of speakers. To be sure, speakers do not always single it out with equal precision. On this point there are differences, either within the same language or from one language to another.

In certain idioms, definite characteristics call the root to the attention of speakers. In German, for instance, the root is fairly uniform; almost always monosyllabic (cf. *streit–*, *bind–*, *haft–*, etc.), it follows certain structural rules; phonemes do not appear haphazardly; certain word-final combinations of consonants, such as occlusive + liquid, are ruled out; *werk–* is possible, *wekr–* is not; we find *helf–*, *werd–*, but not *hefl–*, *wedr–*.

We recall that regular alternations, especially between vowels, tend generally to strengthen rather than to weaken our feeling for roots and subunits. Here also, German with its variable interplay of ablauts (see p. 158) differs greatly from French. Semitic roots exhibit the same characteristic but in even greater proportions. Here the alternations are quite regular and govern a large number of complex oppositions (cf. Hebrew *qāṭal*, *qṭaltem*, *qṭōl*, *qiṭlū*, etc., all forms of the same verb meaning 'kill'). In addition, Semitic roots have a trait similar to German monosyllabism but even more striking. They always include three consonants (see below, pp. 230 ff.).

French is completely different. It has few alternations and, side by side with monosyllabic roots (*roul–*, *march–*, *mang–*), many roots composed of two or even three syllables (*commenc–*, *hésit–*, *épouvant–*). Besides, these roots contain—chiefly in final position—such varied combinations that they cannot be reduced to rules (cf. *tu-er* 'kill,' *régn-er* 'reign,' *guid-er* 'guide,' *grond-er* 'growl,' *souffl-er* 'blow,' *tard-er* 'delay,' *entr-er* 'enter,' *hurl-er* 'bark,' etc.). That the feeling for roots scarcely exists in French should come as no surprise.

The defining of the root has as its counterpart the defining of prefixes and suffixes. The *prefix* goes before the part of the word that is recognized as the radical (e.g. *hupo–* in Greek *hupozeúgnūmi*). The *suffix* is the element added to the root to make a radical (e.g. *zeug-mat–*) or to a first-grade radical to make a second-grade radical (e.g. *zeugmat-io–*). We saw above that the suffix, like the inflectional ending, may be zero. The extracting of the suffix is just one more side to the analysis of the radical.

The suffix sometimes has a concrete meaning, a semantic value, as in *zeuk-tēr*, where *–tēr–* names the agent or performer of an action. At other times the suffix has a mere grammatical function, as in *zeúg-nū* (*–mi*), where *–nū* expresses the idea of the present. The prefix may also play both roles, but our languages rarely give it a grammatical function: e.g. the *ge–* of German past participles (*ge-setzt*, etc.), the perfective prefixes of Slavic (Russian *na-pisát'*, etc.).

The prefix also differs from the suffix through a characteristic which, though fairly general, is not absolute. The prefix is more sharply delimited, for it is easier to separate from the word as a whole. This is due to the very nature of the prefix. A complete word usually remains after the prefix is removed (cf. French *recommencer* 'recommence': *commencer* 'commence,' *indigne* 'unworthy': *digne* 'worthy,' *maladroit* 'unskilled': *adroit* 'skilled,' *contrepoids* 'counterweight': *poids* 'weight,' etc.). Latin, Greek, and German offer even more striking examples. Moreover, many prefixes function as independent words: cf. French *contre* 'against,' *mal* 'ill,' *avant* 'before,' *sur* 'on,' German *unter*, *vor*, etc., and Greek *katá*, *pró*, etc. But the suffix is altogether different. The radical element obtained by removing the suffix is not a complete word: e.g. French *organisation* 'organization': *organis–*, German *Trennung: trenn–*, Greek *zeúgma: zeug–*, etc.[11] Furthermore, the suffix has no independent existence.

The result is that the first part of the radical is usually delimited beforehand. The speaker knows, before he has made any comparisons with other forms, where to draw the line between the prefix and what follows. This is not true of the last part of the word. There one can draw no boundary without first comparing forms that have the same radical or suffix, and the resulting delimitations will vary according to the nature of the terms compared.

Subjectively, suffixes and radicals derive their value solely from syntagmatic and associative oppositions. We can usually find a formative and a radical element in any two opposing parts of a word, provided that possible oppositions exist. In Latin *dictātōrem*, for instance, we shall see the radical *dictātōr-(em)* if we compare it with *consul-em*, *ped-em*, etc.; *dictā-(tōrem)* if we compare it with *lic-tōrem*, *scrip-tōrem*, etc.; and *dic-(tātōrem)* if we think of *pō-tātōrem*, *can-tātōrem*, etc. Generally, and under favorable circumstances, the speaker may make every imaginable division (e.g. *dictāt-ōrem*, from *am-ōrem*, *ard-ōrem*, etc.; *dict-ātōrem*, from *ōr-*

[11] This pattern, though not necessarily applicable to English words derived from Germanic sources (*teach-er*, *sad-ly*, *hope-less*), is characteristic of English words derived from Romance sources (*duch-ess*, *appari-tion*, *cap-able*). [Tr.]

ātōrem, ar-ātōrem, etc.). We know that the results of these spontaneous analyses appear in the analogical formations of each period (see p. 170). Through them, we can single out the subunits (roots, prefixes, suffixes, and endings) which language recognizes and the values which it attaches to them.

3. *Etymology*

Etymology is neither a distinct discipline nor a division of evolutionary linguistics. It is only a special application of the principles that relate to synchronic and diachronic facts. It goes back into the history of words until it finds something to explain them.

To speak of the origin of a word and say that it "comes" from another word may imply several different things: thus French *sel* comes from Latin *sal* through a simple sound change; *labourer* 'plough' comes from Old French *labourer* 'work' solely through a change in meaning; *couver* 'brood' comes from Latin *cubare* 'be in bed' through a change in both meaning and sound; finally, the statement that French *pommier* 'apple-tree' comes from *pomme* 'apple' brings in the relation of grammatical derivation. The first three examples concern diachronic identities; the fourth is based on the synchronic relation of several different terms, and everything that has been said about analogy shows that this relation is the most important part of etymological research.

It is not possible to fix the etymology of *bonus* merely by going back to *dvenos.* But if *bis* is found to go back to *dvis,* implying a relation with *duo,* then the procedure is etymological. The same applies to the comparing of French *oiseau* 'bird' and Latin *avicellus,* for comparison reveals the link between *oiseau* and *avis.*

Etymology is then mainly the explaining of words through the historical study of their relations with other words. To explain means to relate to known terms, and in linguistics, *to explain a word is to relate it to other words,* for there are no necessary relations between sound and meaning (principle of the arbitrary nature of the sign, see p. 67 f.).

Etymology does not simply explain isolated words and stop there. It compiles the history of word families and of families of formative elements—prefixes, suffixes, etc.

Like static and evolutionary linguistics, etymology describes facts. But this description is not methodical, for it follows no fixed course. In compiling the history of a word, etymology borrows its data alternately from phonetics, morphology, semantics, etc. To reach its goal, etymology uses every means placed at its disposal by linguistics, but it is not concerned with the nature of the operations that it is obliged to perform.

PART FOUR

Geographical Linguistics

Chapter I

CONCERNING THE DIVERSITY OF LANGUAGES

As we approach the question of the spatial relations of the linguistic phenomenon, we leave internal linguistics and enter external linguistics. The scope of external linguistics was outlined in Chapter V of the Introduction.

The most striking thing about the study of languages is their diversity—linguistic differences that appear when we pass from one country to another or even from one region to another. Divergences in time often escape the observer, but divergences in space immediately force themselves upon him; even savages grasp them, thanks to their contacts with other tribes that speak a different language. Indeed, these comparisons are what makes a nation aware of its idiom.

We note in passing that this feeling makes primitive people look upon language as a habit or custom like dress or weapons. The term *idiom* rightly designates language as reflecting the traits peculiar to a community (Greek *idiōma* had already acquired the meaning 'special custom'). This notion, though appropriate, becomes misleading when one goes so far as to see language as an attribute, not of the nation, but of race, in the same way as the color of the skin or the shape of the head.

It is also worth noting that each nation believes in the superiority of its own idiom and is quick to regard the man who uses a different language as incapable of speaking. For instance, Greek *bárbaros* apparently meant 'one who stammers' and was related to Latin *balbus;* in Russian, Germans are called *Nêmtsy* 'mutes.'

Geographical diversity was, then, the first observation made in linguistics. It determined the initial form of scientific research in language, even among the Greeks. To be sure, the Greeks were concerned only with the diversity of the different Hellenic dialects, but this was because their interest did not generally go beyond the borders of Greece proper.

Having noticed that two idioms differ, one instinctively looks for similarities. This is a natural tendency of speakers. Peasants like to compare their patois with the one spoken in a neighboring village. People who speak several languages notice their common traits. But for some strange reason science has waited a long time to make use of the results of such observations. For example, the Greeks noticed many resemblances between the Latin vocabulary and their own but were unable to draw any linguistic conclusions.

Scientific observation of linguistic similarities proves that two or more idioms may be akin, i.e. that they have a common origin. A group of related languages makes up a family. Modern linguistics has successively identified several families: the Indo-European, Semitic, Bantu,[1] etc. Comparing these families with each other, in turn, occasionally brings to light older and broader affiliations. There have been attempts to find similarities between Finno-Ugric[2] and Indo-European, between the latter and Semitic, etc., but such comparisons always come up against insuperable barriers. One must not confuse what is probable with what is demonstrable. The universal kinship of languages is not probable, but even if it were true—as the Italian linguist Trombetti[3] believes—it could not be proved because of the excessive number of changes that have intervened.

Beside diversity within related groups, then, there is absolute diversity—differences between languages that have no recognizable or demonstrable kinship. What method should linguistics use in each of these degrees? Let us begin with the second, which is more common. As we have just noted, countless languages and families of

[1] Bantu is a group of languages spoken by South African tribes, mainly the Kaffirs. [Ed.]

[2] Finno-Ugric, which includes—among other languages—Finnish proper or Suomi, Mordvinian, Lapp, etc., is a family of languages spoken in northern Russia and Siberia. Doubtless these languages all go back to a common original idiom. The family is a part of the great Ural-Altaic group of languages, which have no proven common origin although some traits appear in all of them. [Ed.]

[3] See his *L'unità d'origine del linguaggio*, Bologna, 1905. [Ed.]

languages are not related. A good example is Chinese with respect to the Indo-European languages. The fact that they differ does not mean that they cannot be compared, for comparison is always possible and useful; it applies to grammatical organisms and general ways of expressing thought as well as to systems of sound; it also includes diachronic facts, the phonetic evolution of two languages, etc. The possibilities of comparison, though incalculable, are limited by certain constant phonic and psychological data that determine the make-up of any language; reciprocally, the discovery of these constant data is always the main aim of any comparison of related languages.

The other class of differences—those that exist within families of languages—offers an unlimited field for comparison. Two idioms may differ in any degree. They may bear a striking resemblance to each other, like Zend and Sanskrit, or be as entirely dissimilar as Sanskrit and Gaelic. All intermediate degrees are possible: Greek and Latin are more closely related to each other than to Sanskrit, etc. Idioms that differ only slightly are called *dialects*, but this word must be used loosely. We shall see that languages and dialects differ quantitatively, not by nature (see p. 203).

Chapter II

COMPLICATIONS OF GEOGRAPHICAL DIVERSITY

1. *Coexistence of Several Languages at the Same Point*

Up to this point geographical diversity has been presented in its ideal form: there were as many territories as there were different languages. And our method was justifiable, for geographical separation is still the most general force in linguistic diversity. But there are secondary facts that disturb the ideal relationship and cause several languages to coexist in the same territory.

Two things we pass over. First is the real, organic mixture or interpenetration of two idioms that results in a change in the system (cf. English after the Norman Conquest). Second is the political accident of several languages clearly separated in space but included within the boundaries of the same state, as in Switzerland. The only fact that concerns us is that two idioms can exist side by side in the same place without intermingling. This occurs frequently, but is of two kinds.

First, newcomers may superimpose their language on the indigenous language. For instance, in South Africa, two successive colonizations introduced Dutch and English, which now exist alongside several Negro dialects; in the same way, Spanish was implanted in Mexico. Nor are such linguistic encroachments peculiar to modern times. Throughout the centuries nations have intermingled and still kept their idioms distinct. To realize this fact we need only glance at a map of modern Europe: Ireland, with Celtic and English; many of the Irish speak both languages. In Brittany, French and Breton. In the Basque region, French and Spanish as well as Basque. In Finland, Swedish and Finnish have coexisted for a rather long time, and Russian has been added more recently. In Courland and Livonia, Lettish, German and Russian are spoken; German, which was brought in by colonists under the auspices of the Hanseatic League during the Middle Ages, belongs to a special segment of the population; Russian subsequently entered by conquest. Lithuania witnessed the implantation of Polish alongside Lithuanian as a consequence of her former union with Poland, and of Russian as a result of annexation. Until the eighteenth century Slavic and German were used throughout the section of Germany that lies to the east of the Elbe. In other countries languages are even more entangled: in Macedonia every imaginable language is found—Turkish, Bulgarian, Serbian, Greek, Albanian, Rumanian, etc.—and the languages are mixed in different ways in different regions.

Coexisting languages are not always absolutely entangled; there may be a certain relative territorial distribution. Of two languages, one may be spoken in town and the other in the country, but such a distribution is not always clear-cut.

The story was the same in ancient times. A linguistic map of the Roman Empire would show facts like those already described. Toward the close of the Republic, for instance, Campania numbered three or four languages: Oscan, attested by the inscriptions of Pompeii; Greek, the language of the colonists who founded Naples, etc.; Latin; and perhaps even Etruscan, which was the dominant language before the arrival of the Romans. In Carthage, Punic or Phoenician persisted beside Latin (it still existed during the period of the Arab invasion), and Numidian was certainly spoken in Carthaginian territory. One might also suppose that during ancient times unilingual countries in the Mediterranean Basin were the exception.

Invasion is the usual cause of superimposition, but it may also come through peaceful penetration in the form of colonization. Or nomadic tribes may take their dialect with them: that is what the Gypsies did, especially those who settled in Hungary, where they form compact villages; study of their language shows that they must have come from India at some unknown time in the past. In Dobruja, at the mouth of the Danube, scattered Tatar villages show up like tiny specks on the linguistic map of the region.

2. *Literary Language and Local Idiom*

As a further step, linguistic unity may be destroyed when a natural idiom is influenced by a literary language. This never fails to happen whenever a nation reaches a certain stage of civilization. By literary language I mean not only the language of literature but also, in a more general sense, any kind of cultivated language, official or otherwise, that serves the whole community. Given free reign, a language has only dialects, none of which has the advantage over the others, and for this reason it habitually splinters. But as communications improve with a growing civilization, one of the existing dialects is chosen by a tacit convention of some sort to be the vehicle of everything that affects the nation as a whole. The reasons for the choice differ widely. Sometimes preference goes to the dialect of the region where civilization is most advanced or to the province that has political supremacy and wields the central power. Sometimes the court imposes its dialect on the nation. The privileged dialect, after it has been promoted to the rank of official and standard language, seldom remains the same as it was before. It acquires dialectal elements from other regions and becomes more and more composite, though without losing completely its original character. Thus the dialect of the Ile de France is clearly recognizable in literary French and the Toscan in Standard Italian. But the literary language is not imposed from one day to the next, and a majority of the population is found to be bilingual, speaking both the standard language and the local patois. This occurs in many parts of France, like Savoy, where French is an imported language that has not yet eliminated the regional patois, and generally in Germany and Italy, where dialects persist alongside the official languages.

It has been the same with all nations that have reached a certain stage of civilization. The Greeks had their *koinè*, derived from Attic and Ionian, along with coexisting local dialects. Presumably even ancient Babylon had its official language and its regional dialects.

Does a standard language necessarily imply the use of writing? The Homeric poems seem to prove that it does not. Even though they were composed at a time when writing was used little or not at all, their language is conventional and has every characteristic of a literary language.

The facts discussed in this chapter are so common that they might pass as normal forces in the history of languages. But to keep to our purpose we must turn aside from everything that obscures the basic phenomenon of natural geographical diversity and consider it apart from any importation of a foreign language or any formation of a literary language. This schematic simplification seems to go against reality, but the natural fact must first be studied in itself.

Consistently with this principle, we shall say that Brussels is Germanic since it is in the Flemish part of Belgium; though French is spoken there, what matters is the boundary between the Flemish and Walloon territories. Liège is Romance for the same reason: it is in Walloon territory; French is a foreign language that happens to have been superimposed on a dialect of the same stock. Similarly, Brest belongs linguistically to Breton; the French spoken there has nothing in common with the native idiom of Brittany. Berlin, where High German is heard almost exclusively, is Low German, etc.

Chapter III

CAUSES OF GEOGRAPHICAL DIVERSITY

1. *Time, the Basic Cause*

Whereas absolute diversity poses a purely speculative problem (see p. 192 f.), diversity within related languages can be observed and traced back to unity. That Vulgar Latin took different paths in the northern and southern parts of Gaul explains the common origin of French and Provençal.

By simplifying the theoretical situation as much as possible, we can get at the basic cause of differentiation in space. What would happen if a language spoken at one clearly delimited point—e.g. a small island—were transported by colonists to another clearly delimited point—e.g. another island? After a certain length of time various differences affecting vocabulary, grammar, pronunciation and the like would separate the language of the source (S) from the language of the settlement (S′).

It is wrong to imagine that only the transplanted idiom will change while the original idiom remains fixed or vice versa. An innovation may begin on either side or on both sides at the same time. Take a linguistic feature *a* that can be replaced by *b*, *c*, *d*, etc. Differentiation may occur in three different ways:

$$\frac{a \text{ (Source S)}}{a \text{ (Settlement S')}} \begin{cases} \rightarrow \dfrac{b}{a} \\[2ex] \rightarrow \dfrac{a}{c} \\[2ex] \rightarrow \dfrac{b}{c} \end{cases}$$

A one-sided approach will not do, for the innovations of either language are of equal importance.

What created the differences? It is illusory to think that space alone was responsible. By itself, space cannot influence language. On the day following their arrival at S′ the colonists from S spoke exactly the same language as on the preceding day. It is easy to forget about the factor of time because it is less concrete than space, but it is actually the cause of linguistic differentiation. Geographical diversity should be called temporal diversity.

Take two differentiating features *b* and *c*. No speakers have passed from the first to the second or from the second to the first. To discover how unity became diversity, we must go back to the original *a* for which *b* and *c* were substituted: *a* gave way to the later forms *b* and *c*. Hence the following diagram of geographical differentiation which will cover all similar cases:

$$\begin{array}{ccc} \mathrm{S} & & \mathrm{S'} \\ a & \longleftrightarrow & a \\ \downarrow & & \downarrow \\ b & & c \end{array}$$

The separation of the two idioms shows the tangible form of the phenomenon but does not explain it. Undoubtedly divergence in space was a necessary condition—no matter how small the amount—but by itself distance does not create differences. Volume is measured, not by one surface, but by adding a third dimension, depth; similarly, geographical differentiation is pictured completely only when projected in time.

One objection might be that differences in environment, climate, topography, and local customs (e.g. customs of mountaineers contrasted with those of a maritime population) influence language, and that our variations are therefore conditioned geographically. Such influences are open to dispute, however (see p. 147 f.). Even if they could be proved, a further distinction would be in order: *direction of movement*, which is governed in each instance by imponderable forces that can neither be demonstrated nor described, is attributable to environment. At a particular moment and in a particular environment *u* became *ü*. Why did it change at that moment and in that place, and why did it become *ü* instead of *o?* That question we cannot answer. But *change itself* (leaving out the special direction it takes and its particular manifestations)—in short, the instability of language—stems from time alone. Geographical diversity is then a secondary side of the general phenomenon. The unity of related languages is found only in time. Unless the comparative linguist thoroughly assimilates this principle, he is likely to delude himself.

2. *Effect of Time on Continuous Territory*

Now take a unilingual country, i.e. one with a uniform language and a stable population, like Gaul around 450 A.D., when Latin was well established everywhere. What will happen?

(1) Since there is no such thing as absolute immobility in speech (see pp. 75 ff.), the language will no longer be the same after a certain length of time.

(2) Evolution will not be uniform throughout the territory but will vary from zone to zone; no records indicate that any language has ever changed in the same way throughout its territory. Therefore, it is not the diagram:

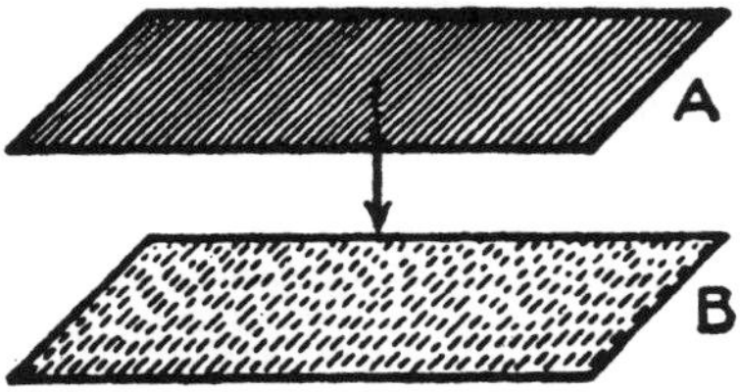

but the diagram:

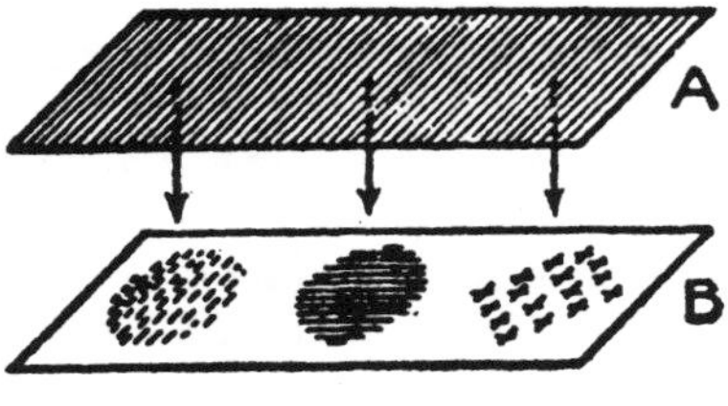

that gives the true picture.

How do differences that result in the most varied dialectal forms originate? What pattern does their evolution follow? Differentiation through time, which is not so simple as it seems at first, has two main characteristics:

(1) Evolution takes the form of successive and precise innovations that include as many partial facts as could be enumerated, described, and classified according to their nature (phonetic, lexicological, morphological, syntactical, etc.).

(2) Each innovation embraces a definite and delimited area. There are two possibilities: either the area of the innovation embraces the whole territory and creates no dialectal differences (the less usual possibility), or the change affects only a part of the territory, each dialectal fact having its special zone (the more common occurrence). We can illustrate with phonetic changes, but other innovations are the same. For instance, while part of a territory may witness the change of *a* to *e:*

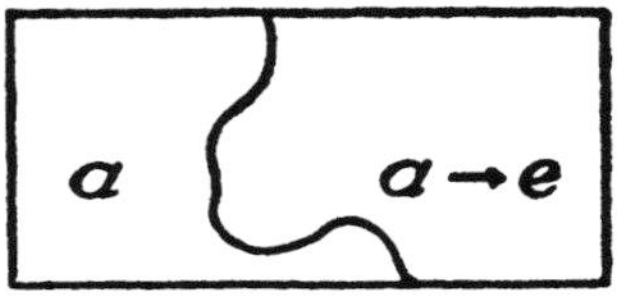

it is possible that on the same territory but within other limits, another change, such as *s* to *z*, will occur:

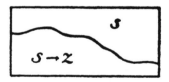

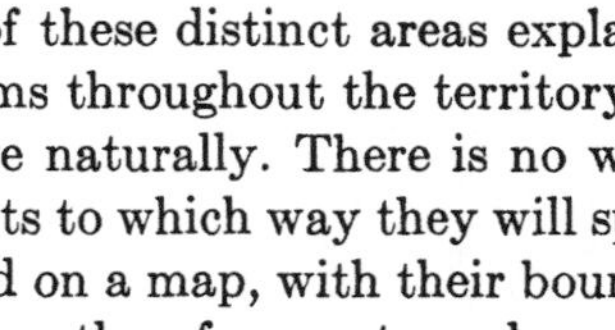

and the existence of these distinct areas explains the diversity of regional speech-forms throughout the territory of a language that is allowed to evolve naturally. There is no way to foresee these zones; nothing points to which way they will spread; all we can do is record them. Laid on a map, with their boundaries crossing and recrossing each other, they form extremely complicated patterns. At times their configuration is paradoxical. Thus *c* and *g* changed before *a* to *tš*, *dž*, then *š*, *ž* (cf. *cantum* → *chant* 'song,' *virga* → *verge* 'rod') throughout northern France except in Picardy and part of Normandy, where *c* and *g* remained intact (cf. Picard *cat* for *chat* 'cat,' *rescapé* for *réchappé*, which was recently adopted by French,[4] *vergue* from *virga*, cited above, etc.).

What is the result of differentiation through time? At one moment in history a single language may reign throughout a particular territory, and five or ten centuries later the inhabitants of two of its extremes probably will not be able to understand each other. At any particular point, however, speakers will still understand the speech-forms of neighboring regions. A traveler going from one end of the country to the other would notice only small dialectal differences from one locality to the next. But the sum of these differences would increase, and eventually he would come to a language that the inhabitants of this starting point would not understand. Or if, starting from a given point in the territory, he traveled outward, now in one direction, now in another, he would find the sum of these differences increasing in each direction, but with one sum differing from the other.

Peculiarities found in the dialects of one village will reappear in neighboring localities, but there is nothing to show exactly how far each peculiarity will reach. For instance, in Douvaine, a locality in the department of Upper-Savoy, the name of Geneva is pronounced *ðenva*. This pronunciation is heard far to the east and to the south, but on the other side of Lake Geneva speakers say *dzenva*. Still, it is not a question of two clearly distinct dialects, for the boundaries of some other phenomenon would be different. In Douvaine, speakers say *daue* for *deux* 'two,' but this pronunciation has a much more restricted zone than *ðenva*. At the foot of the Salève, a few kilometers away, speakers say *due*.

3. *Dialects Have No Natural Boundaries*

The current practice, which differs from ours, is to picture dialects as perfectly defined linguistic types, bounded in all directions and covering distinct zones placed side by side on a map (*a*, *b*, *c*, *d*, etc.). But natural dialectal transformations produce entirely different results. As soon as we studied each phenomenon separately and determined its spread, our old notion had to give way to the new one: there are only natural dialectal features, not natural dialects; in other words, there are as many dialects as there are localities.

[4] See page 156. [Tr.]

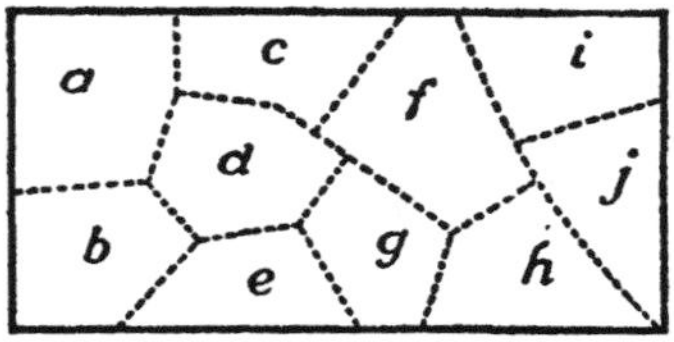

The notion of natural dialects is therefore incompatible with the notion of fixed well-defined zones. This leaves us with two choices: (1) we may define a dialect by the totality of its characteristics—which involves choosing one point on the map and encompassing only the regional speech-forms of a single locality since the same peculiarities will not extend beyond this point; or (2) we may define a dialect by one of its characteristics, and simply map the spread of this characteristic—which obviously is an artificial procedure since the boundaries that we mark off correspond to no dialectal reality.

Research in dialectal characteristics was the point of departure for works on linguistic cartography. The model linguistic atlas is Gilliéron's *Atlas linguistique de la France*. Wenker's map of Germany should also be mentioned.[5] The form of the atlas is predetermined, for we have to study a country region by region, and a map includes only a small number of the dialectal characteristics of each region. One must sift the facts for each region many times to bring to light the phonetic, lexicological, morphological, etc. peculiarities that are superimposed on each other. Such an undertaking requires a staff of experts, well-planned questionnaires, the co-operation of local correspondents, etc. One noteworthy project is the investigation of the patois of French-speaking Switzerland. Linguistic atlases are useful in that they furnish material for works on dialectology. Many recent monographs are based on Gilliéron's *Atlas*.

The boundaries of dialectal characteristics have been called *isogloss lines* or *isoglosses*. This name, coined on the model of *isotherme*, is obscure and inappropriate, for it means 'having the same language.' Since *glosseme* means 'idiomatic character,' the

[5] Cf. also Weigand, *Linguistischer Atlas des dakorumänischen Gebiets* (1909) and Millardet, *Petit atlas linguistique d'une région des Landes* (1910). [S.]

expression *isoglossematic lines*, if practical, would be more appropriate. But I prefer to use *innovating waves*, a descriptive expression that goes back to J. Schmidt. Chapter III will show the reasons for my preference.

A glance at a linguistic atlas will sometimes reveal two or three waves that almost coincide or even overlap in one zone:

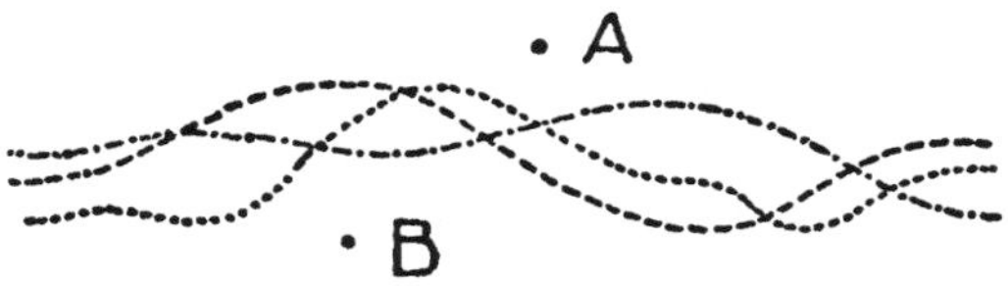

The two points A and B, which are separated by such a zone, obviously have some divergencies and constitute two rather clearly differentiated forms of speech. These concordances, instead of being partial, may characterize the whole perimeter of two or more zones:

A dialect is defined, roughly speaking, by a sufficient accumulation of such concordances. Their foundations are social, political, religious, etc., matters which do not concern us at the moment but which veil, without ever erasing completely, the basic and natural fact of differentiation from zone to zone.

4. *Languages Have No Natural Boundaries*

Precisely how a language differs from a dialect is hard to specify. Often a dialect is called a language because it has produced a literature. This is true of Portuguese and Dutch. Intelligibility also plays a part; everyone would agree that people who do nc' understand each other speak different languages. Still, languages that have evolved over continuous territory and among stable populations exhibit, on a broader scale, the same facts as dialects. Innovating waves appear here too, but with this difference: they embrace a zone common to several languages.

It is impossible, even in our hypothetical examples, to set up boundaries between dialects. The same applies to related languages. The size of the territory makes no difference. We would be unable to say where High German begins and Low German ends, and would find it just as impossible to draw the dividing line between German and Dutch, or between French and Italian. There are extreme points where we may assert, "Here French predominates, here Italian," but in the intermediate regions the distinction would disappear. We might imagine a compact, more restricted zone of transition between two languages—e.g. Provençal between French and Italian—but such a zone simply does not exist. How can we possibly depict an exact linguistic boundary on territory that is covered from one end to the other by gradually differentiated dialects? The dividing lines between languages, like those between dialects, are hidden in transitions. Just as dialects are only arbitrary subdivisions of the total surface of language, so the boundary that is supposed to separate two languages is only a conventional one.

Still, abrupt transitions from one language to another are common, due to circumstances that have destroyed imperceptible transitions. The most disrupting force is the shifting of populations. Nations have always shuttled back and forth. Their migrations, multiplied throughout the centuries, have wrought confusion everywhere, and at many points all trace of linguistic transition has been wiped out. The Indo-European family is typical. At first its languages must have been closely related, with an unbroken chain of linguistic zones. We can reconstruct the broad outlines of the major zones. Slavic shares overlapping characteristics with both Iranian and Germanic, and this conforms with the geographical distribution of the three languages; similarly, Germanic is an intermediate ring that links Slavic and Celtic, which in turn is closely related to Italic; the latter is mid-way between Celtic and Greek. Thus a linguist, without knowing its geographical location, could readily assign each idiom to its proper place. And yet, as soon as we consider a boundary between two groups of idioms (e.g. the Germanic-Slavic boundary), there is an abrupt break, with no transition. The two groups collide instead of overlapping. That is because the intermediate dialects have disappeared. Neither the Slavs nor the Germans were stationary; they emigrated, conquered territory, each at the expense of the other; the neighboring Slavic and Germanic populations of today are not the same as those that were once in contact. If the Italians who live in Calabria settled on the French border, the move would naturally destroy the imperceptible transition between Italian and French. A number of similar facts accounts for the distribution of Proto-Indo-European.

Still other forces help to wipe out transitions. Take the spreading of standard languages at the expense of patois (see pp. 195 ff.). Today literary French (formerly the language of the Ile de France) extends to the border, where it conflicts with official Italian (a generalized form of the Tuscan dialect), and it is only through chance that traditional patois still exist in the western Alps, for along many other linguistic boundaries all trace of intermediate speech-forms has been wiped out.

Chapter IV

SPREAD OF LINGUISTIC WAVES

1. *Intercourse*[6] *and Provincialism*

The laws that govern the spread of linguistic phenomena are the same as those that govern any custom whatsoever, e.g. fashion. In every human collectivity two forces are always working simultaneously and in opposing directions: individualism or *provincialism* [*esprit de clocher*] on the one hand and *intercourse*—communications among men—on the other.

Provincialism keeps a restricted linguistic community faithful to its own traditions. The patterns that the individual acquires

[6] In his lectures Saussure used the English word *intercourse*. [Tr.]

during childhood are strong and persistent. If they alone were at work, these patterns would create an infinite number of peculiarities in speech.

But intercourse, the opposing force, limits their effect. Whereas provincialism makes men sedentary, intercourse obliges them to move about. Intercourse brings passers-by from other localities into a village, displaces a part of the population whenever there is a festival or fair, unites men from different provinces in the army, etc. In a word, it is a unifying force that counteracts the splintering action of provincialism.

Intercourse spreads language and gives it unity. It acts in two ways: negatively, it prevents dialectal splintering by wiping out an innovation whenever and wherever it springs up; positively, it promotes unity by adopting and spreading an innovation. The second form that intercourse may take justifies the use of the word *wave* to designate the geographical boundaries of a dialectal fact (see p. 203), for an isoglossematic line is like the outermost edge of an undulating flood.

Surprisingly enough, we sometimes find that two widely separated dialects within the same language have a common linguistic trait. That is because the change which sprang up at one place on the territory met no obstacle in spreading and gradually extended far beyond its starting point. Nothing impedes the action of intercourse in a linguistic mass within which there are only imperceptible transitions.

The generalizing of a particular fact—regardless of the size of its zone—requires time, and occasionally the time is measurable. Thus the change of *þ* to *d*, which intercourse carried throughout continental Germany, first spread over the south, between 800 and 850 A.D., except for Franconia where *þ* persisted as soft *ð* and did not give way to *d* until a later date. The change of *t* to German *z* (pronounced *ts*) took place within more restricted boundaries and began during a period that preceded the first written documents; it must have started in the Alps around 600 A.D. and spread both north and south as far as Lombardy. The *t* still appears in an eighth-century Thuringian charter. During a later period Germanic *ī* and *ū* were diphthongized (cf. *mein* for *mīn*, *braun* for *brūn*); it took 300 years for this phenomenon, which began in Bohemia around 1400 A.D., to reach the Rhine and cover its present zone.

The foregoing linguistic facts spread through interdialectal influence, and the same is probably true of all waves: they start from one point and radiate. This brings us to a second important observation.

German consonantal mutation is again illustrative. When the phoneme *t* became *ts* at one point in Germanic territory, the new sound tended to radiate from its source, and *ts* became the rival of the original *t* or of other sounds that might have evolved from it at other points. At its source such an innovation is purely phonetic, but elsewhere it becomes established only geographically and through interdialectal influence. Hence the diagram:

t
↓
ts

is valid in all its simplicity for the source and no more. If we try to apply it to propagation, the resulting picture is distorted.

The phonetician must therefore distinguish carefully between sources and affected zones. At its source a phoneme evolves solely on the axis of time. But mere phonetic facts will not explain affected zones, for they result from the interaction of both time and space. Take *ts*, which came from an outside source and replaced *t*. This is an example, not of modification of a traditional prototype, but of imitation of a neighboring dialect, irrespective of the prototype. *Herza* 'heart' came from the Alps and replaced the more archaic form *he*^{r}*ta* in Thuringia. Here we should not speak of phonetic change but of the borrowing of a phoneme.

2. *The Two Forces Reduced to One*

If we focus on a single geographical point—by "point" I mean a very small area comparable to a point (see p. 202), e.g. a village—it is easy to single out what is attributable to each of the two forces, provincialism and intercourse. Any particular fact depends on only one force, never on both; every feature shared with another dialect is due to intercourse; every feature that belongs exclusively to the dialect of the point under consideration is due to provincialism.

But as soon as we turn to a larger area—e.g. a canton—a new difficulty arises. No longer is it possible to say which force is responsible for a given phenomenon. Both forces, though in opposition, are involved in each trait of the idiom. What is distinctive of canton A is common to all its parts. There, the individualistic force prohibits canton A from imitating something from canton B and the latter in turn from imitating A. But the unifying force, intercourse, is also involved, for it shows up in the different parts of A (A^1, A^2, A^3, etc.). On larger areas the two forces therefore work simultaneously but in different proportions. The more intercourse favors an innovation, the farther its zone will reach; as for provincialism, it tends to protect a linguistic fact throughout its zone by defending it against outside competitors. We cannot foresee the final results of the action of the two forces. In Germanic territory, which reached from the Alps to the North Sea, the change from *þ* to *d* was general while the change from *t* to *ts* affected only the south (see p. 206); provincialism created an opposition between the south and the north, but intercourse was responsible for linguistic solidarity within each region. Thus there is basically no difference between this second phenomenon and the first. The same forces are present; only the intensity of their action varies.

Practically, this means that in studying linguistic evolutions we can disregard the individualistic force. That is, we can consider it as the negative side of the unifying force. The latter may be strong enough to unify the whole area. If not, the phenomenon will come to a standstill after covering only a part of the territory. Internally, however, the part that was covered will form a coherent whole. That is why we can reduce everything to the single unifying force without bringing in provincialism, which is nothing more than the force of intercourse peculiar to each region.

3. *Linguistic Differentiation on Separate Territories*

Three things must be realized before one can study profitably a language that develops concurrently on two separate territories: (1) in a unilingual mass cohesiveness is not the same for all phenomena; (2) not all innovations spread; and (3) geographical continuity does not prevent perpetual differentiations.

Such concurrent development is common. When Germanic

crossed over from the continent to the British Isles, for example, there began a twofold evolution. On the one hand were the German dialects and on the other Anglo-Saxon, from which English evolved. Another example is French after it was transplanted to Canada. Discontinuity is not always the effect of colonization or conquest; it may also result from isolation. Rumanian lost contact with the Latin mass through the interposition of Slavic populations. The cause is unimportant; what matters is whether separation plays a role in the history of languages and whether its effects differ from those that appear where there is continuity.

Earlier, in order to point up the preponderant effect of time, we imagined an idiom as it might develop concurrently on two rather limited points—two small islands, in our example—where we might disregard a gradual spread. Now, however, with two territories that cover a broader area, we find once more that a gradual spread brings about dialectal differences. That the two territories are discontinuous does not simplify the problem in the least. We must guard against attributing to separation something that can be explained without it.

This is the mistake that the earliest Indo-European scholars made (see p. 2). Confronted with a great family of languages that had diverged enormously, they failed to realize that the differences could have resulted from something besides geographical splintering. It was easy for them—and for anyone—to imagine different languages in separate localities; in a superficial view no more was needed to explain differentiation. But they went further. They associated nationality with language, using the first to explain the second. Thus they pictured the Slavs, Germans, Celts, etc. as so many swarms of bees from the same hive and imagined that these tribes, torn away from the original stock by migration, had carried Proto-Indo-European over as many different territories.

Only much later was this mistake corrected. Not until 1877 did Johannes Schmidt open the eyes of linguists by proposing the theory of continuity or waves (*Wellentheorie*) in his book *Die Verwandtschaftsverhältnisse der Indogermanen.* Then they saw that local splintering suffices to explain the reciprocal relations of the Indo-European languages, and that it is not necessary to assume that the different nations moved to new places (see p. 204). Dialectal differentiations could and must have arisen before these nations spread out in various directions. The wave theory therefore not only gives a truer picture of Proto-Indo-European; it also reveals the causes of differentiation and the conditions that determine the kinship of languages.

The wave theory opposes the migratory theory but does not necessarily exclude it. In the history of the Indo-European languages there are many examples of nations that lost contact with the main family through migration, and this must have produced special effects. But these effects mingle with those of differentiation where contact is maintained, and the difficulty of identifying them brings us back to the problem of the evolution of an idiom in separate territories.

Take Old English. It broke away from the Germanic trunk as a result of migration. In all probability it would not have its present form if the Saxons had stayed on the continent during the fifth century. But what were the specific effects of separation? It would seem that we should first ask whether such and such a change might not have sprung up just as well where geographical contact was maintained. If the English had occupied Jutland instead of the British Isles, it is possible that some of the facts attributed to absolute separation would have occurred here in a contiguous territory. There is nothing to prove that discontinuity is what enabled English to preserve older þ while the sound became *d* throughout the continent (e.g. English *thing* and German *Ding*). Nor was geographical continuity necessarily responsible for the generalizing of the change in continental Germanic; it might very well have been checked in spite of continuity. The mistake is the usual one of contrasting isolated and continuous dialects. Nothing actually proves that interdialectal influence would have caused *d* to spread throughout our imaginary English colony in Jutland. We have seen that in the linguistic territory of French, for example, *k* (+ *a*) persisted in the angle formed by Picardy and Normandy but became hushing š (*ch*) everywhere else. Isolation is therefore an unsatisfactory and superficial explanation. Differentiation can always be explained without it. What isolation can do, geographical continuity does equally well. If there is a difference between the two classes of phenomena, we cannot grasp it.

But the picture changes when we consider two related idioms not from the negative viewpoint of their differences but from the positive viewpoint of their solidarity. Then we see that separation immediately opens the door to potential severance of every relation whereas geographical continuity supports solidarity even among strikingly different regional speech-forms, provided they are connected by intermediate dialects.

In order to determine degrees of kinship among languages, we must therefore make a rigid distinction between continuity and isolation. Two isolated languages will retain from their common heritage a number of traits that attest their kinship, but since each language will evolve independently, new characteristics that appear in one will not be found in the other (with the exception of certain characteristics that originate after separation and are identical in the two languages through sheer coincidence). What is ruled out in each instance is the spreading of these characteristics through interdialectal influence. A language that has evolved out of touch with related languages generally has a set of traits that distinguish it from them. When this language splinters in turn, its dialects evidence a closer kinship through the common traits that bind them together and set them apart from dialects of the other territory. They actually form a distinct branch, detached from the trunk.

Vastly different are the relations of languages on continuous territory. Their common traits are not necessarily older than the traits that differentiate them. Indeed, an innovation that starts at a given point may spread at any moment and even embrace the whole territory. Besides, innovating zones vary in extent, so that two neighboring idioms may have a common peculiarity without forming a separate group, and each may be related to contiguous idioms through other traits, as is shown by the Indo-European languages.

PART FIVE

Concerning Retrospective Linguistics

Chapter I

THE TWO PERSPECTIVES OF DIACHRONIC LINGUISTICS

Synchronic linguistics has only the perspective of speakers and, consequently, only one method; diachronic linguistics, however, requires both a prospective and a retrospective viewpoint (see p. 90).

The prospective method, which corresponds to the actual course of events, is the one we must use in developing any point concerning the history of a language or of languages. It consists simply of examining the available documents. But all too many problems of diachronic linguistics cannot be met by the prospective method.

In fact, in order to give a detailed history of a language by following its course in time, one would need an infinite number of photographs, taken at different times. Now this requirement has never been met. Romance scholars, for instance, even though they have the advantage of knowing Latin, the point of departure for their research, and of possessing an imposing array of documents covering several successive centuries, are constantly aware of wide gaps in their documentation. They must then discard the prospective method—direct evidence—and work in the opposite direction, using the retrospective method to retrace time. This means choosing a particular period and trying to determine, not how a form developed, but the oldest form that could have given it birth.

The prospective method amounts to simple narration and is based entirely on textual criticism, but the retrospective viewpoint requires a reconstructive method supported by comparison. It is impossible to establish the original form of a single, isolated sign, but the comparing of two different signs that have the same origin (e.g. Latin *pater*, Sanskrit *pitar-* or the radical of Latin *ger-ō* and that of *ges-tus*) immediately brings to light the diachronic unity which relates both signs to a prototype that can be reconstructed inductively. The more numerous the comparisons, the more accurate inductions will be, and the results—if sufficient data are at hand—will be true reconstructions.

The same applies to languages in their totality. We can infer nothing about Basque; because it is isolated, there is nothing with which we can compare it. But by comparing a group of related languages like Greek, Latin, Old Slavic, etc., scholars were able to single out the common original elements and to reconstruct the essentials of Proto-Indo-European as it existed before differentiation in space occurred. What was done for the whole family on a large scale was repeated on a smaller scale—and always by the same procedure—for each of its parts wherever this was necessary and possible. We know numerous Germanic idioms directly, through documents, but we know Proto-Germanic—the source of these different idioms—only indirectly, through the reconstructive method. Using the same method with varying success, linguists have also sought the original unity of other families (see p. 192).

The retrospective method, then, takes us far beyond the oldest documents in tracing the history of a language. Thus it was possible to draw the prospective outline of Latin, whose history hardly begins before the third or fourth century B.C., only after the reconstruction of Proto-Indo-European had given an inkling of what must have happened between the period of original unity and the first known Latin documents.

With respect to reconstruction, evolutionary linguistics is like geology, another historical science. Geology sometimes has to describe stable states (e.g. the present state of Lake Geneva Basin) without considering what might have preceded in time, but its main concern is the chain of events and transformations that make up diachronics. A prospective geology is conceivable, but in reality the viewpoint is usually only retrospective. Before recounting what has occurred at a given point on the earth, the geologist must reconstruct the chain of events and try to determine what is responsible for the present state of that part of the globe.

Not only in method do the two perspectives contrast sharply; in teaching, even, to use them simultaneously in the same exposition is a disadvantage. The study of phonetic changes, for instance, offers two very different pictures, depending on the perspective. Using the prospective viewpoint, we might ask what Classical Latin *ĕ* became in French. We would see that a single sound, by evolving in time, varied and gave rise to several phonemes: cf. *pĕdem* → *pyę* (*pied* 'foot'), *vęntum* → *vã* (*vent* 'wind'), *lĕctum* → *li* (*lit* 'bed'), *nĕcāre* → *nwayę* (*noyer* 'drown'), etc. Against that, if we used the retrospective viewpoint to find what French open *e* stands for in Latin, we would see that this single sound is the terminal point of several originally distinct phonemes: cf. *tęr* (*terre* 'earth') = *tĕrram*, *vęrž* (*verge* 'rod') = *vĭrgam*, *fę* (*fait* 'fact') = *factum*, etc. We could present the evolution of formative elements in two ways, and the two pictures would be just as different; everything that was said about analogical formations (see pp. 169 ff.) is *a priori* proof. Thus the (retrospective) search for the origin of the suffix of French participles in *-é* takes us back to Latin *-ātum;* the Latin suffix is related etymologically to denominative Latin verbs in *-āre*, which go back mainly to feminine substantives in *-a* (cf. *plantāre: planta*, Greek *tīmaō: tīmā́*, etc.); furthermore, *-ātum* would not exist if the Proto-Indo-European suffix *-to-* had not been living and productive in its own right (cf. Greek *klu-tó-s*, Latin *in-clu-tu-s*, Sanskrit *çru-ta-s*, etc.); finally, *-ātum* includes the formative element *-m* of the accusative singular (see p. 154). Conversely, a (prospective) search for the French formations that have the original suffix *-to-* will reveal that there are not only the different suffixes—whether productive or not—of the past participle (*aimé* 'loved' = *amātum*, *fini* 'ended' = *fīnītum*, *clos* 'closed' = *clausum* for **claudtum*, etc.), but also many others like *-u* = *-ūtum* (cf. *cornu* 'horned' = *cornūtum*), *-tif* (learned suffix) = Latin *-tīvum* (cf. *fugitif* = *fugitīvum*, *sensitif*, *négatif*, etc.) and a number of words no longer analyzable, like *point* 'dot' = Latin *punctum*, *dé* 'die' = *datum*, *chétif* 'wretched' = *captīvum*, etc.

Chapter II

THE OLDEST LANGUAGE AND THE PROTOTYPE

In the earliest stages of Indo-European linguistics scholars understood neither the real purpose of comparison nor the importance of the reconstructive method (see p. 3). That explains one of their grossest mistakes: the exaggerated and almost exclusive role that they gave to Sanskrit. Because it was the oldest document of Proto-Indo-European, they promoted Sanskrit to the rank of prototype. To imagine that Proto-Indo-European engendered Sanskrit, Greek, Slavic, Celtic, Italic, etc. is one thing; to substitute one of these languages for Proto-Indo-European is something else entirely. The glaring mistake of the earliest scholars had varied and far-reaching consequences. Doubtless their hypothesis was not stated so categorically as I have implied, but it was tacitly accepted in practice. Bopp wrote that he "did not think that Sanskrit could be the common source," as if there were a possibility of formulating, even while expressing doubt, such a supposition.

This prompts one to ask what is meant by the statement that one language is older than another. Three interpretations are theoretically possible:

(1) "Older" may refer to the beginning, the starting point of a language. But only a little reasoning will show that there is no language to which we can assign an age, for each language is the continuation of what was spoken before it. What is true of humanity is not true of speech; the absolute continuity of its development prevents us from distinguishing generations in it. Gaston Paris was justified in criticizing the conception of daughter languages and mother languages since this assumes interruptions. "Older," in this sense, is meaningless.

(2) "Older" may also indicate that one particular state of a language we are studying is earlier than another state of the same language. Thus the Persian of the Achaemenian inscriptions is

older than the Persian of Firdausi. In a specific case like this, where one idiom has definitely developed from the other and where both are equally well known, we should of course reckon only with the earlier idiom. But unless both conditions are met, priority in time has no importance. Thus Lithuanian, which is attested only since 1540, is no less valuable than Old Slavic, which was recorded in the tenth century, or than the Sanskrit of the Rig Veda for that matter.

(3) Finally, "older" may designate a more archaic language-state, i.e. one with forms that are very close to the forms of the original model, quite apart from any question of dates. In this sense sixteenth-century Lithuanian is older than the Latin of the third century B.C.

Only in the second or third sense is Sanskrit older than other languages. It fits both definitions. On one hand, it is generally agreed that the Vedic hymns antedate the oldest Greek texts; on the other hand—and this is especially important—Sanskrit has a considerable number of archaic features in comparison with those preserved by other languages (see pp. 2 ff.).

But the earliest linguists, because of their confused notion of age, put Sanskrit ahead of the whole family. The result was that later linguists, though cured of the notion that Sanskrit is the mother language, continued to attribute too much importance to the evidence that it furnishes as a collateral language.

In *Les Origines indo-européennes* (see p. 224) A. Pictet, while explicitly recognizing the existence of a primitive nation with its own language, still insists that we must first consult Sanskrit, and that the evidence which this language furnishes is worth more than that of several other Indo-European languages combined. The same delusion has for many years obscured issues of primary importance, such as that of the Proto-Indo-European vocalism.

The mistake has been repeated on a smaller scale and in detail. Those who studied specific branches of Indo-European thought that the earliest known idiom was a complete and satisfactory representative of the whole group and did not try to become better acquainted with the original state. For example, instead of speaking of Germanic, they had no scruples about citing Gothic and stopping there, for Gothic antedates the other Germanic dialects by several centuries; it usurped the role of prototype and became the source of the other dialects. As regards Slavic, they based their research exclusively on Slavonic or Old Slavic, which is attested from the tenth century, because the other Slavic dialects are attested from a later date.

Only on very rare occasions do two specimens of language that have been set down in writing at successive dates represent exactly the same idiom at two moments in its history. More often we find that one of the dialects is not the linguistic successor of the other. Exceptions prove the rule. The most famous exception is the Romance languages with respect to Latin: in tracing French back to Latin, one certainly follows a vertical route; the territory of the Romance languages happens to match the territory where Latin was spoken, and each idiom is no more than a later state of Latin. Persian is another exception to the rule; the Persian of the inscriptions of Darius is the same dialect as the Persian of the Middle Ages. But the opposite occurs much more frequently. The written documents of different periods generally belong to different dialects of the same family. Germanic, for instance, appears successively in the Gothic of Ulfilas (its successor is unknown), then in Old High German texts, later in Anglo-Saxon and Old Norse texts, etc. None of these dialects or groups of dialects is the continuation of the one attested previously. The following diagram, in which letters stand for dialects and dotted lines for successive periods, suggests the usual pattern:

```
..............A....   Period 1
........B..........   Period 2
..C.......D.......    Period 3
................E..   Period 4
```

This pattern is a valuable asset to linguistics. If succession were vertical, the first known dialect (A) would contain everything that we could deduce by analyzing successive states. But by searching for the point of convergence of all the dialects (A, B, C, D, etc.) in the pattern, we may find a form older than A (i.e. a prototype X) and thus avoid confusing A and X.

Chapter III

RECONSTRUCTIONS

1. *Their Nature and Aim*

The sole means of reconstructing is by comparing, and the only aim of comparison is a reconstruction. Our procedure is sterile unless we view the relations of several forms from the perspective of time and succeed in re-establishing a single form. I have repeatedly emphasized this point (see pp. 3 ff. and p. 198 f.). Thus we explain Latin *medius* against Greek *mésos*, without going back to Proto-Indo-European, by positing an older form **methyos* as the source of both *medius* and *mésos*. Or we may compare two forms of the same language rather than two words of different languages: Latin *gerō* and *gestus* go back to a radical **ges-* that was once common to both forms.

We note in passing that comparisons having to do with phonetic changes must always rely heavily on morphological considerations. In examining Latin *patior* and *passus*, I bring in *factus*, *dictus*, etc. because *passus* is a formation of the same class. By basing my conclusion on the morphological relation between *faciō* and *factus*, *dīcō* and *dictus*, etc., I can set up, for an earlier period, the same relation between *patior* and **pat-tus*. Reciprocally, I must use phonetics to throw light on a morphologieal comparison. I can compare Latin *meliōrem* with Greek *hēdiō* because the first form goes back phonetically to **meliosem*, **meliosm*, and the second to **hādioa*, **hādiosa*, **hādiosm*.

Linguistic comparison is not simply a mechanical operation. It implies the bringing together of all relevant data. But it must always result in a conjecture which we can express by some formula and which aims to re-establish something that has preceded; it always results in a reconstruction of forms.

But is the aim of viewing the past to reconstruct the whole, concrete forms of the previous state? Or is reconstruction limited to abstract, partial affirmations about word-parts (e.g. to the observation that Latin _f_ in _fūmus_ stands for Proto-Italic þ, or that the initial element of Greek _állo_ and Latin _aliud_ already existed as _a_ in Proto-Indo-European)? Reconstruction may well confine itself to the second type of research; its analytical method has no aim other than these partial observations. Still, from the sum of isolated facts, we can draw general conclusions. A series of facts similar to those pertaining to _fūmus_ allows us to state with certainty that þ had a place in the phonological system of Proto-Italic; similarly, we can state that the pronominal declension of Proto-Indo-European has a neuter singular ending _–d_, different from the _–m_ of adjectives. We deduce this general morphological fact from a set of isolated observations (cf. Latin _istud_, _aliud_ against _bonum;_ Greek _tó_ = _*tod_, _állo_ = _*allod_ against _kalón;_ English _that_, etc.). We can go even further. It is possible, after we have reconstructed the different facts, to synthesize those relating to the whole form and to reconstruct whole words (e.g. Proto-Indo-European _*alyod_), inflectional paradigms, etc. Synthesis consists of drawing together completely isolated statements. For example, when we compare the different parts of a reconstructed form like _*alyod_, we notice a great difference between the _–d_, which raises a point of grammar, and _a–_, which has no grammatical significance. A reconstructed form is not a solidary whole. It is a sum that we can always analyze phonetically. Each of its parts is revocable and subject to further examination. Therefore, restored forms have always been a faithful reflection of the general conclusions applicable to them. The Proto-Indo-European word for 'horse' was successively posited as _*akvas_, _*ak_$_1$_vas_, _*ek_$_1$_vos_, and finally _*ek_$_1$_wos;_ only _s_ and the number of phonemes have remained undisputed.

The aim of reconstruction is, then, not to restore a form for its own sake—this would be rather ridiculous to say the least—but to crystallize and condense a set of conclusions that seem logically to follow from the results obtained at each moment; in short, its aim is to record the progress of our science. No one has to defend linguists against the rather absurd charge of intending to restore Proto-Indo-European completely as if they wished to use it. They do not have this objective even in studying the languages that are historically attested (one does not study Latin linguistically in order to speak it well). There is even less justification for it in the case of individual words of prehistoric languages.

Reconstruction, though always subject to revision, is necessary for an overall view of the language studied and of its linguistic type. It is an indispensable instrument for depicting with relative ease a great number of general facts, both synchronic and diachronic. The whole set of reconstructions immediately illuminates the broad outlines of Proto-Indo-European. For instance, we know that suffixes were formed from certain elements (*t*, *s*, *r*, etc.) to the exclusion of others, and that the complicated variety of the vocalism of German verbs (cf. *werden, wirst, ward, wurde, worden*) obscures the rules governing one and the same original alternation: *e–o–zero*. The result is that reconstruction is a great help in studying the history of later periods, for without reconstruction it would be much more difficult to explain the changes that have occurred since the prehistoric period.

2. *Relative Accuracy of Reconstructions*

We are absolutely certain of some reconstructed forms, but others are either open to dispute or frankly problematical. We have just seen that the accuracy of whole forms depends on the relative accuracy that we can attribute to the partial restorations that go into the synthesis. On this score two words are almost never identical. Between Proto-Indo-European forms as illuminating as **esti* 'he is' and **didōti* 'he gives,' there is a difference, for the reduplicated vowel of the second form gives room for doubt (cf. Sanskrit *dadāti* and Greek *didōsi*).

There is a general tendency to consider reconstructions less accurate than they actually are. Three facts should fortify our confidence.

The first fact, which is of capital importance, was mentioned earlier (see pp. 39 ff.). We can distinguish clearly the sounds of a particular word, their number, and their delimitation. We have also seen (p. 54) how we should regard the objections that certain linguists squinting into the phonological microscope might raise. In a sequence like *–sn–* there are doubtless furtive or transitional sounds, but to give weight to them is antilinguistic; the average ear does not single them out, and—even more important—speakers always agree on the number of elements in such a sequence. We can therefore state that the Proto-Indo-European form $*ek_1wos$ had only five distinct, differential elements to which speakers had to pay heed.

The second fact has to do with the system of the phonological elements of each language. Any language operates with a clearly delimited gamut of phonemes (see p. 34). The least frequent elements of the Proto-Indo-European system appear in no fewer than a dozen forms—and the most frequent in a thousand—all attested through reconstruction. With this we are sure of knowing them all.

Finally, we do not have to delineate the positive qualities of the phonic units in order to know them. We must consider them as differential entities that are characterized by their being distinct (see p. 119). This is so basic that we could designate the phonic elements of an idiom that is to be reconstructed by numbers or by any signs whatsoever. There is no need for determining the absolute quality of *ĕ* in $*\breve{e}k_1w\breve{o}s$ or for puzzling over whether *ĕ* was open or closed, just how far forward it was articulated, etc. All this is unimportant unless several types of *ĕ* have been identified. The important thing is that we do not confuse it with another element singled out by language (*ă*, *ŏ*, *ē*, etc.). This is another way of saying that the first phoneme of $*\breve{e}k_1w\breve{o}s$ does not differ from the second of **mĕdhyŏs*, the third of **ăgĕ*, etc., and that without specifying its phonic nature, we could catalogue it and assign it a number in the table of Proto-Indo-European phonemes. The reconstructed form $*\breve{e}k_1w\breve{o}s$ means therefore that the Proto-Indo-European equivalent of Latin *equos*, Sanskrit *açva-s*, etc. was composed of five definite phonemes taken from the phonological gamut of the original idiom.

Within the limitations just outlined, reconstructions do retain their full value.

Chapter IV

THE CONTRIBUTION OF LANGUAGE TO ANTHROPOLOGY AND PREHISTORY

1. *Language and Race*

Thanks to his retrospective method, the linguist can go back through the centuries and reconstruct languages that were spoken by certain nations long before their written history began. But might not reconstructions also provide information about the nations themselves—their race, filiation, social relations, customs, institutions, etc.? In short, does language provide some answers to questions that arise in the study of anthropology, ethnography, and prehistory? Many people think so, but I believe this is largely an illusion. Let us examine briefly some parts of the general problem.

First, race. It would be wrong to assume that a common language implies consanguinity, that a family of languages matches an anthropological family. The facts are not so simple. There is, for instance, a Germanic race with distinct anthropological characteristics: blond hair, elongated cranium, high stature, etc.; the Scandinavian is its most perfect example. Still, not all populations who speak Germanic languages fit this description; thus the Swabian from the foot of the Alps differs strikingly from the Scandinavian. Might we at least assume, however, that an idiom belongs exclusively to one race, and that if nations belonging to other races use the idiom, this is only because it has been imposed upon them through conquest? No doubt nations often adopt or are forced to submit to the language of their conquerors (e.g. the Gauls after the victory of the Romans), but this does not explain everything. For instance, even if they had subjugated so many different populations, the Germanic tribes could not have absorbed all of them; we would have to imagine a long period of prehistoric domination and still other unsubstantiated circumstances.

Consanguinity and linguistic community apparently have no necessary connection, and we cannot draw conclusions from one and apply them to the other; consequently, in the numerous instances where anthropological and linguistic evidence do not agree, it is not necessary to set the two types of evidence in opposition or to choose between them; each type retains its own value.

2. *Ethnic Unity*

What can we learn from the evidence furnished by language? Racial unity alone, a secondary force, is in no way necessary for linguistic community. But there is another type of unity—the only crucial type—which is of infinitely greater importance and which is constituted by the social bond: *ethnic unity* [*éthnisme*]. By this I mean a unity based on the multiple relations of religion, civilization, common defense, etc., which spring up even among nations of different races and in the absence of any political bond.

Between ethnic unity and language is established the mutual relation mentioned earlier (see p. 20). The social bond tends to create linguistic community and probably imposes certain traits on the common idiom; conversely, linguistic community is to some extent responsible for ethnic unity. In general, ethnic unity always suffices to explain linguistic community. For example, in the early Middle Ages a Romance ethnic unity, in the absence of any political bond, linked nations of the most varied origins. Reciprocally, on the question of ethnic unity, we must first consult language. The information that it provides takes precedence over everything else. Here is one example. In ancient Italy the Etruscans lived alongside the Latins. If we try to determine what the two nations had in common in the hope of tracing them back to the same origin, we can call up everything that they transmitted (monuments, religious rites, political institutions, etc.) and still lack the assurance that language provides immediately. Four lines of Etruscan are enough to show that the speakers of this language belong to a nation distinct from the ethnic group that spoke Latin.

Thus language—within the limitations indicated—is a historical document. That the Indo-European languages form a family, for example, is proof of a primitive ethnic unity that has been transmitted more or less directly through social filiation to every nation that speaks one of these languages today.

3. *Linguistic Paleontology*

Linguistic unity may allow us to predicate social community, but does language reveal the nature of this common ethnic unity?

For a long time languages were considered an inexhaustible source of documents concerning the nations that spoke them and their prehistory. Adolphe Pictet, a pioneer of Celtism, is known especially for his book *Les Origines indo-européennes* (1859–63). His work has served as a model for many others; it is still the most engaging of all. Pictet looks to the Indo-European languages for data that will reveal the fundamental traits of the civilization of the "Aryans" and believes that he can fix the most varied details: material things (tools, weapons, domesticated animals), social life (whether they were a nomadic or an agricultural nation), family, government, etc. He seeks to identify the cradle of the Aryans, which he places in Bactriana, and studies the flora and fauna of the country that they inhabited. His is the most important undertaking of its type. The science that he founded is called linguistic paleontology.

Other efforts in the same direction have since been made. One of the more recent is Hermann Hirt's *Die Indogermanen* (1905–1907).[1] Basing his research on the theory of J. Schmidt (see p. 209), Hirt tries to identify the country inhabited by the Indo-Europeans. But he does not slight linguistic paleontology. Lexical facts show him that the Indo-Europeans were farmers, and he refuses to place them in southern Russia, which is better suited to nomadic life. The frequency of occurrence of names of trees, especially of certain kinds (fir, birch, beech, oak), makes him think that their country was wooded, and that it was located between the Harz Mountains and the Vistula, more specifically in the region of Brandenburg and Berlin. We should also recall that even before Pictet, Adalbert

[1] Cf. also d'Arbois de Jubainville, *Les premiers habitants de l'Europe* (1877); O. Schrader, *Sprachvergleichung und Urgeschichte* and *Reallexicon der indogermanischen Altertumskunde* (works that appeared a little earlier than the volume by Hirt); and S. Feist, *Europa im Lichte der Vorgeschichte* (1910). [Ed.]

Kuhn and others had used linguistics to reconstruct the mythology and religion of the Indo-Europeans.

Now we cannot expect language to furnish such information for the following reasons:

First is the uncertainty of etymology. Scholars have at last realized how rare are words with well-established origins, and have become more cautious. Here is an example of the rashness that once prevailed. Given *servus* and *servare*, scholars compared the two—they probably had no right to do this—and by giving the first word the meaning "guardian," they were able to conclude that a slave was originally used in the sense of "to guard." Nor is that all. The meanings of words evolve. The meaning of a word often changes whenever a tribe changes its place of abode. Scholars were also wrong in assuming that the absence of a word proves that the primitive society knew nothing of the thing that the word names. Thus the word for "to plow" is not found in the Asiatic languages, but this does not mean that in the beginning plowing was unknown; it might just as well have been discarded or conducted by other procedures known by different names.

The possibility of loan-words is a third cause of uncertainty. An object that is borrowed may bring its name along with it. For instance, hemp came into the Mediterranean world at a very late date, and into the countries to the north even later; each time, the name for hemp came with the plant. In many instances the absence of extralinguistic data does not allow us to ascertain whether the presence of the same word in several languages is due to borrowing or is proof of a common original tradition.

The foregoing limitations do not preclude our distinguishing with no hesitation some general traits and even certain precise data. For example, common terms indicating kinship are abundant and have been transmitted very clearly. They allow us to state that among the Indo-Europeans the family was a complex and stable institution, for their language could express subtleties that ours cannot. In Homer, *einắteres* means "sisters-in-law" with reference to the wives of several brothers, and *galóōi* denotes the relationship between the wife and the sister of the husband. Latin *janitrīces* corresponds to *einắteres* in form and in signification.

Similarly, "brother-in-law" (the husband of the sister) is not named by the same word as "brothers-in-law" (denoting the relationship among the husbands of several sisters). Here we can identify a minute detail, but usually we must be satisfied with general information. The same applies to animals. For important species like the bovine we can rely on the coincidence of Greek *boûs*, German *Kuh*, Sanskrit *gau-s*, etc. and reconstruct the Proto-Indo-European form **$g_2$où-s;* besides, the inflection of the word has the same features in each language, and this would be impossible if it had been borrowed from another language at a later date.

Here we might consider another morphological fact that has the dual characteristic of being limited to a definite zone and of touching upon a point of social organization.

In spite of everything that has been said about the relation of *dominus* and *domus*, linguists do not seem to be completely satisfied, for the use of the suffix *–no–* in forming secondary derivatives is most extraordinary. There are no formations like **oiko-no-s* or **oike-no-s* from *oîkos* in Greek, or **açva-na* from *açva-* in Sanskrit. But this very rarity gives the suffix of *dominus* its value and prominence. Several Germanic words are, I think, quite revealing:

(1) **þeuða-na-z* 'head of the **þeuðō*, king,' Gothic *þiudans*, Old Saxon *thiodan* (**þeuðō*, Gothic *þiuda* = Oscan *touto* 'people').

(2) **druχ-ti-na-z* (partially changed to **druχ-tī-na-z*) 'head of the **druχ-ti-z*, army' (whence the Christian name for the Master, i.e. God), cf. Old Norse *Dróttinn*, Anglo-Saxon *Dryhten*, both with final *–ina-z*.

(3) **kindi-na-z* 'head of the **kindi-z* = Latin *gens*.' Since the head of the *gens* was a vice-ruler with respect to the head of a **þeuðō*, the Germanic word *kindins* (completely lost elsewhere) is used by Ulfilas to name the Roman governor for, in his Germanic way of thinking, the delegate of the emperor was the head of the clan with respect to the *þiudans;* however interesting the association may be from a historical viewpoint, there is no doubt that the word *kindins*, which is wholly unlike everything Roman, indicates a division of the Germanic populations into *kindi-z*.

Thus the secondary suffix *–na–*, when added to any Proto-Germanic theme, means 'head of a certain community.' All that remains now is to observe that in the same way Latin *tribūnus* literally means 'head of the *tribus*,' that *þiudans* means 'head of the *þiuda*,' and finally, that *dominus* means 'head of the *domus*,' the last division of the *touta* = *þiuda*. *Dominus*, with its singular suffix, seems to me to offer almost irrefutable proof not only of linguistic community but also of a community of institutions among the Italic and German ethnic groups.

But again it is worth noting that comparisons between languages rarely yield such characteristic indices.

4. *Linguistic Type and Mind of the Social Group*

Does language, even if it fails to supply much precise and authentic information about the institutions of speakers, serve at least to characterize the mind of the social group that speaks it? A popular notion is that a language reflects the psychology of a nation. But one serious objection opposes this viewpoint: psychological causes do not necessarily underlie linguistic procedures.

The Semitic languages express the relation of a substantival determinant to its noun (cf. French *la parole de Dieu* 'the word of God') by simple juxtaposition. To be sure, the noun that is determined has a special form, called "construct state," and precedes the determinant. Take Hebrew *dab̄ar* 'word' and *'elōhīm*[2] 'God': *dab̄ar 'elōhīm* means 'the word of God.' Should we say that such a syntactical pattern reveals something about the Semitic mind? That would be a rash assertion, for Old French regularly used a similar construction: cf. *le cor Roland* 'Roland's horn,' *les quatre fils Aymon* 'Aymon's four sons,' etc. Now the procedure arose in Romance through sheer chance, morphological as well as phonetic: a sharp reduction of cases forced the new construction on the language. It is entirely possible that a similar accident started Proto-Semitic on the same route. Thus a syntactical fact that is apparently one of its indelible traits gives no accurate clue to the Semitic mind.

Another example: Proto-Indo-European had no compounds with a word-initial verbal element. That German has such compounds (cf. *Bethaus*, *Springbrunnen*, etc.) does not prove that at a given moment the Germans modified a way of thinking inherited from

[2] The symbol ['] designates the alef or glottal stop that corresponds to soft breathing in Greek. [S.]

their ancestors. We have seen (p. 195) that the innovation was due to an accident which was not only material but also negative, the elimination of the *a* in *betahūs*. Everything occurred outside the mind and in the realm of sound changes, which readily impose a tight yoke on thought and force it into the special way that the material state of signs opens to it. A great number of similar observations confirms this conclusion. The psychological character of the linguistic group is unimportant by comparison with the elimination of a vowel, a change of accent, or many other similar things that may at any moment revolutionize the relation between the sign and the idea in any language form whatsoever.

It is always of interest to determine the grammatical character of languages (whether historically attested or reconstructed) and to classify languages according to the procedures that they use for expressing thought. But even after we become acquainted with the structures of languages and classify them, we can draw no accurate conclusions outside the domain of linguistics proper.

Chapter V

LANGUAGE FAMILIES AND LINGUISTIC TYPES[3]

We have just seen that language is not controlled directly by the mind of speakers. Let me emphasize, in concluding, one of the consequences of this principle: no family of languages rightly belongs once and for all to a particular linguistic type.

To ask the type to which a group of languages belongs is to forget that languages evolve; the implication is that there is an element of stability in evolution. How is it possible to impose limitations on an activity that has none?

Of course many people really have in mind the traits of the original idiom when they speak of the characteristics of a family;

[3] This chapter, though it does not deal with retrospective linguistics, is included in Part Five because it serves as a conclusion for the whole work. [Ed.]

their problem is not insoluble since they are dealing with one language and one period. But when we assume that there are permanent traits which neither time nor space can change in any way, we clash head-on with the fundamental principles of evolutionary linguistics. No characteristic has a right to permanent existence; it persists only through sheer luck.

Take the Indo-European family. We know the distinctive traits of the language from which it derives. The sound system of Proto-Indo-European is very simple. There are no complicated clusters of consonants or double consonants, and its monotone system gives rise to an interplay of extremely regular and profoundly grammatical alternations (see p. 157 and p. 220); the tonic accent can in principle be placed on any syllable in a word and therefore has a role in the interplay of grammatical oppositions; quantitative rhythm is based solely on the opposition of long and short syllables; compounds and derivatives are easily formed; nominal and verbal inflections are numerous; and the inflected word with its self-contained determiners is independent in the sentence, allowing much freedom of construction and greatly restricting the number of grammatical words with determinative or relational value (preverbs, prepositions, etc.).

Now it is clear that none of the foregoing traits has been retained in its original form in the different Indo-European languages, and that several of them (e.g. the role of quantitative rhythm and of tonic accent) no longer appear in any member of the group. Some languages have even changed the features of Proto-Indo-European to such an extent that they suggest an entirely different linguistic type (e.g. English, Armenian, Irish, etc.).

It would be more fitting to speak of certain transformations that affect different languages belonging to the same family. For instance, progressive weakening of the inflectional mechanism is characteristic of the Indo-European languages, although they all offer striking differences. Slavic has put up the strongest resistance while English has reduced inflection almost to zero. To offset this, a rather stable word-order has developed, analytical processes of expression have tended to replace synthetic processes, prepositions express case values (see p. 180), auxiliaries have taken the place of compound verbal forms, etc.

We have seen that a trait of the prototype may not appear in some of the derived languages. The reverse is equally true. It is not unusual even to find that the common traits of all the representatives of a family do not appear in the original idiom. This is true of vocalic harmony (i.e. similarity of some type between the timbre of every suffixed vowel and the last vowel of the radical). This salient trait is found in Ural-Altaic (a large group of languages spoken in Europe and Asia and extending from Finland to Manchuria) but is probably due to later developments. Vocalic harmony is then a common trait but not an original one; consequently we cannot invoke it—any more than agglutination—to prove the common origin (highly debatable) of these languages. We also know that Chinese has not always been monosyllabic.

The thing that first strikes us, when we compare the Semitic languages with their reconstructed prototype, is the persistence of certain traits. The Semitic languages seem, more than any other family, to constitute a type, unchangeable and permanent, with traits of the family inherent in each language. The following traits, many of which contrast sharply with those of Proto-Indo-European, set Proto-Semitic apart. Compounds are practically nonexistent. Derivation plays only a small part. The inflectional system is poorly developed (better in Proto-Semitic, however, than in the daughter languages), with the result that strict rules govern word-order. The most notable trait has to do with the structure of the root (see p. 187). It regularly includes three consonants (e.g. *q-ṭ-l* 'kill') which are retained in every form within a given language (cf. Hebrew *qāṭal*, *qāṭlā*, *qṭōl*, *qiṭlī*, etc.), and which do not change from one language to another (cf. Arabic *qatala*, *qutila*, etc.). In other words, consonants express the "concrete sense" or lexical value of words while vowels—with the help of certain prefixes and suffixes, of course—have the exclusive role of indicating grammatical values through the interplay of their alternations (e.g. Hebrew *qāṭal* 'he killed,' *qṭōl* 'to kill'; with a suffix, *qṭāl-ū* 'they killed'; with a prefix, *ji-qṭōl* 'he will kill'; and with both, *ji-qṭl-ū* 'they will kill,' etc.).

Against the foregoing facts, and in spite of the statements that they have elicited, we must defend our principle: there are no unchangeable characteristics. Permanence results from sheer luck; any characteristic that is preserved in time may also disappear with time. But to come back to Semitic. We see that the "law" of the three consonants is not really characteristic of the Semitic family since analogous phenomena appear in other families. In Proto-Indo-European, rigid laws also govern the consonantal structure of roots. For example, two sounds of the series *i, u, r, l, m, n* never follow *e;* a root like **serl* is impossible. The functioning of Semitic vowels is even more instructive. Indo-European has an equally rigid but less rich set of vowels; oppositions like Hebrew *daḇar* 'word,' *ḏḇār-īm* 'words,' *dīḇrē-hem* 'their words,' etc. recall German *Gast: Gäste, fliessen: floss*, etc. In both instances the genesis of the grammatical procedure is the same. Mere phonetic modifications, which are due to blind evolution, result in alternations. The mind seizes upon the alternations, attaches grammatical values to them, and spreads them, using the analogical models which chance phonetic developments provide. The immutability of the three consonants in Semitic is only a general rule, not a hard-and-fast one. We could be sure of this *a priori*, but our view is confirmed by the facts. In Hebrew, for example, the root *'anās-īm* 'men' has the three expected consonants, but its singular *'īs* has only two, for this is the reduced form of the older form that contained three consonants. Even if we agree that Semitic roots are quasi-immutable, this does not mean that they have an inherent characteristic. It means simply that the Semitic languages have suffered fewer phonetic alterations than many others, and that consonants have been better preserved in this group of languages than elsewhere. We are dealing with something evolutionary and phonetic, not something grammatical or permanent. To proclaim the immutability of roots is to say that they have undergone no phonetic change, nothing more, and we cannot vow that changes will never occur. Generally speaking, everything that time has done, time can undo or change.

We now realize that Schleicher was wrong in looking upon language as an organic thing with its own law of evolution, but we continue, without suspecting it, to try to make language organic in another sense by assuming that the "genius" of a race or ethnic group tends constantly to lead language along certain fixed routes.

From the incursions we have made into the borderlands of our science, one lesson stands out. It is wholly negative, but is all the more interesting because it agrees with the fundamental idea of this course: *the true and unique object of linguistics is language studied in and for itself.*

Errata

A few errors of typesetting or translation impede the understanding of Saussure in Baskin's translation. We here give corrections with reference to the currently available French text.

Page 13: Language is "a storehouse filled by the members of a given community through their active use of speaking": to follow more exactly the text (*CLG* 1972, 30), the English text should read "a treasure deposited, by the act of speaking, in each subject belonging to a given community."

Page 15: "indeed, the science of language is possible only if the other elements are excluded": the French says "only if these other elements are not mixed with it [*langue*]" (*CLG* 1972, 31).

Page 22: "just like any other genuine sign": less misleadingly, "just like any native-born [*autochtone*] sign" (cf. *CLG* 1972, 42). The opposition is not between genuine and nongenuine signs but between loanwords and indigenous words. "Language is a system that has its own arrangement": a weak statement. More accurately: "Language is a system that knows only its own order."

Page 55: "3) *Implosive Link*" should be "3) *Explosive Link*" (see *CLG* 1972, 84).

Page 74: "At every moment solidarity with the past checks freedom of choice. We say *man* and *dog*. This does not prevent the existence in the total phenomenon of a bond between the two antithetical forces." The second sentence should read: "We say *man* and *dog* because others before us have said *man* and *dog*" (see *CLG* 1972, 108).

Page 90: "What is said of journalism applies to diachrony: it leads everywhere if one departs from it." The loss of a word causes the old joke to lose its point: it should be rather "it leads everywhere, if only one will get out of it" (see *CLG* 1972, 128).

Page 108: "The linguistic mechanism is geared to differences and identities, the former being only the counterpart of the latter." Here Baskin has misread the expression "*roule sur*": rather than being geared or connected to differences and identities, the linguistic mechanism *runs on* them, as a train runs on rails; the connotation is one of dependency, not just of connection.

Page 117: "But it is quite clear that initially the concept is nothing . . . ": here Baskin seems to have misconstrued the sentence "mais il est bien entendu que ce concept n'a rien d'initial," which should be rendered as "but it is quite clear that this concept has no primacy"; that is, it does not preexist the system of values with which it is interdependent.

Page 119: "The same person can write *t*, for instance, in different ways": this sentence is followed by a blank in Baskin's translation, whereas in *CLG* (1972, 165) and its predecessors the statement is borne out by an illustration (which is here reproduced):

Notes

These notes do not purport to offer an exhaustive interpretation of Saussure's *Course*, only to explain some difficulties and point to later developments first hinted at in it. Tullio de Mauro's annotations in *CLG* (1972) are still unrivaled for their learning and breadth and should be referred to by readers with French or Italian.

Page 1: Wolf "started the movement" in 1777 by refusing to enroll as "student of theology" in the University of Göttingen and insisting on the title "student of philology." Wolf's later work suggesting collective authorship of the Homeric poems (*Prolegomena ad Homerum*, 1795) belongs to the history of both scholarship and Romanticism.

2: Bopp initiated the "independent science" of comparative grammar (so called from his *Vergleichende Grammatik*, 1837), taking as his object of study the parallels among the Indo-European languages.

4: "Schleicher supposed that each language has to pass through those grades separately and in exactly the same way": on August Schleicher's reliance on the model of history as development, derived from Hegel, see Koerner (1983, xxxviii–xxxix).

5: Brugmann, Osthoff, Sievers, Paul, Leskien: all teachers or associates of Saussure's during his studies in Leipzig and Berlin.

6: Saussure's definitions of anthropology (the study of humankind as such) and ethnography (the study of distinct human societies) follow French usage. In English-speaking countries, the boundaries are less distinct.

9: "language [*langue*]," "human speech [*langage*]": here Baskin first confronts a terminological problem that no English-language translator has satisfactorily resolved. Saussure uses *langage* in the sense of "the human faculty of communication": it is the broadest term in the set. *Langue*, as defined later, is the system of norms accepted and used by members of a speech community (what would ordinarily be referred to as "a language"). *Parole*, which makes its first appearance on p. 13, is the act of linguistic expression as performed by an individual trained in (some version of) those norms; for this Baskin often uses "speaking." Saussure is by no means as consistent as he might have been, either in the *CLG* or in his handwritten notes, nor does the translator uniformly follow Saussure's terminology.

16: Roland Barthes in 1957 offered a partial draft of "the science of signs in social life" through his reading of what he called, elaborating a syntax for what Marxism calls "ideology," "myths." "Myth," he said, "is an act of speech [*une parole*]" (1957, 109, translation modified [see *CLG* 1972, 33]; 1993, 683). A "mytheme" such as milk, wine, pro wrestling, saluting the flag, or the Tour de France is a semantic unit drawn from a vocabulary of such items characterized by difference, opposition, and mutual interreference; moreover, it is made up of similar units. Barthes refers often to Saussure, to whose *Course* he had been introduced through Louis Hjelmslev and Algirdas Greimas.

23–32: The section on writing is more than any other part of the *Course* a creation of the editors, who wove together sentences and remarks from different versions of the courses on general linguistics, especially the first (1907–1908). See Engler in *CLG* (1968–1974, 65–89).

32: What Saussure here calls "phonology" is closer to what would later be called "phonetics," that is, a descriptive study of speech sounds. The study of speech sounds as systems of differential units—the application of a theory of their functioning first articulated in Saussure's *Course*—would take the name of phonology or phonemics following the work of Nikolai Trubetzkoy, who defined the phoneme as a minimal opposable unit in such a system (International Congress of Linguists 1933, 109–113; Trubetzkoy 1939). Trubetzkoy's primary inspirations were Baudouin de Courtenay and Saussure. Phonology, in this sense, the study of the phoneme as functional unit, does not occur in the chapter "Phonology" or in the appendix "Principles of Phonology" of Saussure's *Course* but is lightly sketched in the chapters on language system and change (e.g., p. 119). On the history of the term "phoneme," see de Mauro in *CLG* (1972, 421–434).

67: "Signifier" and "signified" have a long history in Western speculations about language: see de Mauro in *CLG* (1972, 380–381).

77: "Speech less speaking": cf. p. 66 above.

79: On the question of Saussure's debt to economics and sociology, see de Mauro in *CLG* (1972, 450–451) and Koerner (1973, 67–71).

80: The graph given here is perpendicular to a more widely circulated visualization indebted to Jakobson and Halle (1956) and to Jakobson (1987, 62–94), representing the axis of time as horizontal and that of simultaneity as vertical.

83: The pairing of "diachronic" and "synchronic" points of view on language is an innovation of Saussure's. "Synchronic" had long been used to describe historical timelines that showed simultaneous events occurring in different places through the device of parallel columns; in linguistics, its earliest use was in the branch of psychophysical phonetic research rejected in the early parts of the *Course* as insufficient to give insight into the mechanism of language. Pierre Jean Rousselot's work with probes that reported variations of movement and pressure in the throat and nose allowed him to break the pronunciation of a single letter into multiple events, some of them occurring simultaneously, others in succession; he described the former as "synchroniques" (Rousselot 1891, 84). The representation of the flow of speech as a "continuous ribbon" segmented only by the mind (e.g., *CGL* 1959, 103–104; *CLG* 1972, 146) may derive similarly from the techniques used in experimental phonetics (Marey 1868, 94; 1878, xiv; Rosapelly 1896; Brain 1998).

86–87: Having no sensory realization of its own, the "zero sign" most clearly exhibits the differential relatedness of elements of a system. Cf. p. 118 and, for a fallacious instance, p. 139.

116: Barthesian "myths" are good examples of different "values" for the same "signification."

232: On these famous concluding lines, see the introduction, pp. xxiii–xxiv. The student course notes from which the editors drew this material are far more tentative and pragmatic in tone. One version reads:

> All linguistics can study is the social product, [i.e.,] language. But this social product is manifested by a great diversity of languages (its concrete object then is the social product deposited in each person's brain). But what is given is languag*es* in the plural.
>
> The first task is to study languages, a diversity of languages. By observing these languages, what is universal can be extracted. The linguist will then examine a set of abstractions: this will be *language*, where we will study what can be observed in different *languages*. Thirdly, the linguist will be concerned with the individual. The execution [of linguistic patterns] has its importance but is not essential. For purposes of study, the general phenomenon and the individual mechanism of execution must not be confused.
>
> (Georges Dégallier, quoted by Engler in *CLG* 1968–1974, 515; also Godel 1957, 65; and see de Mauro in *CLG* 1972, 476–477; Bouquet 1997, 138, 266–267)

Works Cited

Aarsleff, Hans. 1982. *From Locke to Saussure: Essays on the study of language and intellectual history*. Minneapolis: University of Minnesota Press.

Aristotle. 1984. *The complete works of Aristotle*. Ed. Jonathan Barnes. Princeton, N.J.: Princeton University Press.

Arrivé, Michel. 2007. *A la recherche de Ferdinand de Saussure*. Paris: Presses Universitaires de France.

Barthes, Roland. 1957. *Mythologies*. Trans. Annette Lavers. New York: Hill and Wang, 1972.

——. 1993. *Oeuvres complètes*. Ed. Eric Marty. Paris: Seuil.

Baudelaire, Charles. 1863. The painter of modern life. In *"The Painter of Modern Life" and other essays*, trans. Jonathan Mayne, 1–40. London: Phaidon, 1964.

Benveniste, Émile. 1939. The nature of the linguistic sign. In *Problems in general linguistics*, trans. Mary Elizabeth Meek, 43–48. Coral Gables, Fla.: University of Miami Press, 1971.

Bergson, Henri. 1889. *Time and free will: An essay on the immediate data of consciousness*. Trans. F. L. Pogson. New York: Dover, 2001.

Bloom, Harold. 1978. Freud and the poetic sublime. In *Freud: A collection of critical essays*, ed. Perry Meisel, 211–231. Englewood Cliffs, N.J.: Prentice-Hall, 1981.

Bloomfield, Leonard. 1922. Review of Sapir. *The Classical Weekly* 15: 142–143. Reprint, in *A Leonard Bloomfield Anthology*, ed. Charles F. Hockett, 55–58. Chicago: University of Chicago Press, 1987.

——. 1923. Review of Saussure. *Modern Language Journal* 8 (October 1923–May 1924): 317–319. Reprint, in *A Leonard Bloomfield Anthology*, ed. Charles F. Hockett, 63–65. Chicago: University of Chicago Press, 1987.

Boas, Franz, ed. 1911. *Kwakiutl: Handbook of American Indian languages*. Vol. 1. Bureau of American Ethnology, Bulletin 40. Washington, D.C.: Smithsonian Institution.

Bouquet, Simon. 1997. *Introduction à la lecture de Saussure*. Paris: Payot.

——, ed. 2003. *Ferdinand de Saussure*. Paris: Editions de l'Herne.

Bourdieu, Pierre. 1972. *Outline of a theory of practice.* Trans. Richard Nice. Cambridge: Cambridge University Press, 1977.

——. 1979. *Distinction: A social critique of the judgment of taste.* Trans. Richard Nice. Cambridge, Mass.: Harvard University Press, 1984.

——. 1980. *The logic of practice.* Trans. Richard Nice. Stanford, Calif.: Stanford University Press, 1990.

——. 1982. *Ce que parler veut dire: L'économie des échanges linguistiques.* Paris: Fayard.

——. 1992. *The rules of art: Genesis and structure of the literary field.* Trans. Susan Emanuel. Stanford, Calif.: Stanford University Press, 1996.

Bourget, Paul. 1893. *Cosmopolis.* Paris: Lemerre.

Brain, Robert. 1998. Standards and semiotics. In *Inscribing science: Scientific texts and the materiality of communication,* ed. Timothy Lenoir, 249–284. Stanford, Calif.: Stanford University Press.

Buell, Lawrence. 1995. *The environmental imagination: Thoreau, nature writing, and the formation of American culture.* Cambridge, Mass.: Harvard University Press.

Calvet, Louis-Jean. 1975. *Pour et contre Saussure: Vers une linguistique sociale.* Paris: Payot.

Culler, Jonathan. 1976. *Ferdinand de Saussure.* New York: Penguin, 1977.

Derrida, Jacques. 1967a. *Of grammatology.* Trans. Gayatri Chakravorty Spivak. Baltimore, Md.: The Johns Hopkins University Press, 1976.

——. 1967b. Freud and the scene of writing. In *Writing and difference,* trans. Alan Bass, 196–231. Chicago: University of Chicago Press, 1978.

——. 1976. *Signéponge/Signsponge.* Trans. Richard Rand. New York: Columbia University Press, 1984.

Dujardin, Édouard. 1887. *Les lauriers sont coupés.* Paris: Messein, 1924.

——1931. *Interior monologue.* Trans. Anthony Suter. In *"The Bays Are Sere" and "Interior Monologue."* London: Libris, 1991.

Dumas, Alexandre. 1849. *Vingt ans après: Suite des Trois mousquetaires.* Paris: Douor et Mulat.

Eagleton, Terry. 1983. *Literary theory: An introduction.* Oxford: Blackwell.

Eco, Umberto. 1976. *A theory of semiotics.* Bloomington: Indiana University Press.

Egger, Victor. 1881. *La parole intérieure*. Paris: Baillière.
Eliot, T. S. 1919. Tradition and the individual talent. In *Selected Essays*, 13–22. London: Faber, 1951.
Ellmann, Richard. 1959. *James Joyce*. New York: Oxford University Press, 1976.
Fanon, Frantz. 1952. *Black skin, white masks*. Trans. Charles Lam Markmann. New York: Grove Press, 1967.
Fechner, Gustav. 1860. *Elements of psychophysics*. Trans. Helmut E. Adler. New York: Holt, Rinehart and Winston, 1996.
Freud, Sigmund. All references are from *The standard edition of the complete psychological works of Sigmund Freud*, ed. James Strachey. 24 vols. London: The Institute of Psycho-Analysis and the Hogarth Press, 1953–1974.
Genette, Gérard. 1966. *Figures*. Paris: Seuil.
Gilroy, Paul. 2004. *After empire: Multiculture or postcolonial melancholia*. London: Routledge.
Harris, Roy. 1980. *The language makers*. Ithaca, N.Y.: Cornell University Press.
——. 1987. *Reading Saussure: A critical commentary on the* Cours de linguistique générale. London: Duckworth.
——. 2001. *Saussure and his interpreters*. New York: New York University Press.
Heath, Stephen. 1972. Ambiviolences: Notes for reading Joyce. In *Poststructuralist Joyce: Essays from the French*, ed. Derek Attridge and Daniel Ferrer, 31–68. Cambridge: Cambridge University Press, 1984.
Hume, David. 1748. *An essay concerning human understanding*. Oxford: Oxford University Press, 1999.
International Congress of Linguists. 1933. *Actes du deuxième Congrès International de Linguistes, Genève, 25–29 août 1931*. Paris: Maisonneuve.
Jakobson, Roman. 1949a. The phonetic and grammatical aspects of language in their interrelations. In *On language*, ed. Linda R. Waugh and Monique Monville-Burston, 395–406. Cambridge, Mass.: Harvard University Press.
——. 1949b. Current issues of general linguistics. In *On language*, ed. Linda R. Waugh and Monique Monville-Burston, 49–55. Cambridge, Mass.: Harvard University Press, 1990.
——. 1987. *Language in literature*. Ed. Krystyna Pomorska and Stephen Rudy. Cambridge, Mass.: Harvard University Press.

Jakobson, Roman, and Morris Halle. 1956. *Fundamentals of language.* The Hague: Mouton.

James, William. 1890. *Principles of psychology.* 2 vols. New York: Dover, 1950.

Jameson, Fredric. 1972. *The prison-house of language: A critical account of structuralism and Russian formalism.* Princeton, N.J.: Princeton University Press.

Johnson, Samuel. 1751. The advantages of living in a garret. *The Rambler* 117. Reprint, in *The Rambler,* 3 vols., 2:269–275. London: Joyce Gold, 1806.

——. 1755. Preface to *Dictionary of the English language.* In *Selected writings,* ed. Patrick Cruttwell, 235–243. London: Penguin, 1968.

Joseph, John E. In press. *Pure difference: A life of Ferdinand de Saussure, 1857–1913.* Oxford: Oxford University Press.

Koerner, E. F. K. 1972. *Bibliographia Saussureana 1870–1970.* Metuchen, N.J.: Scarecrow Press.

——. 1973. *Ferdinand de Saussure: Origin and development of his linguistic thought in Western studies of language.* Braunschweig: Vieweg.

——. 1983. The Schleicherian paradigm in linguistics. In *Die Sprachen Europas in systematischer Übersicht,* by August Schleicher, ed. E. F. K. Koerner, xxiii–lxxi. Amsterdam: John Benjamins.

Koerner, Konrad. 1988. *Saussurean studies / Études saussuriennes.* Geneva: Slatkine.

Laqueur, Thomas. 2003. *Solitary sex: A cultural history of masturbation.* New York: Zone Books.

Lévi-Strauss, Claude. 1955. *Tristes tropiques.* Trans. John Weightman and Doreen Weightman. New York: Atheneum, 1974.

Marey, Étienne-Jules. 1868. *Du mouvement dans les fonctions de la vie, leçons faites au Collège de France.* Paris: Baillière.

——. 1878. *La méthode graphique dans les sciences expérimentales, et principalement en physiologie et en médicine.* Paris: Masson.

Médina, J. 1985. Charles Bally: de Bergson à Saussure. In *Le sujet entre langue et parole(s),* special issue, *Langages* 19, no. 77 (March 1985): 95–104.

Mounin, Georges. 1968. *Saussure ou le structuralisme sans le savoir.* Paris: Seghers.

Ogden, C. K., and I. A. Richards. 1923. *The meaning of meaning.* New York: Harcourt, Brace & World.

Richards, I. A. 1936. *The philosophy of rhetoric*. Oxford: Oxford University Press.

Rosapelly, Charles. 1896. Nouvelles recherches sur le rôle du larynx dans les consonnes sourdes et sonores. *Mémoires de la Société de Linguistique de Paris* 9: 488–499.

Rousselot, Pierre Jean. 1891. *Les modifications phonétiques du langage, étudiées dans le patois d'une famille de Cellefrouin (Charente)*. Paris: Welter.

Sanders, Carol, ed. 2004. *The Cambridge companion to Saussure*. Cambridge: Cambridge University Press.

Santone, Laura. 1999. *Voci dall'abisso: nuovi elementi sulla genesi del monologo interiore*. Bari: Edipuglia.

——. 2009. *Egger, Dujardin, Joyce: microscopia della voce nel monologo interiore*. Rome: Bulzoni.

Sartre, Jean-Paul. 1966. Jean-Paul Sartre répond. *L'Arc* 30: 87–96.

Trubetzkoy, Nikolai Sergeyevich. 1939. *Grundzüge der Phonologie*. Prague: Ministry of Education of the Czechoslovak Republic.

Vansina, Jan. 1961. *Oral tradition: A study in historical methodology*. Trans. H. M. Wright. Chicago: Aldine, 1965.

Vološinov, V. N. 1929. *Marxism and the philosophy of language*. Trans. Ladislav Matejka and I. R. Titunik. Cambridge, Mass.: Harvard University Press, 1986.

Wordsworth, William. 1800–1802. Preface to *Lyrical ballads*, ed. R. L. Brett and A. R. Jones. London: Methuen, 1971.

Index